A Head of My Time

A Head of My Time

of My

Time

Change through a Business Life

George Stephens

authorHOUSE®

AuthorHouse™ UK Ltd.
1663 Liberty Drive
Bloomington, IN 47403 USA
www.authorhouse.co.uk
Phone: 0800.197.4150

Published by AuthorHouse 06/11/2014

ISBN: 978-1-4969-8094-6 (sc)
ISBN: 978-1-4969-8093-9 (hc)
ISBN: 978-1-4969-8095-3 (e)

Contents

Chapter 1 Arriving in the City—1963 1

Chapter 2 Direction and Perspective Change—1965 19

Chapter 3 Investment Marketing Begins—1966 29

Chapter 4 'Go-Go' Days!—1970 45

Chapter 5 Jim Slater's Perception of His Business 75

Chapter 6 Isle of Man—1979 85

Chapter 7 City Establishment: Cultural Change—1982 102

Chapter 8 The Fidelity Years: Eastern Promise—1986 147

Chapter 9 European Creativity 179

Chapter 10 Perpetual, but not for long—1992 194

Chapter 11 Greece: Surprise Posting—1995 199

Chapter 12 Time to Go It Alone—1997 216

Chapter 13 Self-Employed with a Greek Idea 221

Chapter 14 My Hastings Battles—2004 239

Introduction

These are memoirs of my working life from 1963 to 2010. I began writing them in the final months of my career when my workload was being reduced and found I had time on my hands. They were mostly completed within eighteen months, but I have also worked on them from time to time since then.

These memoirs track chronologically how I came to be involved in an area of business, investment management, which has grown from being a business of several million pounds to one of many billions. They give some insight into how life was at various times in my working years, both inside and outside of my various places of work; I only make general mention of some of the technicalities of the work I was doing.

Mostly, the product concepts and ideas I worked on with colleagues and developed to market effectively were innovative. That was what gave me the most satisfaction. Many of the ideas were ahead of their time. Some were modestly but nevertheless sufficiently successful, and many of them have since become widely adopted, even common-place, for example, multi-class funds, no-load funds, own-labelling, investment-linked life insurance and pensions products, renewal commission, portfolio management for fund investors, cross-border funds, international product design and distribution from non-UK offices, and Islamic funds.

For the most part, my working life was fun, stimulating, and occasionally humorous. I had my ups and downs, including redundancies and euphoria. I visited many parts of the world in Europe, including Scandinavia, the Middle East, South-East Asia, and the United States. I met many interesting people along the way and saw their different ways of life, customs, and geography.

The lesson I learned early was to make my own career decisions about the opportunities to advance myself that might come my way. I did not wait for senior colleagues to think about me, let alone know or remember me, for promotion or advancement.

It has been an enjoyable experience writing these memoirs, especially for the early to late-middle years of a creative working life. I'd like to think this career has not only been good for me but for the many thousands in many countries who have been direct and indirect beneficiaries. My thanks go to all those mentioned in this book who helped make this possible.

May 2014

Chapter 1

Arriving in the City

Throughout my career I handled everyday clerical administrative tasks at the outset for about eighteen months, and again, towards the end, for a similar period at Hastings Direct, leading up to my retirement in July 2010. For all the rest of my working life – almost fifty years – I undertook or created more fulfilling roles which could broadly be listed under the heading of 'marketing'. This is a memoir of that working career, the people I have worked with, some of the characters I met along the way, places I visited, and some of my more memorable achievements and experiences.

When I began work, the six-day working week was beginning to come to an end. Fortunately, I never had to work on Saturdays, which was regarded as something of a perk at the time and something only the better companies could offer. All this changed when I ended my working days forty-seven years later at Hastings Direct, where Saturday working was the norm for most departments. This was compensated for by having a 'shift day' in the week preceding the Saturday to be worked. I always hated being on the Saturday shift even though I had had a day off in lieu earlier in the week.

Somehow my career always seemed destined to be involved with financial services. As a child I can remember listening to the lunchtime news on the BBC Home Service (later Radio 4) and hearing reports of how much National Savings had increased in the previous month (£6 million net or so, as I recall). I never really understood it at the time, but I do remember thinking that 'savings' must be important. My father had opened a savings account for me with a Friendly Society whose agent

1

collected money from savers at a house in Plassey Street, near where I grew up in Clive Place, Penarth before going to boarding school in Sussex. One day father said that if I wanted to I could withdraw the accumulated monies he had paid in for some years – a few pence per month. Whatever the modest sum was that I withdrew to close the account, I appreciated that saving was probably a good idea: you should not spend everything you earned (and later when it became easy to obtain, more than you had in credit)!

My general interest in financial services was later aroused at school by the elder brother of a very good school friend of mine, Stephen Swift, who himself later became a director of UBS Asset Management in London and Hong Kong. Stephen's brother worked for Lloyds BOLSA (Bank of London and South America), a subsidiary of Lloyds Bank. Barclays also had an international subsidiary, Barclays Bank (DCO), which appealed to me. Barclays Bank (DCO) was at that time the world's largest multinational bank with a branch network that spanned the Middle East, Africa, the Mediterranean, and the British West Indies. The combination of working with people and being involved with, if not actually travelling to, foreign parts held great appeal to me.

I had unsuccessful interviews with several nonfinancial services companies. Unilever interviewed me in their head office at the northern end of Blackfriars Bridge as a management trainee; I applied to the BBC to become a news reporter or camera man, as the idea of travel appealed, but I never received a reply; I applied for a position with the Ottoman Bank at the London Bridge end of King William Street, where I did get an interview but nothing more, and so on.

An unexpected offer of an interview with a Lloyd's of London insurance broker held great attraction and appeal for me. At least it would fulfil the interest I had in working with people. It came about through my housemaster at Christ's Hospital, who was related by marriage to a director of the company.

I travelled to London in May 1963 for my interview with Mr 'Jock' Holford at C.T. Bowring & Co., one of the largest firms of Lloyd's brokers and over one hundred years old. I attended the interview at 52 Leadenhall Street in my school uniform – blue-coat, knee breeches, and yellow socks. As I walked up Cornhill I was followed by two City gents who recognised the uniform. 'He's a Christ's Hospital boy,' one of them remarked. Each of these men was probably no older than forty, but they wore bowler hats and carried tightly rolled black umbrellas. That was the standard dress for many men who worked in the City regardless of position and status. What might have been different was whether the suit was two-piece, or three-piece, pin stripe or plain, off-the-peg or tailor-made; there were numerous city tailors in such places as Lime Street, Gresham Street, Fenchurch Street, and Little Britain. Most suits were either a tone of grey-black or blue, never brown.

At a second interview during the summer term (again in full school uniform) I again met Holford. On this occasion I was shown The Room: the Lloyd's underwriting room but more of a large open hall with a large first floor balcony. I was entertained to lunch in the Captain's Room. This was all rather splendid, with a highly polished old ship's brass bell and many paintings on the walls of old cargo sailing ships, as well as of *Lutine*, Lloyd's own sixty-foot ocean-racing yacht. We were joined by a number of quite eminent-looking colleagues of Holford's age who seemed to share a rather alien language and a good-sized brandy each. Holford, I learned, travelled from Broxbourne, a place I had barely heard of, but being told his house was in Hertfordshire and fronted onto a river, I thought that maybe one day I might be able to live somewhere similar. Aspiration!

I left school in late July 1963, and since I had already realised that long summer holidays would be a thing of the past and not being under any pressure to start immediately, I decided to enjoy my last long holiday opportunity. I began my career in September in a third-floor office at 22 Billiter Street overlooking the corner with Fenchurch Street. My office manager was a Mr Kimber, who sat in a partitioned office with windows overlooking his domain. Our office was responsible for processing paper for business brokered in The Room at Lloyd's, 'the biggest insurance market in the world' I was told. It was in a building which was across the road and around a corner in Lloyd's Avenue. Mr Kimber was a rather stern-faced man with a black moustache. He wore a single-breasted two-piece grey suit and a bowler hat. He was probably in his early fifties and gave the impression of having never worked or done anything else within the company.

I was just eighteen and London was new to me. I had arrived from Penarth, a small coastal town near Cardiff the day before and had spent the night in a rather elegant mews house occupied by two male friends of Denis Curthoys, director of the National Opera Company of Wales, in Old Barrack Yard, just off Knightsbridge close to The Grenadier pub. I had met Denis for the first time on The Welsh Dragon, a train from London Paddington to Cardiff, when I was auditioning (successfully) for the Glamorgan Youth Orchestra as a French horn player a couple of years before. We all spent the evening listening to Shirley Bassey records and went to bed rather later than I would have preferred for my first working day.

Suit jackets would be removed occasionally in the office but were always worn when outside. It was traditional for regimental ties to be worn on Fridays, and usually club, striped, plain (but never red or yellow), or polka-dot ties on other days. Yellow ties were considered totally taboo as they indicated questionable sexual orientation! After a few weeks I realised that the better-dressed men wore stiff white detached studded collars with plain perfectly laundered coloured or sometimes striped shirts. The detached collars came in a variety of styles, peculiarly called 'Windsor', 'Oxford', 'Classic' and so on. They had to be starched and laundered by Collars of Wembley, who would collect and deliver these collars in purpose-made square brown cardboard boxes direct to offices throughout the City every week at a cost of 9d (4.5p) per collar. I couldn't afford that, and in any case all my shirts were mostly drip-dry, white, single-button cuffs, with collar attached.

Walking from Bank underground station to the office in Billiter Street gave me the option of walking up Cornhill into Leadenhall Street and down Billiter Street or of arriving via Lombard Street across Gracechurch Street and then into Fenchurch Street. The latter was the more interesting route, because most of the old and varied Lombard Street buildings were festooned with historic, hanging signs. All the national banks had offices in the street as well as some foreign ones, and money brokers, and some still hung where now long-gone banks had been. It was a narrow street that made it possible to easily imagine what City life had been like centuries ago. At that time, there were none of the restaurants, bars, and cafes that appeared as the banks moved out in the early 2000's. At the eastern end of the street on the corner with Gracechurch Street was Barclays' grand head office which had stood there since 1864. In the mid 1960's it was knocked down and rebuilt with a new modern design and subsequently was replaced again just fifty years later. It was a sign of things to come with City buildings.

I sat next to my mentor Brian, a ginger-haired quietly spoken and apparently unruffable man in his mid-thirties, always white-shirted. We sat on rather small chairs on casters, Brian at the end and me in the middle of a row of three metal plastic-topped desks, facing another row of three similar desks – all in the same grey colour as the lino-like floor, the walls, and the metal office partitions. The office had several similar double rows of desks and accommodated more than forty people. Overhead we had newly installed fluorescent lighting.

Everyone around me was older. My colleagues appeared generally happy, routinely exchanging comments about the weather, soccer, the latest pop music, or occasionally a film they had seen. Office conversation never changed very much. Most of the people I worked amongst commuted into Fenchurch Street or Liverpool Street stations. This meant they lived to the east, in Essex, a county I knew nothing about, or in Colchester. (How far away was that?) Or they came from Southend, Braintree, Ilford, or Barking. (Is that a place, I thought, or was I mad?)

Of all the people nearby one stood out. Christine was a very large, freckle-faced girl in her early twenties. She wasn't a beauty, but she was very self-confident. She always seemed happy and had natural red hair which she kept short. To my amazement, I learned she threw the shot put and belonged to an athletics club near Hornchurch, where she lived and represented her county Essex. She was also a keen follower of pop music. The Dave Clark Five and the Swinging Blue Jeans were her favourite pop groups.

I can't remember much about the work I did in this office, other than it was unstimulating and repetitious. The office language and terminology, let alone the concept of insurance, were all alien to me.

I had at an early point been given a 'welcome' interview by Mr Kimber. He told me two things: that my position would be reviewed in three months' time and that in the meantime to 'keep your eyes and ears open, but your mouth shut!' I thought of my training period as a sort of Thomas Cook Office Tour. I have pondered from time to time what possible deeper message lay behind Kimber's advice, but I was, nevertheless, very grateful for it. As my life in general and my business life in particular developed, acting as a piece of mental blotting paper (for those who can remember what that was) would prove to be a very useful and valuable skill.

My thinking was that, since I was employed as a Lloyd's trainee broker, I didn't expect to stay too long before being moved to another department to 'learn the business' over time, without the need to know everything immediately. Anyway, after three months clerical work no follow-up meeting had taken place with Mr Kimber, so I gathered up the courage to ask for one, which to my surprise was granted quite soon afterwards. From this I learned a lesson: if I was to get on and make progress in my career, I'd probably have to push rather than wait or expect things to happen.

In due course I moved to another office, this time without any prompting on my part, within the head office building at 52 Leadenhall Street. My new manager was a Mr Eric Borgonon, an assistant director reporting to 'Jock' Holford who had recruited me. Borgonon, a man in his fifties, was rather slight in build but military in appearance, with a clipped moustache, always wearing a chalk pin-stripe three-piece double-breasted suit, with, of course, a bowler hat and a black rolled umbrella. We had the same furniture as my previous office, but there were no windows to throw any natural light, as I recall. I sat beside Len, a pipe-smoking man in his sixties, who would introduce me to North American facultative reinsurance. He was an Associate of the Chartered Insurance Institute. Len commuted via London Bridge station from a flat near Croydon, and he too wore three-piece suits and had a bowler hat and had a tightly rolled umbrella.

I gave some thought about studying for the ACII (Associate of the Chartered Insurance Institute) qualification by correspondence course. In fact, I made several starts at achieving this, including enrolling for evening classes at the Moorgate Institute, but I found the process of reading, paper writing, studying, and the exams (which I always hated) too much grind and bind.

Len was a mine of information about the company, the department, and its work, having worked within it for many years. He had a twinkling eye and a happy disposition. He was a numismatist and often brought old coins into the office for me to look at. On one occasion he produced a groat, an English silver coin worth four English pennies which ceased being produced in the late nineteenth century. On other occasions he showed me silver sixpenny pieces, florins, and half-crowns, and explained the various pure silver contents of each. The metal composition of these coins, Len told me, had changed from being 50% silver, 40%

copper, 10% nickel, in 1920 to being removed totally from all silver coins, from 1947 to become 75% copper, 25% nickel. The removal of all silver content meant that most of the earlier coins disappeared from circulation fairly quickly, and were sought by collectors. Len also liked farthings, because of the wren depicted on the reverse side. He also spoke of his wife fondly.

Len never really showed or told me whether I was doing a good job or not, but his ability to add up long columns of figures – either in pounds, shillings, and pence or US dollars and cents – was phenomenal. The daily work entailed accounting for premiums and commissions for reassurers to the last penny (or cent) for other insurers in the United States. Names such as Niagara Insurance, John Hancock, Fireman's Fund, and Carpenters come to mind. However, the quarterly audit in large heavily bound books was the sort of repetitive work I didn't find particularly stimulating. Obviously, any errors I made could be easily found, as columns and rows of numbers always had to reconcile, so accuracy and attention to detail were paramount – both attributes I was to need later throughout my career.

Numerical speed and accuracy was improved literally overnight with the arrival of an 'electronic' (as it was called) calculator. Up until that point, some people had been using slide rules – something I never mastered. Others used the only mechanical calculator available which had a barrel to which various small movable sliders were attached. This was mounted on a carriage that was turned by hand and moved in a way rather similar to an ancient abacus. The new electronic machine was an ANITA. It measured about fourteen inches square and five or eight inches high. It was indeed the first electronic desktop calculator. Everyone in the office shared it, but it remained in one place. The numerals lit up wired numbers in a display panel and, depending on the calculation, would take long enough that one could observe the numbers being created from the circuitry. It was extremely quick in comparison to anything else being used, and it was accurate. This was the beginning of a new age of electronic calculators!

Another newly invented piece of office equipment was a floor-standing box of a machine that could copy documents one at a time in black and white if they were placed face downwards on a glass screen. Often it was placed in its own small room because it was so large. It was made by Rank Xerox, and it was so successful and ultimately so universal that it created a new verb. To 'Xerox' something became common usage, as did 'photocopy' as a noun or verb. Other, mostly Japanese, manufacturers entered the market very soon afterwards. Hitherto copies had been produced on duplicating machines – Roneo and Gestetner were the leading makes. Copies of documents were made by hand by rolling a drum, which had been covered in a 'skin' of fine paper onto which whatever was to be copied had been typed or drawn, over sheets of paper. Typewriters (mostly manual, but a few electric) were still very much the standard method of writing correspondence for business matters to be distributed or posted. Almost all secretaries, and certainly all senior ones, could take shorthand.

The Pitman system was the most popular secretarial shorthand. It appeared to be a series of hieroglyphics to me, of handwritten strokes made on a small notepad usually in pencil but some times biro, known then as 'a ball-point pen'. In fact it was a series of abbreviations for words and common phrases, which could allow someone well-trained in the system to write as quickly as people speak. This could be as high as 180 words per minute! Most secretaries could manage 80 to 120 words per minute.

I moved into the Treaty Department after six months with Len. The manager of my new office was Mr Gladwell, a fairly portly, white-haired, and rather distinguished man in his late fifties, who always wore a dark pinstripe suit. I didn't have a specific mentor here where another form of reinsurance was administered. Again natural daylight was absent, but the most noticeable change was that the mostly male employees here seemed better spoken than in my previous offices. Frequent visits by our own brokers (only male in those days) to this office to discuss the technicalities of both new risks and claims seemed to provide the stimulus for more active engagement with the work.

Gladwell's assistant manager was Ken Stoddart, one of several Stoddarts in the business (as I discovered later) who were related to the Bowring family, a long-established Lloyd's family with generations of Lloyd's membership. Both families had several members working within 'CTB' - the Bowring Group. Some were underwriters at Lloyd's in Lloyd's building. Michael Bowring, in his late twenties, worked within my new department, not seemingly very hard, and Ken Stoddart, in his forties, didn't seem too bright but was very friendly. He owned a twenty-six foot yacht and asked me one day if I'd like to crew on it in a race from Lymington to Poole and back to Cowes. The weather on the westward stretch was cold and against the wind and tide, which meant a lot of pulling on the sheets and sail changes. Having reached Poole Bar, the furthest point, we turned around, set our spinnaker, and lay out on the deck in bright warm sunshine – perfect sailing weather!

That evening we had all been invited to dinner at the Royal Yacht Squadron in black tie, but to get ashore we had to climb across other yachts, trying not to disturb their crew members below deck. The dinner was very good and the wine flowed. What no one had remembered, however, was that the tide would have gone out by the time we wanted to return, and climbing onto and across other grounded yachts didn't seem too wise. Our yacht was still afloat, however, and the only way to get to it was on an inflatable dinghy in the dark and with most of us feeling slightly 'tired'. It was a memorable moment.

It also became apparent that people in my new office, mostly male and in their forties, commuted from generally rather more appealing places – Sevenoaks, Bromley, Beckenham, Tunbridge Wells, and Brighton for instance, so I presumed that they were probably better paid. Mike Bowring commuted from Cuckfield, in deepest Sussex and Ken Stoddart from Godalming which was in real stockbroker belt. The realisation that at the end of my training I would be a Lloyd's broker coming to discuss business with my new colleagues encouraged me to think that my salary would begin to reflect this environment before too long.

Being a trainee broker who had brought into the business as a protégée of 'Jock' Holford, a main board director, on the introduction of Morton Peto, my housemaster at school and his brother-in-law, didn't make it easy for me to make friends. I recall a young Irishman, Rory, a heavily bespectacled fellow in his early twenties, was always having a laugh and a joke with his work mates. They all smoked cigarettes or panatelas in the office, as did my co-workers in the other offices I had worked in. Some people, such as Len, even smoked a pipe! Rory, who was popular with many of his colleagues, spent some the standard one hour for lunch with me – but as my income was set at £360 per annum, free cash for fun lunches or a pint of beer let alone two was restricted. His attempts at friendship didn't last, as my limited ability to reciprocate his invitations, let alone accept them, became obvious.

Another colleague in his twenties was Richard Lawrence, a smart dresser, quietly spoken, who travelled from Banstead. He and I had little to do with each other in the office, being in different sections, though we were doing pretty much the same job. He had been a clerk for a few years and had progressed from within a rather stolid group to become a deputy section head, which I thought quite an achievement for someone of his age. From time to time he and I would have lunch at the Lime Club, a members-only luncheon club in the basement of a building in Lime Street in Leadenhall Market. It was not particularly expensive, and the cooking was not very inspiring, being traditional, often over-cooked English fare, but it was away from the hustle and bustle of the office and somewhere where we could pass our lunch hour happily. Regulars at the club would typically be older men who mostly seemed to enjoy plenty of alcohol with their lunch – especially on Fridays. It was disappointing when Richard chose to leave Bowrings to become a loss adjuster, though he would be useful to me in this capacity some years later.

Occasionally I would take myself to the Christ's Hospital Club in Great Tower Street for lunch. I felt some compulsion to go there from time to time to support in a small way the City heritage and connections of my school, Christ's Hospital, and it was cheap. It had a rather scruffy dining room in the eaves above offices from which some school administrative functions were run, and in which I had been interviewed and examined (physically and mentally) prior to going to the school in 1956. The food was pretty dire, nobody spoke much to anybody else, let alone to an infrequent diner like me, and it had no licence.

During my time at Bowrings I suffered two bouts of incapacitating illness which kept me away from the office for six weeks each time. The first occasion in the spring of 1964 was the more serious, in that three problems occurred simultaneously. I had lymphangitis, osteomyelitis, and cellulitis, which was an extremely painful combination of ailments, centred on my right lower shin.

At this time I was living in an all-male hostel in Hampstead called HYELM (Hostel for Young Employees of Limited Means). HYELM had a number of houses quite close to each other at the top of Fitzjohns Avenue in Hampstead. I shared a room with two others, (a John Lewis management trainee, a student at Westminster University, training to be a chef,) at 11 Arkwright Road, a four-storey detached house, which was about 200 yards away from the main building where the dining room, laundry and ironing facilities were. My bedroom overlooked the steep road and gardens outside. One of the other residents on my landing was John Dudbridge, a trainee wine salesman at Fortnum and Mason. After I had been bed bound and had not eaten for two or three days, I was still not particularly hungry and had a high temperature. John produced an enormous carton of fresh raspberries for me, which he had brought back from a weekend visit to his parents in High Halden, Kent. It was a very memorable and touching gesture.

Resting in bed in the hope that the leg would settle down and recover with aspirin didn't work. I was unable to stand because of the intense pain. The infected blood in the leg had caused it to balloon up to my groin, where a gland stopped it spreading to the rest of my body. I was taken to the Royal Free Hospital in Hampstead and told that had the groin gland not done its job, I could have been very seriously ill. The most likely cause had been a knock I received on my leg while playing for the Old Blues on their home ground at Fairlop, about as far east on the Underground tube system as it is possible to get on the Central line.

In the Royal Free I was given penicillin injections three times a day by an extremely attractive French nurse. During the five days I was there, she would often joke about having to take my pyjamas down so that she could have a good target on my thigh or backside to see and aim at. 'Please let me see your skin' was her standard line, delivered in a seductive French accent. Sometimes she would throw the needle rather like a dart and other times insert it gently, and always with a cheeky smile afterwards.

Having been told by the consultant not to consider playing contact sports for fear of triggering another bout of the same problems, I rather stupidly began playing rugby again for the Honourable Artillery Company (HAC) in the autumn of 1965. Sure enough, I received an innocent knock on the lower shin through shin pads and had to take more time off work again. I wasn't referred to the hospital this time, as the inflammation was caught and treated immediately. I did, however, take the advice and never played rugby or cricket again. The centre of the infection on the shin bone has remained extremely sensitive to bumps, nudges, and pressure for the rest of my life.

11

After eighteen months with CTB, I was appointed a junior broker in The Room at Lloyd's. I became used to the smell of the place – unlike anything I've known before or since. It was a mixture of disinfectant and carbolic soap, not unlike Germolene, an antiseptic cream! It was quite acrid and not at all pleasant, but somehow 'clean'.

I was given a call number, which would be called by the Lloyd's ushers on the speaker system – used when a broker was wanted by another person in the Room. Mine was Bowring Stephens MP40, and it was written into my brown leather slip wallet. I was to be involved in non-marine business on the first floor level of The Room, a wide gallery overlooking the ground floor.

With my promotion came a salary raise to £520 per annum – £10 a week before tax! I took pleasure in the fact that I had made the transition from trainee to junior broker more quickly than my director's previous protégée Bob Ballantine, whom most of my colleagues regarded as a 'golden boy'. In fact, Bob was to oversee my activity in the Room for several months, where my initial task consisted of visiting brokers and telling them about claims being made on policies (or 'slips') they had underwritten.

Later I would visit underwriters at companies in the Lloyd's market, all located in offices in the streets around the Lloyd's building. They operated in much the same way as Lloyd's underwriters. Usually their offices were modern, warm and comfortable and often spaciously modern. It was perfectly possible to negotiate a route from one office to another through passageways within interconnecting buildings, with only brief dashes to be made outside in alleyways, across streets, and under railway bridges around Fenchurch Street station, if it was wet.

Around that eastern part of the City is a street called Crutched Friars. It and the narrow streets and alley ways that surround it were used mainly for the warehousing of imported items from the London docks which were still actively busy and not too far away, in railway archway spaces behind large wooden doors, as they probably had been for many decades. The area was poorly lit and criss-crossed overhead by railway tracks going into Fenchurch Street. It was easy to picture this area as it would have been in Dickensian times. The atmosphere was made even more so by the strong smell of rat poison and other noxious disinfectants.

By walking everywhere, I visited some of the offices further afield and taught myself the layout of the City. War-damaged buildings were still very much in evidence, their sides blown away by bomb blasts in the Blitz, exposing the innards of what had been offices or living accommodation. Areas of open scrub land, known as bomb sites, were still covered with mounds of rubble and overgrown with buddleia bushes, small trees, and grass. This walking has meant that the City has never felt 'foreign' to me. Indeed, it is familiar terrain, even if many of the older and distinguished buildings, which had stood for one hundred years or more, have been replaced by modern and, on the whole, very attractive new ones.

I learned to drive by taking lessons with the British School of Motoring branch in Fenchurch Street. Starting driving lessons in a small car at the end of a working day meant dealing with rush hour traffic. I well remember one occasion when I had to confront heavy goods vehicles from London Docks in a one way system at Aldgate, coming continuously towards me with right of way at a junction I wished to enter. "How long are y'er going to wait 'ere?" enquired the Cockney instructor. "Use y'er weight son or we'll be here all night,' he rather forcefully implored!

Leadenhall Market, which was close to the office, was a fascinating place to walk at lunch time. I would pass the shops of long-established City meat traders, and a few fishmongers. They took pride in making the year-round open-air displays as attractive as possible under the overhanging hooded lights. In the game season, pheasants, rabbits, and various smaller birds including pigeons would be tied by their feet and suspended so that the blood could be drained onto a white marble sloping counter top. I was shocked when I first saw a pound of meat with a price of £1 on one of my walks!

The market wasn't pedestrianised, so vehicles drove through, but the predominant feature on the roads were the black painted bicycles with their wicker baskets on the front wheel and behind the seat. They were ridden by all the shops' delivery boys wearing dark blue aprons. Underneath the bicycles' crossbars would be a painted panel sign showing the shop name, description, and telephone number.

Apart from the butcher shops there was a Robert Dyas shop selling hardware and household goods and a music shop selling the new invention of Compact Discs as well as LP's. CD's were becoming increasingly popular and sold in slim plastic covers. Cassette tapes which had preceded these as a more robust way of being able to store and play recorded music than on vinyl discs were also sold in plastic cases. It crossed my mind that someone would make a financial fortune from making and supplying these, but it wouldn't be me.

In walking around the City, I also learned of the existence and whereabouts of some of the City's old established and historic shipping and trading companies, such as the Hudson's Bay Fur Company. There were centuries-old banks such as Kleinwort Benson, which occupied a large post-war building in Fenchurch Street (since demolished to make way for a new structure known as the 'phone building'). The tailoring firms are almost all long gone now through amalgamations, takeovers, or simply going out of business. Names such as Gieves & Hawkes, Horne Bros, Dunne & Co., all gentleman's outfitters, Wooderson on the corner of Wood Street and Cheapside for shirts and ties, and others in in Fenchurch Street, Gresham Street and Moorgate, have all disappeared, mostly redeveloped and occupied by banks from all over the world or have been turned into bars, and even a shopping mall.

My training and focus had remained on North American non-marine business, all of which was conducted in the Gallery, or Non-Marine Room in Lloyd's Building. The ground floor, or Marine Room, was where marine business was underwritten which included aircraft, being ships' hull and marine liability insurance. The claims I had to show to the brokers reflected my apprentice status in that I was left with the smallest lines to be acknowledged for claims settlement. Some of the claims were truly huge, running into hundreds of millions of dollars; earthquakes, hurricanes, oil refinery disasters, and huge warehouse fires were some of the most memorable. Inevitably, telling underwriters of their liabilities wasn't always pleasant. Some of the individuals were notoriously difficult and treated me as a new boy with disdain. Had I not worked for CTB, life could have been really unpleasant. I suspect that the prospect of being offered 'decent' (i.e. profitable) business was always an enticement for underwriters to take some of the 'rubbish' or poorer quality business. Anyway, life generally seemed to be pretty good now.

Whilst I was working in this department, the company announced it would go public. Although I knew precious little about such things then, I recall phoning my father from a call box from HYELM, on the evening of the day I heard with the news. He said, surprisingly, that he would make an application. I think the issue price was 119d. (pre-decimal pence) or it might have been £1.19s.0d. (one pound, nineteen shillings), and father bought a couple of thousand shares. Over the years they did extremely well, and he held on to them long after I had left the business, often remarking what a good investment they were.

The company also built a new building close to the Tower of London to house and consolidate its expanding business. It was only a few stories high, but it was built in an angular S-shape. Situated perhaps a quarter of a mile from The Room, as opposed to about 200 yards from the previous head office in Leadenhall Street, my usual lunchtime sandwich could now be eaten listening to the debates and diatribes delivered at Speakers' Corner on Tower Hill most weeks and in all weathers. Only later did I realise how famous some of the speakers were or would become: Michael Foot, Chad Varah, Trevor Huddleston, Lord Stansgate later to become Anthony Wedgewood Benn and Donald (later Lord) Soper, nick-named 'Doctor Soap-box', are just a few examples.

Other lunchtime activities included walking to Petticoat Lane and looking at the street stalls and household product demonstrations by the market traders. These were all very convincing and delivered by true Cockneys. An occasional visit to the Houndsditch Warehouse was another nearby excursion. It was a discount department store, full of mostly household items and clothing – pretty dull for a young man in the City, but a distraction and a change from sitting in the office.

To put it simply, risk underwriting was usually achieved by a senior broker from the firm going to a lead underwriting syndicate that specialised in the type of insurance risk being brokered – buildings, contents, factory machinery, oil refineries, art collections, and personal features occasionally, such as a pianist's fingers, and so on. Often, it seemed to me, R.W. Sturge, on behalf of a collection of different underwriters, would write the risk on behalf of all the syndicate members on a 'slip' by stamping it. Sometimes smaller underwriters, such as Kiln, would express frustration that they couldn't 'write the line' they wanted for what were perceived as the better risks. This process, however, saved time in having uncomplicated risks covered, but it meant that smaller underwriters with less ability to meet potentially large claims had to have utmost trust in the lead underwriter, because they were never being consulted.

For large risks, several slips were issued so as to spread the insurance cover as widely as possible in the market, and each underwriter, in addition to stamping the slip on behalf of his syndicate, each of which had its own 'box-number, had to show the percentage of the risk he was prepared to accept. Sometimes more than fifty underwriting firms would have to see the risk slip to get the risk covered. However, for a really popular insurance risk (i.e. a high premium and a low risk of claim – for example, someone's hands, legs, or teeth!) known as a 'good' risk, we, as the broker, would try to persuade the bigger underwriters to accept that the risk would be oversubscribed. There would then be a pro rata adjustment to get the underwritten figure down to one hundred per cent so that everyone would at least get some benefit – so long as no claim was ultimately made!

The individual underwriters, representing their syndicates, sat in 'boxes'. Each individual sat on a bench, which could take three or four seated people facing towards another bench, but divided by shelves of box files which recorded the syndicate's business, and reference books. New business was accepted on one side, claims on the other. Depending on the size of the underwriting syndicate, each firm would have one or more 'boxes'. It was a way and style of conducting business that had changed very little since the founding of Lloyd's in a city coffee house in 1688.

In due course I began to broker new business, as opposed to presenting claims. This was usually more fun and interesting than telling underwriters about claims they had to meet, but as a new boy in the Room, I was again only ever given risks to complete which had had most of the risk underwritten by underwriting syndicates already. The slip was usually an A4 landscape piece of thin card folded twice. It was an innocuous document in itself, typewritten with details of the risk, its location, the insured value, and the excesses, together with other technical details involving reassurance. However, it represented enormous obligations on everyone who stamped and signed, sometimes with quill pen, their participation on it.

Whether taking around claims or new business, it was usually necessary to queue at underwriters' boxes. This could take up hours as brokers ahead of me engaged in discussions, arguments, joke telling, or sometimes just social gossip with the underwriters. Queuing for underwriters to return from lunches of sometimes indeterminate length (especially on a Friday) or waiting for them to appear on Monday mornings after a weekend in the country was all par for the course. This aspect of Lloyd's life distressed me, as did the realisation that it would take me years to make a really good income obtain through promotion. The majority of the people I was amongst in the Room probably had independent means. Many were members of long-established Lloyd's families, whose traditions and family loyalty would be obstacles to conventional promotion. This all told me that a long-term career to reach financial success here was not something I could wait nor have the patience for.

As far as I could tell everyone left the office on the dot at 5:30 p.m. Certainly in the clerical and administrative offices where I worked there was no hint of being invited for a pub visit before catching the train home from Fenchurch Street or Liverpool Street.

I had never envisaged a career in an office. My aspiration, in whatever sphere I worked, was to be creative in some way, ideally with a travel component. Several times a week I would look at classified advertisements in newspapers I found lying on empty Underground seats, the *Evening Standard* or *Evening News,* or which I borrowed in the office. I could not afford to buy my own paper from the newspaper sellers who stood at seemingly every street corner, with the cry 'Paper, paper! Read all about it!' I never applied for any of the jobs advertised, probably because I had come to realise how lucky I was to have what I had. It was, after all, a position with undoubted but very long-term potential in a rather specialised business, at Lloyd's within the City of London. My office environment was warm, my work colleagues were all 'good sorts', but it remained something far removed from anything any of my school friends from my home town, Penarth, could have envisaged me doing.

One of my bedroom neighbours, and a good friend, in HYELM was Paul Burnett. His family lived in Bembridge on the Isle of Wight, and he was employed by Canada Life as a life assurance salesman, having briefly been a captain in the army. He told me quite a bit about the cold-calling and family-and-friends approach to getting life policies sold, and the potentially high rewards from bonus payments. At some point I went to his Canada Life UK head office in Trafalgar Square and met up with his manager for an informal interview and assessment. He, like all managers in his and (as I was to find out) all companies selling life insurance direct, was keen to build as large a team of agents as possible and take a cut of the sales commission.

Considerable promises of future potential prosperity were made, and examples from existing salesmen were given, should high sales be achieved. It was a tempting thought initially, but the idea of cold calling and canvassing family and connections for business didn't appeal to me.

Later I received an approach to work for Towry Law, a firm of life assurance brokers, without the need to make cold calls but instead to follow up on qualified leads, and with prospects of improving my income. This put me in a bit of a spin. My head was turned by in-house client support for complex tax and legal solutions combined with the security of life cover to pay for school fees or to mitigate unnecessary tax payments, usually at death or within a specified number of years. Their business was in another area of which I had very little knowledge, so I would be starting again from the bottom. I would be leaving the great CTB, but how to do so was another matter.

Chapter 2

Direction and Perspective Change

Telling Mr Borgonon of my decision to leave CTB wasn't going to be easy. I had been there only two years, and the tag of 'protégée' was still shining bright, though perhaps not quite as brightly as I had now begun to make my way up the career ladder. After days of deliberation about how, when, and where I would break the news to him, I seized the moment in the gallery of the Room one mid-morning. Borgonon had a shifty-sidewise walk and a slightly French-looking, haughty look, as if he had just taken snuff – which he might well have done! He was always difficult to approach at the best of times, and being nervous wasn't helping! Anyway, I approached him across the black and white chess board tiled floor and asked if I could speak to him briefly.

'What is it, dear boy?' he enquired.

'I have decided I wish to leave Bowrings, sir.'

'How come? I thought you were doing rather well here.'

Immediately I started to wonder whether I was making the best move. For the first time ever he had given me some praise, though in a curious way. Maybe I should rethink things. And in a flash I had. None of my reasons for wanting to leave had changed, so I continued.

'I'm sorry I shan't be staying longer,' I blurted out, 'but I want to move on, sir.'

'Well, I'll have to discuss it with Mr Holford, the main board director, and if you hear nothing from either me or him, you can leave in four weeks.'

We shook hands and went our separate ways. I didn't hear any more from him or anyone else, and I left my first employer in November 1965.

The next stage of my career started with my arrival at a firm of life assurance brokers, Towry Law & Co., Ltd. I had been meeting with John Dyson, one of the firm's directors, over the past several weeks on Friday evenings after Bowrings had closed for the day. These discussions had taken place in The Square Rigger pub on the north-west side of the old, known as 'new', London Bridge opened in 1831, opposite Adelaide House where my mother had worked years previously. The latest London Bridge was built between 1967 and 1973, and the 'new' one sold to an American oil magnate who, it was rumoured believed he had bought Tower Bridge to span a canal in Arizona!

My meetings with John had begun as a result of having met John socially. Quite where I had met him, I can't remember, even though socialising was distinctly unusual on my salary after travel and hostel boarding costs had been met. I also felt distinctly disloyal, feeling I was letting down all those who had given me an enviable chance to work at Lloyd's of London in one of the most respected and oldest brokerages.

John was in some ways an enigma. He wasn't public-school educated, but he spoke with a distinctly cultured and well-modulated voice. He was sure that I would be a success; he suggested that if I succeeded in broking life insurance and investment-linked products (which were a comparatively new concept at the time) to clients of the firm, I could make a good income with every prospect of good bonuses. So I decided to make the move.

I shared an office with John at 5 St Paul's Churchyard, overlooking the northern side of St Paul's Cathedral. The small office building was built in the early twentieth century close to the entrance to St Paul's underground station. The offices were above a Moyses Stevens florist shop and had a rickety self-operated lift, which few male members of staff used, preferring to get to the offices on the third to fifth floors by striding or running up the stairs several steps at a time.

It was an amazing location. I frequently gazed out from my second-floor office trying to take in the privilege of having the view of the cathedral, even if it was being stone-washed by a company whose plastic sheeting with the name 'Szerelemy' on it covered most of the side that I could see for most of my time there.

'TL' was a real eye-opener. It was pretty much everything Bowrings wasn't, being young, dynamic, and go-getting. There was a collective enthusiasm to do well, to achieve results, and above all to give unquestionably good advice. It was nothing for us to work late into the night preparing lengthy schedules, initially hand-written and then typed, of detailed recommendations for clients who had appointments the following day. Electric typewriters were now the norm. It was here that I first came across a word processor, a device which some senior secretaries had. These electric machines could memorise standard paragraphs for letters, and at the push of a button, preselected paragraphs could be typed.

The business had been set up about five years previously by Hon. C.T.H. (Cecil) Law and Nigel Paget-Brown. Other directors included Lord Ellenborough, Cecil's brother. He rarely appeared in the offices but was on the note paper, I suppose to show 'class'. Clive Seeley was a former Guards officer and a mad-hatter. Clive Scott-Hopkins ('Scottie') was reputed to be the most successful life assurance salesman in the country; he lived near Maidenhead and usually travelled in with Richard Cockroft, another director. Other than John, these were all Old Etonians, and it showed! But there were other directors who were not Old Etonians. Don Griffiths concentrated on mortgage business; David Rouse, who sadly died young with heart problems, was financial director; Peter Harris, a former barrister, was a leading authority on Estate Duty (inheritance tax) planning; and Clive Williams from North Wales seemed to have no special responsibilities but talked well and encouraged me a lot. A subsidiary company brokered home insurance policies under its managing director Alasdair Holbein, a very intense Jew if ever I saw one.

Everyone wore well-cut bespoke tailored suits, double-cuffed shirts with link chain cufflinks, and classically styled lace-up black shoes. From that time on, that became my standard office dress wherever I worked.

The company obtained business mostly from referrals by existing clients, as well as from small classified advertisements in *The Times* (which in those days – until 1967 – appeared on the front page) and from personal advertisements in the *Daily Telegraph* and their Sunday sister papers. This was a unique approach. As far as I know, we were the only company to target individual ads specifically at particular professions, and for a period it was highly successful.

It was nothing for several of these directors to be working until 8:00 p.m. or much later most nights, and I was expected to do the same. The company was driven by success and achievement. It was admired not only by its competitors but also by the company 'inspectors' (basically, servicing agents) from the life assurance companies whose products we used because of the amount of business they received from us. We strived to ensure we had the very best and quickest service. It was a thoroughly professional business, and high standards were expected from all who worked there in every respect. And although one or two might have had insurance (ACII) or secretarial (ACIS) qualifications, all of this was achieved without any of us having any relevant business or financial intermediary qualifications, which weren't at that time a statutory requirement!

The process of learning the business was to watch and listen and then have verbal tests. I recalled Mr Kimber's comments a few years earlier. As time went on, I began to make my own appointments from leads provided from the company's advertising in *The Times* and *Daily Telegraph*. Each director was responsible for a different area of the country, and I joined John in looking after the Home Counties. The typical client was usually pretty well-heeled and professional. Titled folk, landed gentry, and inherited wealth were significant parts of the business. These clients usually needed effective tax planning for their assets and ultimately protection from taxes on their death, then known as 'death', or 'Estate Duty'. As a new boy, however, I dealt with much smaller cases, often helping newly qualified accountants, lawyers, military officers, and doctors to obtain their first mortgages and to plan for school fees, and pensions in later years.

It was in this area of financial planning that I found the concept of investment and saving, with or without life assurance that was to become the focus of my career from now on.

Soon after I started there, I arrived at the office wearing a gabardine raincoat my mother had bought for me. I hung it up on the coat stand in the shared office. John arrived in the office a few minutes later.

'Don't ever let me see that coat in here again!' he exclaimed. 'It is the most appalling thing I have ever seen. Do you understand, George?'

I felt rather insulted. 'Okay, but what is the problem?'

'Just look at it. It is truly dreadful!'

There was no point in discussing it any more. In retrospect, he was right. The coat was pretty awful! It was brown and made of textured polymer material that would change different shades of brown, almost shimmering, as it moved. It was also rather stiff and knee-length. I think my mother had bought it for me because at the time gabardine coats were quite popular. But they were not really attractive for an up-market City business with a self-conscious professional image! Anyway, the experience made me aware of my dress and appearance and of the standards expected, and I never had any further problems of that type.

In a way I overreacted to this sartorial criticism. Although I could barely afford it, I had an overcoat made to measure by a small tailor in Little Britain, a narrow street off the west end of London Wall. It was a blue cashmere coat with a velvet collar, about knee length and very waisted in an Edwardian frock-coat style. I felt rather self-conscious in it, and I remember the tailor telling me that sitting down in it would spoil it, as would putting anything in any of the pockets. Father, rather disparagingly, said that it was the sort of thing my grandfather would have worn. Standing while travelling on the tube when there were plenty of seats available was a practice that didn't last long. The coat was horrifically expensive, but I thought it would last a few years, and I made sure it did.

It led to the purchase over the years of a few suits, some two-piece some three, as well as a rather loud and large sports jacket, predominantly cream but with large yellow and brown checks. In retrospect this was a rather ostentatious jacket, again very waisted, and quite full length. It came from Drew & Co., a long-established small tailoring business in Lime Street, who had been recommended to me by a number of colleagues. At that time, Horne Bros. and Dunn & Co would make suits for a reasonable price, but I felt I wanted something better than from a high street retailer.

Stories became legion about some of my colleagues. Scottie used to dictate so many letters in a day that he couldn't carry them all in his briefcase to sign on his way home. He was often to be seen going home with not only a large and bulging briefcase but also several plastic shopping bags obviously crammed full of private correspondence. (There was no Data Protection Act in those days!) He would always travel to Paddington in a taxi, signing letters until he reached Paddington, when he would be seen desperately holding on to pink office copies, whilst stuffing a post box with filled envelopes. Often pink carbon copy letters could be seen fluttering along the platforms. The signing would continue on the train all the way home.

He only showed anything remotely personal about his private life when his brother who had been Member of Parliament (MP) for North Cornwall since 1959 was re-elected having lost his seat in 1966, to be MP for West Derbyshire at a 1967 by-election. Clive was over the moon and champagne was ordered and liberally enjoyed.

Clive was a superb salesman when talking to clients directly who came to meet him in the office; he said he never had time to go out and meet them. He would also talk incessantly on the telephone. 'No' was just not in his vocabulary. His lines were well rehearsed and his verbal flow almost unstoppable – all delivered in the most seductive and rounded old-Etonian tones. Ultimately the pressure took its toll and he suffered two heart attacks, but he continued working in this way until well into his seventies before finally deciding to work from home near Maidenhead.

Clive Seeley was a social animal in London, a practical joker and a keen card player. He had a wonderful sense of fun, told jokes ('dear boy') with panache, and gurgled with laughter like a drain most of the time. Life was for living, and he made sure as best he could that everyone else enjoyed it the same way. He always wore his Brigade of Guards regimental tie. Sometime later I heard he was gay.

After a few months with the firm, I left the office overlooking St Paul's to become Clive's assistant. I was now an 'Assistant Life Manager'! This entailed picking up the pieces of Clive's unfinished business. If the case wasn't of a particular type or size, he'd pass it over and expect me to complete it. He expected a one hundred per cent closing rate and was distinctly unhappy if that didn't happen, no matter what reason.

My new office looked down the length of Cheapside towards the Mansion House and the Royal Exchange, but sitting in the same room as Clive meant living with constant noise. Clive's Old Etonian tones were incessant on the telephone or dictating into a small dictation machine (known as a 'Dictaphone') or giving instructions to either of two secretaries. This was extremely wearing, but it was a good way to learn something about the business and about how to handle both easy and difficult clients. Hearing Charles's antics in the corridor with his fellow directors or their secretaries after he had made a sale was a happy distraction – to me if not to Clive!

Clive had three telephones on his desk and could hold two conversations at once. For instance, when calling a life office on one line for a policy premium quote, he would keep a client on hold on the other line. No return calls for him!

The way phone numbers in London worked at that time was interesting. Different districts had their own area codes. Numbers were accessed by turning a dial with a finger inserted in the appropriate hole on the front of a desktop telephone, which was usually black, occasionally grey, and sometimes beige. As now, the letters ABC and number 1 shared the same position, and so on through the alphabet and numbers 1 to 0 clockwise on the dial. A Mayfair number would be dialled as 'MAY', Bayswater as 'BAY', and so on, but some areas had codes that seemed to have no relevance to their location. (Why would 'Flaxman' be part of Fulham?) Most districts had obvious abbreviations: PUT(ney), KNI(tsbridge), BAL(ham), etc. It wasn't until many years later that these codes really became numbers so that 'Mayfair' became '628', Bayswater '228', and Putney '788'. All London numbers dialled from outside London were prefixed '01'.

One medium-sized life assurance company, London & Manchester, offered fifteen, twenty or twenty-five year policies linked to unit trusts (similar to OEICS today). In addition, the life company was able to offer mortgages, provided it had sufficient funds available, at an interest rate of around seven and a half per cent. It was a leader in this field. The idea was that, dependent on a deduction based on the proposer's age, a known portion of the premium would be paid into the life policy while the balance would be used to pay off the interest on the loan secured by the life coverage, in anticipation that the growth of the investments would not only pay off the mortgage and accumulated mortgage interest but also produce a tax-free capital sum at maturity. The premiums for this type of policy were less than for what had hitherto been available, a with-profits policy, but the returns were unknown and relied on an act of faith that stock markets would go up!

Typically, the better with-profits policies would pay an annual or triennial bonus of a declared percentage rate, applied to the premiums paid, and sometimes on already declared bonuses as well. These bonus rates were based on the life company's investment performance, which was generally announced at the end of the year in December. Once declared, these bonuses were guaranteed. In future years, added to these would be a 'maturity bonus', which would not be guaranteed until policy maturity and would be an additional sum paid on top of the already declared annual or triennial bonuses.

The unit-linked policies were usually sold in conjunction with with-profits endowment policies to fund school fees as far ahead of their need as possible. It wasn't unusual for clients to start these policies as soon as they knew a baby was expected and so hopefully gain the benefits of investing for the longest possible period before drawing from the policy as school fees became payable. At that time all premiums paid into life assurance policies, other than for term assurance policies, attracted life assurance premium relief at a rate of seventeen and a half per cent, which made saving in this way extremely attractive.

My interest in life assurance and its uses for investment and in unitised funds in particular was well and truly born. One of the biggest attractions to me was that unit-linked performance could be transparently measured and costs known. With-profits policies were totally opaque: bonus declarations were only an indication of investment performance, and only the bare minimum was given to policyholders in order to remain competitive with their peers. Investment management costs were unknown.

My own investments began in a small way with the purchase of Great Britain stamps from a shop in a parade running underneath our offices along the north side of Saint Paul's in a pedestrianised walkway that linked Cheapside with Paternoster Square. Over a few months I built up an almost complete collection of mint unused stamps going back to Edward Vll, except for 'faults', which were always out of my range pricewise. As well as these, I had another collection of the same stamps in used condition, and this collection also included some stamps from Queen Victoria.

One day I went to this shop (which was a family business) and found they had a Prussian blue stamp, which was one of a small series issued to mark the silver jubilee of King George V and Queen Mary. For many years controversy swirled as to whether the Prussian blue stamps were in fact proof stamps that had been inadvertently perforated or correct issue stamps that were printed in the wrong colour. The 2½d stamp was submitted in two colours (ultramarine and Prussian blue) to the King for final approval. King George chose ultramarine. The accumulated evidence strongly supports an error in printing colour. It appears that a large number of 2½d stamps were printed in Prussian blue (turquoise) by mistake. Most were destroyed. Six sheets of 240 stamps were identified for destruction, but three of these were mistakenly included in an order to Upper Edmonton Post Office and a fourth sent to an unknown post office. All three Edmonton sheets were sold. The remaining two sheets in stock were destroyed. It is not known what happened to the stamps from the fourth sheet. Thus, no more than 480 Prussian blue stamps were available for sale.

I took the plunge and paid £180, the catalogue value, for one of these stamps in mint condition and unused. My intention, as with the rest of the collection, was to keep it for as long as I could for investment purposes. Sometime later I wanted it authenticated to be sure that it was not a forgery. I went to Stanley Gibbons who had a block of four in stock. They were most interested in it but uncertain. They showed me their stamps and compared them to mine. To my eyes they were identical. If it was forgery, they said, it was the best they had ever seen. They put it into a small white grease-proof paper bag and took it away to send it to the Authentication Committee of the Royal Philatelic Society of London. This was with the full knowledge of the stamp dealer from whom I had bought it, who said that if it was proven not to be genuine, he would refund the cost. He said he personally knew several members of the expert committee.

A few weeks later I received their analysis, and my doubts were confirmed. The colour had been achieved by applying some chemical to an ultramarine stamp, a process which had also removed some of the adhesive on the back, so it was pretty convincing.

I got my money back, but shortly afterwards, being somewhat disillusioned with the experience, I sold my collections for only a modest profit. It is never a good market when such things have to be sold! (I did subsequently develop a collection of first-day covers, not for their investment potential, but as a potential legacy.)

Outside my working life, a significant event occurred when Barclaycard (later to become Visa) was launched in 1966. This was a credit card issued by Barclays Bank offering the familiar credit card facilities of today. The first credit card issued in the United Kingdom had been Diners Club in 1962, followed by American Express in 1963, but Barclaycard was the first credit card designed for mass use by 'the man in the street' as opposed to the very well-heeled.

For the most part, people were initially rather confused by the idea of being able to use a plastic card to pay for something you could own straight away without physically handing over cash. Barclaycard was the only high street bank credit card until 1972, when a consortium of High Street banks including National Westminster Bank, Midland Bank (later to become HSBC), Lloyds TSB, and Williams & Glyn's Bank (now the Royal Bank of Scotland) offered the Access credit card. This too changed its name: to MasterCard in 2002.

People had mixed views as to whether buying things 'on tick' in this way was a good thing or not. The also fairly new weekend colour magazines of the serious newspapers of the late 1960s carried endless coloured advertising promoting the card and the perceived benefits of suddenly being able to buy something without hire-purchase contracts. Applying for and using a few thousand pounds worth of instant credit appealed to many people, but for me, the monthly repayment obligation at astonishingly high rates of interest of 20% and more made me think the concept was a responsibility I didn't want and couldn't afford – at least for the time being.

Chapter 3

Investment Marketing Begins

The unit trust business, although first established in the 1930s, had not yet become a significant business in its own right, but I thought it offered me a future, not least because its products were transparent, its charges disclosed, and its valuations easy to calculate. All these features were to become of overriding importance in years to come. In a way I was ahead of my time. By comparison with traditional with-profits products of conventional life companies, they were a revelation. I successfully responded to an advertisement in the *Daily Telegraph* to become a trainee manager with Save & Prosper Group – at the time the second largest unit trust manager in the market, with £460m under management. I was interviewed by Mr Stan Baker and Mr Fred Trott at the company's administrative offices at Arodene House, in Ilford, Essex.

So this is Essex! Welcome!

Arodene House was a mid-sixties four-storey building facing a Gaumont cinema situated at the Gants Hill roundabout on Eastern Avenue, an arterial road into London through the East End from Essex. The local community had a significant number of Jewish residents, and near the office was a parade of shops which included a wonderful Jewish family bakery called Louis. They baked bread and made fresh cakes with copious quantities of cream every day. Their donuts were exquisite. On another corner of the roundabout, reached by a pedestrian subway, was the Cherry Tree restaurant – a lunchtime favourite of one of my managers, Roger Young. Valentines Park, an Essex County cricket ground was very nearby, but I never went there.

I began at Save & Prosper in April, 1966 with another trainee, Miles Edge, who was slightly older than I, the son of a timber merchant from Craven Arms, Shropshire. Miles was married to a glamorous, outgoing, and voluptuous auburn-haired Greek girl, Anastasia (Anna). They lived in South Kensington, while I was living by this time in Belsize Park. Miles was a kindred spirit and good company. He invited me to his wonderful wedding in Craven Arms parish church. We progressed in our own ways and on separate paths within the company. Sadly, I learned later that his marriage had failed, but not before I had holidayed with them in a cottage in Cadgwith, Cornwall with Polly, another office colleague. This was around the time of the Russian invasion of Czechoslovakia in August 1968.

A third management trainee, who had joined a few months earlier, was Julian Tregonning, an ex-naval lieutenant who had been invalided out because of a serious leg injury. Julian too was good fun, but he seemed a bit of over familiar, always using first names when talking about or with board members – David Maitland, the managing director, Jeremy Hepplethwaite, the finance director, and Chomeley Messer, the legal director. He spent his career in the unit trust and investment industry and became a board member of NY Mellon Bank, in a career with remarkable similarities to the one we both had started together. Some forty years later I met Julian shortly after he had retired. He claimed to have a contact list of 2,500 people around the world, having been involved with setting up Flemings businesses in and throughout South America, and Jersey and with Mellon Bank in the Far East. He had been master of the Grocers Company and a member of their Court of Assistants (or Board).

Stan Baker was the general manager based at Gants Hill. He never saw me or spoke to me again after my interview with him. Fred Trott, a happy smiling man, was administration manager and supervised my training. This consisted of doing what I again called a Cook's tour of the various departments based in Arodene House. We were definitely not in pin-stripe public-school country! Nevertheless, all the people were approachable and helpful. The company was to become a pioneer of what become known as equity-linked life assurance.

An inherent attraction of such policies with monthly sums invested over many years was a phenomenon known as 'pound cost averaging'. If the same amount of money is invested each month, when fund prices are down you get more for your money than when prices are up. This technique irons out the ups and downs of a fund price over time, giving you a number of shares bought at an overall average price, and takes away the worry of timing purchases perfectly. Regular investing in this way is ideal for people starting out or who want to take their first steps towards building a portfolio of funds for their long-term future.

Hitherto S&P had obtained its business via City stockbrokers and bank trustee departments. 'Block offer' advertisements were beginning to become a feature in weekend newspapers, which my later employers, Slater, Walker, were to exploit very successfully. S&P's largest fund Investment Trust Units (ITU) were frequently advertised under the slogan 'Speculate to Accumulate'. As this marketing wasn't an area of the business I was directly involved with, I never knew how successful or otherwise it was. Other well-known funds at the time were Scotbits (Scottish banking, insurance, and trust companies) and Scotyields, a high income fund.

By this time (1968) I had moved with John Dudbridge (mentioned earlier from HYELM) to a one-bedroom flat in Belsize Park. John was now working for a wine shipper L.R. Voigt, famous for importing Mateus Rose. This was a very popular, almost fashionable Portuguese rosé wine sold in a wicker basket around an oval-shaped, green bottle. He would later move on to Fortnum & Mason as a wine salesman and end up as director of a wine merchant's in Banbury selling wine to Oxford colleges.

Travelling by Tube (1s 3d or 6.5p each way) from Belsize Park to Gants Hill (eighteen stops with a change at Bank station) took about an hour and gave me an opportunity to read the City pages from discarded newspapers as comprehensively as I could. I found information about shares or equities easier to understand than bonds and gilts, and it has remained so ever since. Tickets to travel had to be bought either from ticket machines or from the station ticket office. Nobody checked them either on the train or as one entered the platform. Not buying a ticket for the full journey was commonplace. Arriving at a destination without a ticket meant that you could claim a shorter journey than the one actually taken to the ticket inspector, thus saving some expense: not something I ever did, but witnessed frequently.

Once on board, you could enter (unlawfully) through doors at the end of each carriage. Smoking was allowed anywhere: on the trains, on the platforms, even on the escalators! In retrospect it is surprising there weren't fires every day. The carriages had opening slat windows at the top within wooden frames. They were always dusty and dirty. At busy times several people at once would hold on to the straps that hung on either side of the gangways. There was no air-conditioning other than the open windows, so personal smells were difficult to avoid, especially in summer!

Carriage lighting came from small round ceiling-mounted electric light bulbs, but it was always light enough for everyone to be able to sit and reading a broadsheet newspaper with elbows resting on the arm-rests between the seats. Those standing had evolved a way of having a paper folded so that they could strap-hang and read the paper as the train rocked from side to side through the tunnels. Not for them the pleasures of early morning TV or computers or mobile phones! My money was tight, so in the mornings I'd try to find a discarded morning paper and in the evenings a tabloid-sized *Evening Standard,* which I preferred to the broad-sheet *Evening News.*

Stations likewise were always pretty dirty with chewing gum trodden in on the floors. They were dimly lit by recently installed and widely spaced fluorescent lighting strips suspended from the white enamelled tiles, which also covered the walls where advertisements were not covering them.

Before I became involved in life insurance products, I spent my first period in the Dealing Department, where investors and agents would telephone their buying and selling instructions for units in the trust(s) of their choice. Daily dealing prices were calculated at these offices and sent by facsimile machine to the head office in Cornhill to be displayed on a board there which was in the customer centre. This was managed by an old army-type named George McGowan – definitely pin-stripe, bowler, handlebar moustache, and a Surrey man!

The Muirhead facsimile machine used for sending documents to head office was a rather large device that faxed documents by telephone line to another machine. However, it was extremely temperamental and required the receiving machine to be set to receiving mode for the whole exercise to work. The daily faxing of one A4 sheet, then known as a 'Telefax', would often take more than twenty minutes and involved several attempts to get the two machines to recognise each other. As time went by, fax transmissions would become instantaneous, and some twenty years later, they would be overtaken by email.

After several months I moved to the Correspondence Department, managed by Terry Johnson. This work suited me, because I was now dealing with customers, albeit by correspondence. I was able to use the dictation skills I had learned at Towry Law, and in the days before the existence of word processors, this sometimes meant that quite lengthy letters would be dictated repeatedly, and never uninterestingly, several times a day. Pauline Brown was my unofficial secretary. She was one of several secretaries for three correspondents of whom I was one, with Miles and Bill Ramsbotham who had been with the company many years. Pauline, lets say preferred to work with me if she could. She was a bright and bubbly, unhappily married local girl about five years older than I, who, as was the fashion at the time, wore high heels and plenty of make-up and displayed an attractive, firm cleavage. Repeating already dictated paragraphs for similar letters with 'Polly' sitting in front or to the side of me was always fun. We worked well together and were known to get a lot of work completed.

In 1968 the company launched on a trial basis an innovative life assurance product linked to its unit trusts. Depending on policyholder age, a greater or smaller amount of each premium would pay for life coverage, with the balance being invested. A small direct sales team had been established in a branch office in Birmingham managed by Ian Gibson, a rather conscientiously active Scotsman, who normally lived in Tunbridge Wells. Ian reported to Frank Kearney, an Irishman who had previously worked for Canada Life, a direct sales-force life company. He was based at the Cornhill head office.

Kearney was a short, rotund, bouncy sort of guy, and although I didn't have much direct contact with him, he enthused people around him, was always on the move, and was never short of a word. The rumour was that he was having an affair with his secretary, an attractive dark-haired woman in her late twenties (name not recalled). This was almost certainly confirmed when Vicky, my first wife, and I were returning from a holiday in San Agustin, Majorca and found we were sharing a crowded Palma airport departure lounge with both of them and no Mrs Kearney in sight! Mr Kimber's words were applied!

Anyway, I was transferred from the Correspondence Department to a small new department to handle this new life insurance product. The knowledge of life assurance I had gained at Towry Law and my other customer-focussed skills were going to be useful in the new Customer Relations Department, which was also based at Gants Hill and was being managed by Roger Stearn, an accountant by training. Roger had taken over the office from Colin Hawtin who had been promoted to head office and later was to leave altogether to become one of the first employees of the nascent Financial Services Authority. At about the same time Miles, who had also been working there, was transferred to the Cornhill head office to work alongside George McGowan at the customer services desk. I sensed that Gants Hill might become a long-term pigeon hole, which worried me a little. I wasn't close to the centre of the action, and my two fellow trainees had made it to head office. This made me somewhat concerned at being located in a backwater, even though I was doing interesting work.

Within a few days of a trial sales team starting in Birmingham, Ian Gibson, the curly-headed Scotsman who was the manager of the branch there, appeared in the Gants Hill office clutching the first proposal form for the first sale. He had personally made the sale and quickly became extremely successful. He said he had brought the papers by train from Birmingham as he didn't trust the mail and to ensure it was all processed correctly and efficiently. Everybody was very excited. In the following years this innovative product was to be copied by other similar companies, and the unit-linked life assurance industry was born! They were very exciting times, even if I wasn't physically in the City. Anyway, the air was better out in the sticks, but commuting for over an hour took too long for my liking. On balance, I would have liked to be moved to head office in the City.

The only time I went to the City from Gants Hill was to spend sometimes several days each month with three other colleagues at British Linen Bank, later to become part of the Bank of Scotland in 1969, and later Lloyds Bank in 1999. British Linen Bank was one of the company's bankers and was the trustee for several of the trusts. The bank was located in Threadneedle Street, and we would check standing order payment slips for the amount being paid and for the correct insurance policy. The pink slips of paper were carbon copies of originals, showing the policy number, the amount paid, and the name of the policyholder. Sometimes these were difficult to decipher and had to be kept back for further scrutiny at the end of the day. They were difficult to read because the black carbon-backed paper used to copy the originally typed details onto two or more layers of paper with carbon paper in between each one would wear out, or the original typed impression hadn't been hard enough. It was extremely dull and repetitive work.

The company became keen to expand its innovative product range, and within a few further months I was summoned to St Helen's Place, just off Bishopsgate. This was Save & Prosper's head office. The building was connected to the offices of Robert Fleming & Co., a significant merchant bank that had a substantial equity stake in Save & Prosper; later it took over completely. The new white stone-faced building stood in a pedestrianised square in the shadow of the Commercial Union Tower, a brand new twenty-storey building that was to be demolished and replaced within thirty years. The building was slightly at odds with, St. Helen's, a 12th century church which contains more monuments than any other church in Greater London except Westminster Abbey. William Shakespeare worshipped there.

The head office reception area was manned by George McGowan and Nancy Haslam, both long-term servants of the company. They were both almost incapable of being flustered by people or circumstance, and they always provided an excellent welcome to all visitors. Anyway, I was to meet 'TME' – Mark Dunn.

Mark was Business Development Director and had the responsibility to do just that! He was in his early forties and travelled from Kent, where he lived in a Georgian terraced house in Wye and later in an Elizabethan manor house on the western outskirts of Canterbury. Typically, he wore a double-breasted grey dog-tooth three-piece suit with gold watch chain and breast pocket handkerchief or a flower freshly picked from the garden in his buttonhole. He carried a rolled umbrella but wore no bowler hat. He was quick mentally, an original and lateral thinker, cultured, and for me, thoroughly stimulating and motivational company. He had previously worked for Interpublic and Burston Marstellar, both huge worldwide PR companies. He had an astonishing ability to chair meetings effectively to an unwritten agenda using his public relations skills. I became his assistant and accompanied him to meetings inside and outside the office.

Working with the S&P's actuaries (Bacon & Woodrow), Mark decided that a unit-linked Personal Pension Plan (PPP) for the self-employed should be developed. It was a product way ahead of its time but one which we believed would, after initial doubts and bewilderment, prove to be successful. The structure of the product was significantly more complicated than unit-linked life assurance, as it not only had to create a pot of money at retirement age but it also had to produce a reasonably stable, possibly growing, income thereafter. I became involved with its development; again my perceived expertise or knowledge from Towry Law was a benefit. After several months of work the product was ready for launch, but how was it to be promoted? I prepared a manual presentation in a Nyrex folder with coloured charts, graphs, and tables to help convey how this technically complex product could meet the retirement pension needs of self-employed clients.

Part of the development process was to assess the likely competition. At the time Abbey Life was the most aggressive. This was a new life company established in 1961 by Mark Weinberg (later knighted) and others, of whom Mike Wilson was the most high-profile, being the City inspector promoting the company's unit-linked life products to City intermediaries. It had been a very successful company and received significant business from the likes of Towry Law and Julian Gibbs (more of JG later), who focussed on private individuals rather than on corporate business. Mark and Mike, however, both had only very small equity shareholdings in Abbey and foreseeing the growth in the business in years to come, both left and set up another company known as Hambros Life in 1971, with the backing of Hambros Bank, a leading merchant bank in which they would have a more significant investment and potential.

As part of the effort to monitor the competition, S&P had a Statistics Department. The manager was Mike Crosbie, a man in his late forties, with Mike Hockings (mid-twenties) as his assistant. They were ably helped by Jeannie, who later became Mrs Hockings. The company owned the minimum investment, typically £100, in all the competitors' funds it wanted to monitor. Crosbie was a true statistician, using sophisticated mathematical formulae to analyse fund data in depth using a slide rule and basic mathematical disciplines, which only became available more generally with the arrival of computers some twenty years later. He was a genial and understanding man, with a ready smile and twinkling eye. Hockings also was a true investment ideas man and later became editor of *Planned Savings*, the leading monthly publication for all personal investment and savings topics.

I was asked, when visiting insurance brokers, to assess how successful the new unit-linked business was. Abbey Life had been the pioneer, and after the management shake-up, to form Hambros Life, Mark was intrigued to know more about this new company. To this end, on one occasion I photographed documents on a broker's desk when he was called away. It all felt a bit surreal, if rather underhanded and dishonest or perhaps even unlawful. We were particularly interested to see how the brochures were laid out, because at the time the whole product concept was still very new, and Hambros seemed to have quickly become by far the most dominant player in the market.

Initially, and rather obviously, we decided to promote our pension plan to stockbrokers. They were largely attracted to the product for themselves, being usually classed as being self-employed, but also to suitable clients, not least because they would receive three per cent commission on premiums received, with a trail commission of one quarter of a per cent for five years based on the accumulated value, as well as reciprocal stock market brokering business on reaching agreed volume sales. This package of potential income compared to just one and a quarter per cent commission on unit trust sales.

Rather untypically for Mark, this ultimately important commission element of the process hadn't been thought through. Frank Kearney was unwilling to distract his growing network of sales offices and newly recruited salesmen with a significantly more complicated product. In addition PPP had a clearly defined, and in his view restricted, target audience (only self-employed people). In addition, the initial commission for the salesman wasn't as high, although in the longer run, with annual commissions, it paid more. He also argued that PPP was a competitive product to the life policy, which could provide a capital sum at retirement that could then be used to buy an annuity, albeit from another provider.

Mark's angle was simple. Having created the pot of money and being in the position of earning management fees from it, why then allow it to be transferred to a third party and so lose the income from management fees? I thought it was a no-brainer, but a marketing solution had to be found. It was.

We were able to find the appropriate, usually private client-focussed partner within each firm not by contacting the existing consultant force (mentioned below) who were generally un-cooperative towards my and the company's wishes, but by referring to the Stock Exchange Members'

Book. Getting hold of one of these was not easy as they were only issued to Stock Exchange members. My books were usually a year out of date and were passed on when the new annual edition was issued. Contact was then made by telephone.

Save & Prosper had for many years employed retired military officers to be regional consultants. Their job was to service agents (stockbrokers, insurance brokers, accountants, solicitors, and others) for their investment needs on behalf of their clients. The work carried a significant social element, with lunchtime entertaining high on the list of their duties. The City was obviously a plumb area to cover, and Brigadier Mellor was the man there. He and the other consultants across the United Kingdom reported to Ralph (RDG) Davidson (ex-Navy), who in turn reported directly to David Maitland, the managing director.

Between the field consultants of Davidson and Kearney's direct sales force – cold calling for business from a developing branch network – there was a separate office tucked away in a room overlooking an open atrium lined with white enamelled brick. In this room worked chalk-stripe-suited, legally minded, humourless, and quiet Graham Turner with Harry Verney, an old-Etonian, tall, slim, and naturally well-spoken albeit with a slight lisp. His family lived near Alton in Hampshire and was a direct relative of Florence Nightingale. He led a fairly frantic social life that included the organisation of the annual St Andrew's Ball at either the Grosvenor House Hotel or the Dorchester, a big social event in the London calendar.

The role of these two was to evaluate new ideas and assess market potential whilst discussing projects within the building with different departments. I didn't stay with them long, because the decision to proceed with the Personal Pension Plan was being taken, and I was to be the front man in the market place.

Davidson's view was that his army of consultants wouldn't want to become involved in promoting the Personal Pension Plan (PPP), just as they weren't involved with the life product, known as the Save, Insure, and Prosper Plan (SIP). The direct sales team was barred from visiting these professionals unless by approved invitation. Obviously, access to the professional agent market was paramount in obtaining sales, and it was decided that I should be the one to do this in collaboration with the existing regional consultants. It was a delicate balancing act, not to double-book appointments within days if not on the same day with key agents. It led to some frustrations on my side and some irritations elsewhere.

Things eventually came to a head. The old regional consultant force became less significant, and my developing and more product-knowledgeable team became the company's representative outfit. I recruited internally from the existing direct sales force, and in relatively quick time I was obtaining not just PPP business from stockbrokers and other agents' clients but individual and personal business from them as well. I took it upon myself to look after City stockbrokers and thoroughly enjoyed this development work and formed several good friendships. Additionally, I visited high street insurance brokers throughout the South-East.

One of the more unusual occurrences whilst I was working at S&P was an invitation from a broker in Hay Hill, Mayfair, who specialised in arranging business insurance cover for vending machines. Coincidentally, it was a small UK general insurance subsidiary of C.T. Bowring! The invitation was to the Annual Vending Machine Show held at the Grosvenor House Hotel in Park Lane. I decided to attend the show, in part because I wanted to show interest in the broker's core business. And who knows? I might have been able to promote PPPs to exhibiting companies for their staff. (At that time, this was an unusual concept, as most businesses with pension schemes offered Final Salary Schemes, while a few had Money Purchase Schemes). Also, I had little idea about the scale and scope of vending machines and what they could do.

The exhibition was held downstairs from the main lobby, and entrance was gained through revolving doors with glass panels. As I went to push on one of these, a very attractive brunette girl was exiting through the revolving door I had deliberately selected, and we 'clocked' each other, smiled, and each continued on our respective ways. For me to 'clock' anyone was completely out of character, but I was genuinely taken by this girl's looks, generous smile and diamond eyes.

I returned to my flat, having looked at machines that could dispense chips, chewing gum, drinks, chocolates – in fact almost anything that could fit into a good-sized handbag. The girl's face was imprinted on my mind, and I decided, again unusually for me and never repeated, to contact the show organisers to find out who she was, on which stand she could be found, and the telephone number to reach her at the show. My description of her was sufficient to get me answers.

I then had to decide whether I was going to try to contact her or not and just let the episode pass by. And anyway, why should a fabulously attractive girl want to meet up with someone like me, let alone talk over the phone to a stranger? Anyway, I did call her that afternoon when I had returned to my flat off Baker Street, reckoning that if I left it until the next day or later, she might have forgotten our glances through the glass revolving door.

Remarkably I got through to the exhibition stand, found out her name and asked to speak to her by name, Jennifer (Jenny) Lewis. Without much conversation she agreed to meet again the next day at the show. After the show closed, we got along fine, even though she had been Miss United Kingdom the previous year and second (or in beauty parade parlance, first runner-up) in Miss World and Miss Universe. What I learned over the next eighteen months about this business and about her world as a model and film actress was interesting and quite different from the world I knew. I admired her for her hard work, determination, and no-nonsense approach to her career. She had a small role in *On a Clear Day You Can See for Ever*, a feature film starring Barbara Streisand, which was partly filmed in Brighton, as well as in many fashion/couture photo-shoots with the likes of a young David Bailey.

On one occasion Jenny had a photo shoot with photographer, Mike Marchant, a friend of Willie Welch's, who was retained by Gulf Oil as their publicity photographer. Gulf Oil sponsored a racing car team which entered the Le Mans 24 hour race with a team of Ford GT40's, and won the race four years in succession. These had distinctive pale blue and orange paintwork. In 1969 the car won the race with Jacky Ickx being one of the drivers. He was a rather good looking Belgian, who invited us both to Brands Hatch for a day of testing. Jenny and I went together but I came home alone …

One of the interesting things about calling at different offices was to observe how visitors were greeted. It wasn't at all unusual to arrive and find the receptionist was also the telephonist, operating from a small, booth-like office without natural light near the front door, where cold drafts of wind would circulate from the street outside. Almost invariably women, they would speak to visitors through a sliding glass window.

Often the booth would be smoke-filled. The receptionist would be facing a panel of holes and cables, each with a jack plug at its end which would be inserted to give a line to an outgoing caller. This would then light up a red bulb, but it would have to be tugged out at the end of a call when the red light turned green.

Considerable dexterity was needed to ensure that people wanting a line to make a telephone call could have one and that no cables were left inserted a second longer than necessary. Occasionally the receptionist would be asked to dial a number (literally dialling a number on a rotating wheel) for some office big-wig, and when the call had been connected, the cables would be attached and the call 'put through'. At busy times these boards, which were positioned vertically in front of the operator, looked to be a complete jumble of leads and wires, but somehow the operator knew what was going on and occasionally would pull several cables from the board with great skill in a complete rush, only for them to all fall into individual holes in a shelf where they rested until being flicked out and inserted again.

In addition to this work, the telephonist/receptionist might also be the telex operator, or at least the telex operator would be in the same room. Their work was both to receive and send telex messages on rolls of paper about one inch wide onto which holes had been punched which corresponded to letters of the alphabet. All these had to be read and then distributed. The work appeared to get busier as the day went on, so that when most offices closed at 5:30 or 6:00 p.m. there was invariably a stampede to get work done.

A leading insurance broker of the time, Julian Gibbs & Co., referred to earlier, offered a similar upmarket approach to clients as Towry Law. Getting an appointment to see Julian was extremely difficult, busy as he was with his business and writing a weekly column in the Saturday *Daily Telegraph*, in which the company advertised, and doing occasional broadcasts. On one occasion Julian invited me to lunch at his home in Trevor Square just off Knightsbridge. I duly arrived and climbed the small staircase to the front door of the elegant Georgian four-storey townhouse. To my initial surprise, the door was opened by a butler dressed in black waiter attire who was almost the same colour as the clothes he was wearing. I couldn't but help be taken aback, not only at this but the entire set-up. Julian, quietly spoken and not in the least ostentatious personally, and I dined alone in an elegant room from beautiful glass and china. The food and wines equalled the ambience and were served by a waitress and another butler.

Some other intermediaries specialising in pensions were visited outside London. Wilfrid T. Fry, founded in 1898 in Worthing where Graham Banks and John Elkins were the leading lights, offered an excellent service; they had a link with ex-servicemen's associations. Noble Lowndes in Croydon and Lowndes Lambert in the City also gave excellent new business support.

Another recollection was the variety of lifts encountered. Few buildings were more than five storeys high. In the larger office buildings, it wasn't unusual for the lift to be controlled by a lift man or operator. Not infrequently, these men were from the Corps of Commissionaires and wore an Army-blues type of uniform with a white Marines-style peaked cap. They would smoke whether they were operating or not, in or out of the lift. These men would open and close sliding concertina metal doors that looked similar to garden trellis. You would board through a 'trellis' metal door which had been moved to the side (or sometimes two which parted in the middle) and ask the lift-man to take you to the company you were visiting, and away the lift would go, each floor passing by inches away just through the expanded metal of the folding doors. The lift man would know all the companies in his building and more often than not everyone who worked there.

In smaller buildings, some lifts without operators had the same door mechanism, but you would operate it yourself. In others, movement up or down was achieved by pulling on a thick rope in the corner of the lift cabin. You stopped by having first pressed a button to the floor required on a usually highly polished brass panel before yanking on the rope to get 'lift off'. These lifts could sometimes be fitted in out-of-the-way places on the ground floor. They could be very small and were not necessarily square. I recall a triangular lift at the offices of McAnally Montgomery, stockbrokers, in Queen Victoria Street.

The final part of my time at Save & Prosper from late 1968 was spent in a branch office of the direct sales force in High Holborn, which was managed by Stuart Frystone. He had a sales team of about fifteen people of all ages and backgrounds. One of the best branch salesmen was Raoul de Rohan, who claimed that his family had invented the wooden pencil in Czechoslovakia, which was a good story but untrue! He was a keen skier and was involved with the Ski Club of Great

Britain, spending annual vacations in smart Swiss ski resorts, including Zermatt where his family had a chalet.

Another memorable salesman in Stuart's office was a short upright man, Harold Margolis. Harold was a charming Jew, always smartly dressed and smiling. He was invariably the top salesman of the week or month, and consequently because a salesman's salary was wholly commission based after their initial salary had been tapered off had been exhausted, was the best paid. He regarded his job as providing a social need or benefit. He cold-called relentlessly, found reasons why saving in a life assurance policy would benefit the customer and then sold the policy like crazy. He was a great example to the branch salesmen – especially the younger ones who sometimes only took the job whilst looking for another one.

My position in the office was rather irregular, as my work was totally different from that of the direct sales force, although there was a time when it was thought that some of the salesmen could be deployed within national department stores to promote investment centres which I would manage. This thought was way ahead of its time, but the company was unable to allocate anything like the resources and support necessary to make it work. A few futile attempts were made, but the salesmen regarded being in a store for a few hours as rather a waste of their time compared to their usual activity of cold calling and developing their client base in an area that suited them. This area was known as a 'patch', and it was supposed to be exclusive to one salesman, not to be trespassed on by others.

Stuart and I became good friends, and I spent several weekends near Marden in Kent where he lived happily with his wife, going to several, almost Bacchanalian, parties. I was enjoying bachelorhood to the full. 'Soss' James became a good weekend friend who lived nearby and introduced me to a wide circle of her mostly married country-living friends. Dame Edith Evans lived in a large house opposite Soss's cottage.

However, at work I wasn't happy being out of the swim of things in High Holborn away from head office. It looked as if the company had decided I had found my niche developing sales for the Personal Pension Plan and had no need to be near or in head office. I began to get unsettled and wanting to move on. My wish was partly fulfilled by being recalled to the City to work from Dashwood House in Old

Broad Street. Here I could liaise more easily with head office personnel at St. Helen's Place with my product development work: but there was surprise in store!

As a sad footnote to this experience with Save & Prosper and despite all this innovation and dynamism, the company was sold several times by a succession of owners from 2000. It had stopped issuing new business in 1998. Following various mergers and takeovers Save & Prosper unit trust funds were, re-branded as JP Morgan Fleming, later JP Morgan Asset Management. In December 2010, Chesnara plc announced that it had completed the acquisition of the business which then totally disappeared from view. On reflection it is an example of how established City names were to evaporate over the following years, either through poor management as in S&P's case, or opportunities created by new City regulation and legislation.

Chapter 4

'Go-Go' Days!

In mid-1969 Mark Dunn, very unexpectedly, left S&P to join a relatively new City business, Slater, Walker Securities Ltd. I was more than surprised, but my work had taken me away from him on a daily business as I had begun to report to Ralph Davidson. I felt secure being pretty much my own boss for the first time and happy to manage my time from my new office in Dashwood House. It was a typical pre-war, possibly even Victorian, rabbit warren of an office building whose public areas were decorated with ceramic tiles of white and very unattractive patterned greens and browns. The public area floors and staircases were covered with green flecked linoleum, and bare light bulbs hung from long electric flexes from high ceilings within the narrow passageways.

One evening in January 1970 I was at my Melcombe Street flat, just off Baker Street and opposite the Tube station, when I received a telephone call from Mark asking me if I would like to join him at Slater, Walker. SW had by this time launched a couple of unit trusts, INVAN (an abbreviation for 'Investment Analysis'), known in the vernacular of the time as a 'go-go' capital growth trust, and the Slater, Walker Unit Trust, an accumulation fund. 'Go-go' funds were in vogue because a few had achieved remarkable capital growth in relatively short periods of management. INVAN was the leader of this group and both the SW funds had established outstanding capital growth performances.

Mark was again Development Director for the investment management subsidiary of this publicly quoted secondary bank. Mark offered me a significant salary increase to around £1,500 per annum and the opportunity to join the business at an early stage and likely to be going places. It all sounded almost too good to be true, but after a few days' reflection I decided that SW didn't offer the established institutional security I had enjoyed at Bowrings or Save & Prosper, so I declined.

A few months later Mark called again to repeat his offer. He asked me to reconsider but told me that there would be no changes to the original offer. This time I accepted. In retrospect, I think the extra few months had given me the opportunity to look at likely career developments where I was. I had come to believe that I could possibly stay for really quite a long time as so many of my colleagues had done and not progress very far. I preferred to think that there would be some more dynamism at SW. I wasn't yet married, so I could reasonably afford not to take the safer option. There was also the possibility of again being relocated out in the Essex sticks if I stayed!

By the time I joined Slater, Walker Investments in April 1970, the company's banking business was already involved in corporate finance, private banking, and property. The investment management company was physically separate from all the other activities, but we did receive visits from the bank and property divisions. One of these, I recall, was by a rather smooth-talking and smooth-looking man, Greville Howard (a grandson of the seventeenth Earl of Suffolk), who, it later transpired, was a close friend of Lord Lucan. Lucan disappeared in 1974 in mysterious surroundings after murdering his housemaid in their house in Eaton Terrace, apparently instead of his wife. The wife escaped with some injuries. Howard would later become Baron Howard of Rising after donating large sums to the Conservative Party, but not until after he had been private secretary to Enoch Powell and later PA to Sir James Goldsmith, who was to become Chairman of Slater, Walker in 1972.

The company would soon also enter the life assurance industry, initially in the UK, and later still would have a Guernsey-based life assurance company run by Arthur Pierce, a Bahamian actuary. The main focus of the business was investment in its broadest sense. Getting fees for managing assets was what the business was ultimately all about. These fees, enhanced by some judicious trading of stocks and shares on the company's account, gained the company a huge popular following, which in some ways became a self-feeding success story. The company monitored, perhaps even manipulated, its own share price closely and daily.

With a salary of £1,500, I joined Mark at SW in their offices in London Wall Buildings. Working with Mark was great fun and stimulating. We sometimes lunched at the Travellers Club in Pall Mall, which was the first of many eye-opening experiences my career would introduce me to from that point on. The managing director was Jim Nichols, and Brian Banks was investment director. Both were formerly Messel's stockbrokers and were primarily responsible for the investment and administration of investment portfolios, including unit trusts. Eric Farrell was dealing director and Alan Maidment financial director. It was a small department of about twenty people.

I was to work alongside Christopher Neville, who had read Music at university. He had joined earlier in the year from EMI, where he had been PA to the company chairman, Sir Joseph Lockwood. EMI, a major British multinational music recording and publishing business, was about as remote from being a financial services business as possible.

Although very personable, he almost inevitably had no knowledge of the City, its traditions, or of the industry he now found himself in. In many ways this was probably part of his appeal to the stockbrokers he and I were going to visit, just as I had been doing at Save & Prosper. We divided the country as equally as we could, each having a number of City stockbroker firms as our core clientele. In addition Chris took the North-West and South-West, while I took on the Midlands, Scotland, and Wales. We each were given a company car: Chris, a yellow 2000E Ford Cortina MkII with a black vinyl roof, and I, for some reason, a 1600E navy blue one, later replaced with a dark metallic green Cortina Mkll two-litre version with a black vinyl roof.

Mark's ability to think outside the box was shown one day when M&G (the oldest unit trust management company, founded in the 1930s) launched a public offering for a split-level investment trust. These investment vehicles were rarely offered, but essentially they offered investors a choice between receiving either income or capital growth. The income shares entitled investors to most (or all) of the income generated from the assets of the trust until the wind-up date (usually ten years from launch), with some capital protection. The capital shares on the other hand entitled investors to most (or all) of the remaining assets after prior ranking share classes had been paid; this was a very high risk. Mark's idea was to subscribe for the whole offering of income shares, which would be invested in the Slater, Walker High Income Trust, effectively removing any investment management in that holding to M&G who had an excellent reputation in this area. Needless to say, our investment managers were not enthused and didn't support the somewhat opportunistic idea!

Mark enjoyed his lunches to discuss his ideas. His favourites included Sweetings (usually on a Friday for fish), the Jamaica Inn, and the George and Vulture, all long-established restaurants serving classic English menus. Barrington House in Aldermanbury and his club, the Travellers in Pall Mall, were other places where he could go for more discreet meetings. When not eating out, he'd have lunch in the directors' board room – more of this later – to which I and a few others of my rank would occasionally be invited to attend or bring guests.

Soon after joining SW, my life began to take on a new dimension, both career-wise and socially. Through John Dyson I had met a number of City professionals, one of whom was Derek Lidstone, a stockbroker – the first I ever knew. Derek drove an Aston Martin DB3. He and I met occasionally either in Coates Wine Bar in London Wall or in Gows, another wine bar in Old Broad Street at lunch times. On one occasion he asked me attend a party in Albert Court Mansions in Knightsbridge adjacent to the Royal Albert Hall. The party was for the twenty-first birthday of Judith, granddaughter of the recently retired *Times* editor, William Haley.

One of the discussions at the party was about Poseidon, an Australian gold mining company whose share price was rocketing. I had never heard of the company, but it transpired that SW held a large holding in the company in one of its unit trusts, which was consequently attracting a good deal of positive publicity and from which a large investment profit was made. I felt comfortable and encouraged to think I was joining a team of winners!

After years in the planning and public preparation, the United Kingdom decimalised its currency in February 1971. Strangely, London Transport and British Rail started using the new arrangements on the fourteenth and the rest of the country's businesses a day later. It was the only time there seemed to be plenty of inspectors at the entry points of the Underground. Baker Street, which was my departure point now, being the location for several London Transport offices, operated smoothly; the ticket machines all displayed the new decimalised fares and everything was going well.

Nobody seemed to have much difficulty in understanding that a pound would now have one hundred 'new' pence as opposed to 240 'old' pence. For a time prices were known as 'new pee'. 5p, for example, was equivalent to 1/- (a shilling), and for a while all prices were shown in both old and new currency. It wasn't uncommon however for people to question why prices seemed to be being rounded up, rather than down when converting old to new prices, thus creating artificial price inflation.

In the autumn of 1971 I bought a three-bedroom detached house at 8 Byng Road, Tunbridge Wells from David White, a colleague at Slater, Walker for £8,250. He had moved just a few streets away to a larger property. I travelled by train (usually getting a seat) to London Bridge. As with the Underground, people could smoke throughout the train, and only later were specific smoking coaches introduced which were always filled with the fog of smoke.

Once a week I drove to London and parked at the HAC in City Road so that I could drive home after practice with the HAC band, which I had joined from school playing the French horn. Invariably, I would pick up a colleague, Alan Page from his flat in Beckenham. He was a keen Beckenham Hockey Club player, who knew of my mate from HYELM Willie Welch, a county standard player who played for Spencer, another leading club based in Tooting. Alan was a thoroughly good guy, and I enjoyed his helpful business and social company greatly. He also knew a route through south-east London which avoided much of the Old Kent Road and other bottle necks to get us over Tower Bridge with minimum delays.

Long before all the regional stock exchanges in the United Kingdom were amalgamated into one, I set myself the challenge to visit as many of them as I could. Most of the regional markets in such places as Birmingham, Cardiff, Manchester, Glasgow, Edinburgh, and Belfast were wood-panelled and were to be found within red-brick Victorian buildings. They all reeked of local history, pipe smoke, and enterprise. I would base myself for the Birmingham and Manchester visits at the Slater, Walker's bank's offices, which in both cases were in majestic Victorian office buildings once owned by the Bank of England.

One of the characters In Manchester was Geoff Ashworth, a partner in Ashworth Sons & Barrett, a local stockbroking firm. Geoff knew Jim Slater, and his firm was used for company share dealing away from the London market. Meetings always took place in his 'other office' – a rather good restaurant where he was a regular and known to all the attractive waitresses on first-name terms.

In Birmingham the senior partner of Smith Keen Barnett, a large stockbroking firm, was Anthony Beaumont-Dark, later knighted, who was outspoken about pretty much everything, including immigration, South African apartheid, Roman Catholicism, contraception, and much else. When he became a Member of Parliament in 1979, he became a notorious backbencher. He made his mark by suggesting that the half-penny (0.5p) piece should be dropped as coinage as it was costing more to make than to use. One of the consequences of this was that a second-class postage stamp went from 12.5p to 13p, but other prices were rounded down! It was helpful that he was a friend of Peter Walker, the 'Walker' in Slater, Walker and also a Tory MP, for the amount of business he could place with SW.

The old London Stock Exchange in Throgmorton Avenue, with it hexagonal 'pitches' and open dealing system, was to disappear itself in the 1970s with the arrival of 'Big Bang'. Prior to this, I would occasionally visit the glass-fronted visitors' gallery to look down on the dealing activity – not all of it serious. Many a time someone would play a practical joke on an unsuspecting member, usually after lunch. One's newspaper might be set of fire as one read it, or occasionally a de-bagging might take place for some 'offence'. One day after lunch, I walked across the Floor myself, as a challenge from one of my stockbroker friends. I dreaded the thought of being caught and either being given a figurative or quite possibly a literal dressing down as a 'stranger'. This word would be shouted out by anyone on the Floor if they suspected such a person, and business would come to a halt whilst the offender was suitably treated. I survived intact!

Slater's investment business began to grow, and in 1971 we all moved to Leith House in Gresham Street, on the corner with Wood Street. My office initially was on the third floor, which was an open-plan space, but with the dealing director, Eric Farrell, and his assistants, Bob Dellow and Rick, sharing a glass-partitioned section at one end. Theirs was a busy office with multiple stock market price screens, telephone handsets, flashing console lights, and constant talking to the markets. Jim Slater was often on the line giving instructions and checking deals. The company stockbroker was Joseph Sebag & Co., and it was very apparent that they shared enormous confidences with our dealers in building and unwinding investment positions in companies. Later I moved to the top (fifth) floor, a bright and airy office which I shared with Roger Porter, manager of the private clients' section and ex-Sebags private client portfolio manager, Martyn Page, and Alan Page.

I enjoyed building relationships with my professional contacts. One such was with a firm called Foster & Braithwaite in Throgmorton Avenue. My contact was Richard Luffman, a good looking man with a ruddy face as if from taking long country walks, who was seemingly always happy and laughing. I attended his wedding to a very attractive Guatemalan girl in Norfolk where he had grown up, and where his parents still lived. Richard was to discover she had an affair within a couple of years and shot himself. We used to enjoy many a lunch in Bow Wine Vaults in Bow Lane, where in 1974 he and I constructed a £1,500 portfolio of 15 sector-leading stocks when the stock market was flat on its back. Had I actually made the investment then, I would have become extremely rich indeed – one of several financial opportunities that either didn't go my way or that I failed to take in life. A colleague of his was Michael Savory, an amiable, extremely bright, if intense young man who was always keen to do and give business. He later became Lord Mayor of London.

Derek Greenwood, a private client partner at Teather & Greenwood, stockbrokers, was another interesting contact. T&G were specialist brokers to many privately owned water companies. His repeated view in the early 1970s was that these companies were a 'steal', meaning that they were cheap and paid good dividends and that it was only a matter of time before they'd be consolidated into a relatively small number of regional water boards and make substantial capital gains. Between 1974 and 1985, the water industry consisted of ten state-owned regional water authorities that supplied three quarters of England and Wales, and twenty-nine privately owned statutory water companies. The ten water authorities were privatised in December 1989 after the introduction of a new regulatory framework. The process, part of Margaret Thatcher's privatisation programme, netted billions to the Exchequer, along with other utility asset privatisations. I never had the resources to benefit from this revolution in managing the country's affairs!

Another good chum was Fred Carr, a stockbroker at Capel Cure Myers, based on Holborn Viaduct. Fred was a larger-than-life character and an Oxford rowing blue. He and Robin Boyle, also a member of his firm who later went to Hoare Govett to set up a specialist fund advisory service, were two of the first truly knowledgeable experts on unit trusts I met, and I embraced them. They appreciated that their firm would receive investment business from us, not necessarily just for the investment of monies invested in our funds they had bought (to keep our investment ideas at least reasonably disguised), but that there would be reciprocal business too, and so they would build their commission income.

In the summer of 1971 Fred was to meet up with Vicky, later my first wife, and me at a house we were renting with another couple, Dawn and Jeremy North. The house overlooked Cassis, a few miles to the east of Marseilles and famous for its *callanque* cliff scenery. Vicky found Fred's personality and looks very attractive. He had driven from England via Aix-en-Provence in a Mini. We had a few hilarious hours before Fred disappeared towards Monte Carlo. He and his Oxford companions bought a post card of a local scene and posted it to the Bishop of Worcester. He said he did this every year, not because he knew the Bishop, but because it was a harmless prank they had started while up at Oxford which he hoped provided the Bishop with some annual amusement and intriguing interest.

Fred became quite a figure in the City. He spent his career in stockbroking and investment management, ultimately (from 1993 to 2004) as chief executive of Carr Sheppards Crosthwaite, a big stockbroking house. This company was a merger (a phenomenon created by 'Big Bang' mentioned later) of three significant stockbroking companies, W.I. Carr, Shepherds and Chase, and Henderson Crossthwaite – all old established businesses. He later became chairman of a number of investment trusts, as well as a consultant to Investec Bank (UK) Limited.

Two more good contacts were Roy Williams, known as the Mad Major, a stock jobber with Pinchin Denny, and Robert 'Bob' Tipping, a stockbroker with L. Messel & Co. Roy was a lover of all things Spanish and in many ways looked and strutted his way about like a bull-fighter.

He had a very straight back and would throw back his head *paso doble* style and had a sidling walk. He and Robert were pretty inseparable and always had lunch together in the Long Room, a Joe Lyons restaurant in Throgmorton Street opposite the London Stock Exchange. They both lived near Abridge, a small village in Essex, and were snappy dressers and rather smooth looking. We were all about the same age (in our early to mid-twenties), and the two of them seemed to spend most of their waking hours testing each other on current stock prices and dealing sizes.

Usually when we met for a convivial lunch, several G & T's were quaffed in the Long Room, followed by a good steak, salad, and chips. There would be frequent interruptions at the table by other diners, all of whom were from the 'market'. Ginge was one, a more senior jobber in the same firm as Roy, who commuted from Herne Bay, close to my parents' home in Chislet.

I attended a house-warming weekend at a thatched country cottage Roy bought later near Bishop's Stortford. It was an attractive typical 'Essex pink' colour washed, hundreds of years old, timber-framed building surrounded by a garden and orchard. We saw a preproduction Concorde fly over on a test flight, beautiful but noisy – the first time most of us had seen one. That evening we had an excellent barbecue and danced the night away to the Four Tops and the Beach Boys. We all slept on bare floor boards, in sleeping bags. I had taken a girl there for the weekend, Mary Drayson, the daughter of a partner of Greenwells, a large firm of stockbrokers where Graham Stewart, who made up this stock market threesome, worked. We had paired up for the night, but there were no fireworks!

Roy surprised us in the morning by providing sledgehammers, pick-axes, and spades with the request to knock down some internal walls. We had no idea whether the ones he wanted down were load-bearing or not, so we happily set to. We presumed the house wasn't listed, although it might well have been, it was so old! We left in the early afternoon with the house still standing. My relationship with Mary ended soon afterwards, but not before I was invited to her parents' house for lunch one Saturday in Sunningdale. Everything was elegant and comfortable, as would be expected: beautiful china, lovely traditional furniture, and so on. The one exception, which Mary's mother apologised for, was that the cream to put on the strawberries was in a carton which hardly matched the fine silverware.

Graham had an attractive sister named Annabel who worked at Belinda Belleville, a top dress designer just off Sloane Avenue, in Pavilion Road, SW3. (Her business later merged with David Sassoon's to be known as Belville-Sassoon and designed many dresses for Diana, Princess of Wales.) Annabel was a petite, bubbly, busty girl. Several times a group of us – John Dyson, Roy Williams, Graham Stewart, and our current girlfriends – would go to the Garrison night club at the bottom of Park Lane near the Dorchester to dance the night away. Later we would move on to the Black Sheep Club in Shepherds Lane to round things off. It was all way out of my league, but somehow I managed to keep my end up.

Most stockbroker firms at the time (the late 1960s and early 1970s) did not accept the unit trust concept and believed they could provide even quite low-value clients with a spread of investments outside a unit trust 'wrapper' and could earn commission on switching clients' monies from time to time. They conducted their business from sometimes quite gentile surroundings. In winter, the partners of a small two-partner firm at one end of the scale, Davey & Candy, in Throgmorton Avenue, would sit in small offices on large leather chairs in front of blazing coal fires, which were regularly topped up by staff. At the other end of the scale, L. Messel, a large firm with probably forty partners, was based in a centrally heated and air-conditioned new tower, Winchester House in London Wall. They would have afternoon tea and freshly made sandwiches and cakes served every afternoon in their 'Partners Room' on a high floor with great views out over the City.

In addition to my basic work as a rep, I was responsible for calculating fund performances and their relative daily and annual performance against various indices. I gave these to Brian Banks and Jim Nicholls each day. Another colleague, Chris Poll, was also consulted about competitor funds' performances. This later became such an involved activity that he left Slaters and set up a company which undertook to monitor the performance of all unit trusts against themselves and major indices. The company, Micropal, became by far and away the largest and most important fund performance measurement service and the benchmark against which subsequent competitor services would be judged. When it was sold to Morningstar, a US funds research company, Chris made millions.

There was significant growth at this time in putting investment management information onto computer screens – particularly stock market information for stockbrokers and investment managers. Almost all computers were made by IBM. They were bulky battleship-grey objects that sat on the desks of the dealers. Everyone else was using paper and pencil or pen for routine clerical and administrative work. Some of the dealers had two screens to look at showing different sectors or market information. The substantial cost of these computers was paid for by giving stockbrokers business on which they received commission – known as 'soft payments'. In fact 'soft commissions' was commonplace for the payment of stockbrokers' company research and other services.

The idea of using screens to get information to the public also began to develop. Through one of my stock-broking contacts, Hoare Govett, I was asked to look at a service called Ceefax (homonymous with "See Facts"). This showed information on a series of standard television screens, accessed by inputting a three-figure number from a menu page, which would then make the screen scroll through to show that page. I visited their offices in Finsbury Circus and was both intrigued and impressed. They were looking for capital to build and expand the business. Slaters declined the offer and opportunity. It was an early forerunner of how TV channel and page selection would become, and it remained a useful and popular service for everyone, investment professionals and public alike, (from 1974 until 2012 when it closed with the arrival of digitisation), who wanted to look up any current information, from sports to news, without using the Internet which had started from small beginnings in 1990.

With Mark I also became involved with the advertising of 'fixed-price offers' for funds in the weekend newspapers. Ideally we wanted 'page dominant' bottom right-hand spaces. This meant that the advertisement had to be fifteen inches high and six columns wide. In those days it was possible to invite investors to subscribe for units by filling in a coupon and sending it to us with a cheque for the amount being invested at a predetermined price. This was what was known as a fixed-price offer.

Some newspapers were printed on more absorbent paper than others, which could be detrimental to the effectiveness of the advertisement in that paper, because fountain pink ink would splodge or run. The Express group newspapers were the worst, and because of their huge circulations of several million, advertising there cost a lot. Sometimes we would use less successful papers simply to obtain visibility. We knew that people often took several weekend papers and one of them could do the trick and produce a result. All of this was closely monitored. One of the roles of the advertising agent was to get as much space-buying discount as possible. Generally, advertising in the *Daily Telegraph* produced the best results, followed by the *Sunday Times*, the *Observer*, and the *Times*. The *Daily Mail* also sometimes did well. The mass circulation papers such as *The News of the World* or the *Sunday Express* were never economic despite huge readership in the millions.

We absorbed any increase or decrease in underlying unit price up to a limit. Invariably we had built up a book of 'old' units from investors who had sold out, which would be resold to new investors responding to our advertising. This became a very profitable activity. If these were all sold, 'new' units would be created at a back-dated unit price of up to three trading days (if the market had risen in the meantime), which again made more profit. With SW's successful investment results and reputation it was not uncommon for several million pounds to be received through the post for investment in response, and within days, to a weekend's campaign.

When Mark Dunn had departed he set up the London Document Exchange with Henry Seymour. Henry was also employed at the company's advertising agents, Mitfords, which was based near the Old Bailey. It was known as Mitfords because the chairman was Lord 'Clem' Redesdale, who was related to the Mitford sisters. Clem's role was not too significant, as he spent most of his time in the House of Lords or having children. He had seven! He was as friendly and 'ordinary' a man as you could wish to meet. On one occasion whilst driving from Edinburgh to London, I stopped for dinner and overnight accommodation at the Percy Arms Hotel a rather run-of-the mill hotel in Otterburn, near his family home in Northumberland. To my amazement, Clem and his wife Sarah were also having dinner there. His estates are in that area, and he couldn't have been more charming and interested in what I had been doing in the area (Territorial Army duties). He later became a vice-president of Chase Manhattan Bank in London.

The London Document Exchange was a typically innovative Mark concept, and eventually he sold out for a large sum. When it was first established, it provided a way for solicitors, for whom it was originally designed, to take and collect documents daily for other firms at a central point in secure lockable document safes without using the Royal Mail. The first two were in Leadenhall Market and Chancery Lane. Members paid a fee, and the service took off. Its success attracted other types of professions to join in; in a matter of months 'DXs' were being established all over the country. It continues to operate in the UK and internationally and is not now solely confined to the legal profession.

With Mark gone and Christopher established in a branch office in Murray Square, Edinburgh (which I had identified on one of my visits to Edinburgh stockbrokers), I became responsible for advertising and printing. Typically, either Brian Banks or Jim Nicholls would say on a Monday or Tuesday morning, sometimes after a conversation with Jim Slater (the company's founder, chairman, and investment guru), that we should run an advertisement for one of the funds or from time to time launch a new fund. If it was an existing fund, a plausible sales message would have to be drafted and approved by all three of these directors. It would then have to be approved by the fund's trustee, National Westminster Trustees, and the finally by Wilf Burnett, an ex-RAF squadron leader.

Burnett ran a small office as secretary of the AUTM – Association of Unit Trust Managers, in Finsbury Circus. The AUTM was our industry regulator. Burnett's office never seemed occupied by more than him and his secretary. Consequently, I was never sure whether he personally vetted and approved every member's publications, and advertisements before publication or not, (or referred them to another party). He was always well versed in what was permitted, how best the sales message could be expressed (sometimes in conflict with what had been agreed elsewhere), and to offer suggestions and advice. How he would fit in with the demands of today's financial regulators can only be guessed at!

Whilst this approval process was underway, the advertisement had to be drafted and space booked within an agreed budget with the national weekend papers. We used a specialist, four-partner advertising agency close to the Old Bailey now owned by Nick Royds. Royds was an international yachtsman, and keen Sunningdale golfer who had bought the Mitfords business. Henry Seymour, who lived in Hyde Park Square, and whose mother had been a lady in waiting to Queen Elizabeth, the Queen Mother, was responsible for buying space; Tim Miller, who lived in mansion block of flats in Islington, was an enthusiastic rally car driver and copywriter; Mike Selvey was designer; and Claire a delightful, funny, petite, attractive and unhappily married secretary, living in Harrow, was a general dog's body cum secretary. Sadly, Tim died some years later in his Caterham 7 at Brands Hatch racing circuit.

We all got on fantastically well. Meetings were frequent, focussed, dynamic and productive, and usually led to significant profits. The style adopted was simple. A reverse-type company name strap line would appear at the top. Tim and I would draft a sales message in a large font, followed by a succinct rationale for why investment was justified. Then approval would be sought from by Brian Banks, Jim Nicholls and finally Jim Slater, who would often have ultra-prescient comments to make. Occasionally, Tim and one or more of his colleagues and I would lunch, usually at the Coal Hole, a Davy's wine bar opposite Chancery Lane in High Holborn, which was also close to new offices they had moved to from Limeburner Street near the Old Bailey. Our usual lunchtime drink was a bottle of Dopft, a Gewurztraminer white wine from Alsace, to accompany our standard choice of pork or game pie and salad.

I occasionally had lunch with Henry, usually at the Turf Club in Pall Mall. Henry was also a racehorse owner whose trainer, Guy Harwood, was based in Pulborough. I can't remember one occasion when I didn't come face to face with the Duke of Norfolk, the Queen's uncle, in the high ceilinged bar surrounded by marvellous equine paintings. The Duke would be seated in a rather slumped way on a long red sofa with his companions with pre-lunch cocktails to hand. Henry was always full of good-spirited fun and useful beyond measure in establishing personal friendships whilst getting the job done successfully.

By Thursday evening prior to a weekend advertisement appearing, the advertisement copy had to have been approved by all parties and had to be ready to be sent by the advertising agents, who would have advised us by then how best to spend our budget in the selected newspapers that would be carrying the advertisement. There it would be set in hot metal for proofs to be seen and approved on Friday morning. There was no leeway for making amendments at that stage or for the advertisements to be 'pulled' (not printed) in the selected Saturday and Sunday papers.

Many a Thursday night was spent in a pub waiting for first proof blocks to be made by the newspapers for us to approve before the printing presses rolled.

It could all be quite stressful, to say the least. Nobody could afford to hold up the process at any point unless for some unavoidable reason. First-time accuracy was essential at each stage. Occasionally, of course, things didn't go well for one reason or another – especially when units were being offered at a fixed price that couldn't be held because of market movements.

Jim Slater was an interesting man. He commuted from a private gated housing estate in Esher. He had founded the business with the MP, Peter Walker, later to become Lord Walker. They started the business in Hertford Street in Mayfair in the late 1960s, later moving to a 1960s office block (Petershill House) in St Paul's Churchyard. Jim occupied a spacious but sparsely furnished office on the first floor overlooking the square. He would hold meetings there with a window always open and without central heating regardless of the weather outside. On occasion it was quite cold, but he would say, 'We make our own heat in here.' And that was that. He also had total intolerance for pencil tapping or anything else that he found distracting to his very intense and focussed concentration on the job in hand.

The building had a health club in the basement which I visited several times a week, primarily for its sun-bed and sauna and also because sandwiches and cold drinks were provided free of charge. I usually went with Bob Dellow, a practical joker and, like Brian and Jim, an enthusiastic golfer. He was a few years older than me and worked as Eric Farrell's assistant in the dealing room. He was known to fancy the pants off almost any girl in a skirt, and his reputation on all fronts was significant! The facilities were overseen by a white-suited manager who could provide massages and, it was said, had been employed by Cunard on the *QE2*. He was called into action one day when Bob and I had a sun-bed session during which one of the extremely hot bulbs fell onto my left testicle, where it seemed to weld itself to my skin. Bob thought it was the funniest thing he had seen and fell about laughing while I was terror struck! The health club manager assisted in prying the thin glass from my body, leaving a very pink and delicate area which he smothered with some cream or lotion.

When Slater, Walker ran into difficulties in the secondary banking crisis of 1972 and was 'saved' by the Bank of England's 'lifeboat' scheme, the bank and most of its other operations were cut back, but the *raison d'être* for the whole enterprise, investment management, was retained in full. At this time it was an almost everyday occurrence for one or other of the golfers in our office – all senior employees – to produce a putting machine. A putting competition would then be held, usually lasting hours throughout the afternoon. The winner could choose the distance to be putted, and it was common to have rolling golf balls run the twenty-plus yards of the carpeted office. Favoured members of staff would join in.

On one of these idle days the National Trust came up for discussion, and Brian suggested I ought to join. I thought about it for a while. At £240 or so, it seemed it a bit out of my range. On the other hand, a life time's membership at this price might not be such a bad thing with a family possible in my future. So I joined and received a silver medallion and a membership card – a green folding card covered in faux-leather. It was one of the best things I have ever bought, and I have subsequently given life memberships to family members – but for rather more money than mine cost!

One of the favoured members of staff was Annie Mackie, who was employed as the directors' boardroom cook. She was trained at *Le Cordon Bleu* and provided three-course lunches daily, often with wine for the directors and invited guests. Occasionally I would be allowed to invite stockbrokers in to be wined and dined in the small but elegantly furnished board room.

Annie was a petite, happy-go-lucky, fair-haired girl, married happily at the time to David Mackie, who was later to become senior partner of Allen and Olgivie at their offices in Old Change where he was a founding proponent of *pro bono* legal work in the UK. They lived after marriage in a small three-bedroom house in a new estate in Bow, long before the development of Canary Wharf, and later moved to a detached house off Roehampton Lane in Putney. Sometime later they divorced, and Annie moved to a small flat off Kingston Hill. She was always up for a laugh and flirted fairly outrageously with Bob Dellow and Brian. On one occasion at a Christmas party in Leith House one of these two put a mirror on the floor near to where Annie was dispensing food and drink. That was a step too far, and shortly afterwards Annie left to set up her own catering business.

In 1974 the UK stock market fell by seventy-three per cent, one of its worst ever falls. Things were so bad that, according to some, the end of capitalism was nigh. One of the consequences of this dramatic period was that fund management groups were being sold. Within a matter of months SW had acquired two other fund groups, Jessel Britannia and the National Group. The additional £250 million or so of assets under management had been purchased for not much more than £1 million. We ended up with forty-four unit trusts, several of which had the same investment management objective. The range would have to be rationalised through mergers, eventually down to twenty-one. Brian Banks was heard to say one day that if capitalism is dead, then buying these two fund groups was either going to either be very cheap or the final nail in the coffin!

When the first acquisition (that of Jessel) was announced, I visited Keith Crowley, my opposite number, at his offices in Fenchurch Street. Our meeting wasn't wholly satisfactory. I came away thinking that Keith was making plans to become the overall marketing boss after the amalgamation took place. I was concerned that I shouldn't be edged out. In the event, Keith did join our offices in Leith House, where I had moved to the top floor. Relations were cool between us; he brought with him a team of people to service professional agents. One day he came to see me in my fourth-floor office and immediately launched into a tirade of personal accusations about how surly, truculent and unco-operative I was being. This was all news to me, coming from someone who had only been in the business for two years after retiring as a V-bomber pilot. As far as I was concerned, and those I reported to, I was doing a good job.

The rationalisation of forty-four funds, several with almost identical investment aims, objectives, and portfolio content, became a significant management operation. Ron Stone, who had joined from Jessel, and David (DLP) Hill were the two directors who undertook this task. It required a quorum of unit-holder investors in the funds being merged to vote on the proposal. At first this operation was slow, not least because everyone was learning on the job; no one in the industry had previously tried to merge more than two funds together, but now we were sometimes merging three or four at a time. First we had to select the best performing fund to be the principal and surviving trust in order to retain the investment performance record for use in future marketing. The production of a letter, a new prospectus, and voting papers was a major undertaking; distribution of these papers had to be coordinated with the half-yearly manager's reports and accounts to save postage, whilst ensuring that any adjustment to these dates should be spread throughout the year so as to avoid management and administrative overload. The trust amalgamation and merger programme took almost two years.

With the largest investment range of unitised funds in the market, I proposed that we create a 'Unit Trust Portfolio Management Service', an idea now replicated worldwide. This would be managed alongside the discretionary service, managed by Alan and Martyn Page (who were not related). The minimum sum for this new and innovative service was £25,000 compared to the £100.000 required for discretionary management. It also provided scope for discretionary use when exposure in foreign markets in particular was needed, but the costs of foreign share purchase, let alone access to foreign currency within the then existing foreign currency exchange controls which were still in force, were restricted.

During 1974, in addition to buying the two fund groups, Jim Slater had told Brian Banks that he wanted to launch a unit trust to be known as Slater, Walker Assets Trust to invest in companies with undervalued share prices compared to their underlying asset values. This was a typical Jim master-stroke: simple, obvious, and a potential good performer when the stock market recovered, which it did by 150 per cent in 1975. Jim had made his investment reputation as a specialist in identifying companies whose assets were more than the value of their shares. He had also made substantial profits by asset-stripping these companies, although he always denied the practice. This was a business model which others began to follow but which also began to cause increasing negative publicity in the financial press. Jim's response was to say, 'We make money, not things!'

The trouble with launching a new unit trust in the depths of a stock market crash was obvious. Nobody would be interested in making investments when the immediate outlook seemed so bleak. I proposed that Christopher and I should visit our stockbroker and bank trustee connections and offer to pay them an enhanced commission of a quarter per cent on top of the regulated initial commission of 1¼ per cent in return for them underwriting the launch with a commitment to buy a volume of units which would be allocated to their clients. The beauty of this arrangement was that everyone would be a winner. The company's launch costs would be proportionate to the amount of money invested in the fund, the brokers would receive commission when business was almost non-existent, and investors would be investing at the bottom of the market.

As an additional incentive, we offered to pay an on-going annual commission for investment balances held within the trust from the annual management charge of 1.25 per cent. This would hopefully get around one of the principal obstacles stockbrokers faced when putting clients into funds, namely, the loss of broking commission or management income. This was in addition to the promise to use participating stockbrokers for investment business in a ratio based on the volume of money invested.

Jim Slater was so enthused with the concept that he accompanied me to several meetings with some of his favoured stockbrokers. Small talk wasn't part of Jim's make-up, but those who met him on these occasions always showed immense interest in what he had to say and treated him with considerable respect, deference, and awe. What he had to say was always insightful, usually thought-provoking, and, in the way he put things, unarguable and logical. A copy of one of his speeches follows this chapter.

The *Financial Times* unit trust correspondent David Lewis headlined his Saturday column one week with the headline 'Slater, Walker Stirs up a Hornet's Nest', which only served to increase the amount of investor interest. Jim Slater was delighted with the concept and subsequent kafuffle. By the end of the launch period of about two weeks we had attracted £5 million for investment. At the time we said this was all that could be invested in the identified opportunities. Later we made 'limited offers' for this fund. As a marketing concept it was based on the fact that the investment managers could only identify a limited number of investment opportunities at the time these offers were open, whilst it also generated a desire by investors to get involved in a product with proven success.

Shortly afterwards, the payment of extra underwriting commissions was deemed outside the rules of the Unit Trust Association, which supervised the management, administration, and marketing of unit trust companies' funds from Finsbury Circus. Quite why was lost on me. I couldn't see how it could be remotely against anyone's interests if it was offered for enhanced sales performance – which could be easily proven. The renewal commission arrangement, however, was allowed to continue for forty years in a number of products across many product lines in the financial service industry.

Exactly how all the investments in our UK invested funds' portfolios were selected was a grey area to me. Our in-house research resources were tiny and confined to the UK. Stockbrokers provided theirs. My strong suspicion was that, despite the proclaimed Chinese Wall between Petershill House, and Leith House (which indeed was why the two activities were kept physically separate), it was perfectly easy for head office's business research to reveal suitable investments for Brian Banks' team to pursue. In this way, the share price for Jim's banking customers could be under-pinned, whilst the funds' performances benefited from the exposure the bank's clients could get via the financial media. Certainly, Eric Farrell, the dealing director, and Jim Slater gave a daily update of investment positions and prices for strategic holdings held by the bank and of the funds.

Later we were to launch the Professional Trust, a general growth trust. It was aimed at first-time investors who had never invested in unit trusts before but who could invest a minimum of £5,000 – twenty times the usual minimum at the time – and it was another innovative concept for the industry. The fund had lower management charges than a traditional fund and provided quarterly management reports instead of at the usual half-yearly. The trust's launch offer was made via the weekend financial press and attracted over £12 million, with many cheques being drawn from building society accounts. This was just the market we had been hoping to tap into. It was one that offered potentially large amounts of money that might be transferred to equity funds provided the rationale could be presented well.

Liaising with our advertising agency was part of my job I thoroughly enjoyed. The preparation of a new advertisement for an existing fund or for a new service was an opportunity to brief these gentlemen on the concept of what was needed, and then for all the copywriters, layout specialists, and 'ideas men' to put in their two pennyworth. We never had as much time as everyone would have liked, which was a good driver for getting minds focussed and things done. The creative buzz was always very energising – especially when a fresh idea had been developed that was accepted by my superiors, who inevitably all thought either that they had had the idea themselves or that they had an even better one (which almost always would not have worked).

In the mid-1970s I had the offer to borrow a British racing green Rover 2000 from an Honourable Artillery Company (HAC) friend of mine, Winthrop Brainerd. He was a gregarious bachelor and related to one of the early settlers in the US, and offered it to me for the Christmas period, as he, being a Queen's Messenger, would be away in Nepal, Thailand, and the Far East. The only condition was that it would be available for his collection at Heathrow when he returned and it should be in pristine, valeted condition. I was thrilled to have use of this car, which had a flag mast on the offside front wing and a royal household flag in the glove pocket! Unfortunately, I was hit from behind at a traffic light junction and had to drive the car to my parents' house in Chislet near Canterbury with a damaged rear wing and misshapen boot lid: with flag flying of course!

Apart from the embarrassment of having to tell my parents what had happened, although it was no fault of mine, I urgently needed the car to be mended at a time when most repair shops would be closed. Fortunately, my mother knew the owner of Swayle Motors, a Ford dealer in Sittingbourne, who was able to get the car repaired and resprayed. It was delivered back to Heathrow in pristine order.

Some weeks later I met Brainerd in the Suttling Room bar at the HAC. 'What happened to my car?' he enquired. While I hesitated, he went on, 'I heard you had an accident from someone I met when I was in Katmandhu High Street!' I had nowhere to hide and owned up. He wasn't happy, and to this day I have no idea how he got to know about the accident long before the days of Internet and mobile phones.

During my time Slater, Walker, I received an enquiry from Christopher Gilchrist, a trade press writer, who wanted to write a book about unit trusts and needed a sponsor. At a cost of £5,000 he would write and publish an authoritative book which that be targeted at consumers and professionals alike. It would be titled *Unit Trusts: What Every Investor Should Know*. The only previous book on the subject, *The Management of Unit Trusts*, had been written by Oliver Stutchbury in 1964. He was a former chief executive of Save & Prosper, and the book was only of interest to institutional and industry people. We thought

Christopher's book would have longevity and be good for our corporate image and at a cost well below the cost of a quarter page advertisement in a weekend newspaper. It would have good and potentially effective resonance to our traditional promotions. More than that, we would receive a proportion of each book sold at £2.50.

Slaters also formed a Jersey fund management business in 1974 – a busy year! Richard Wilkinson was the managing director, ably supported by Richard 'Butch' (anything but!) Paling and Douglas Aitken (ex-Save & Prosper and also owner of a Gloucestershire old people's home). The Jersey business had been founded on a Jersey-based fund set up by Hugh James, a bespectacled, smartly dressed, and slightly gnomish young man. He had found marketing and promotion of his fund difficult despite having established a good performance record based on his own research and investment dealing. Slaters' had bought the fund, the Growth Investors Fund, and changed its name with the prefix Slater, Walker. The fund had a board of directors which included Hugh van Cutsem, son of a successful race-horse owner from Norfolk and a society figure and a close friend of Prince Charles. Hugh's two sons were pages for Prince Charles's wedding to Lady Diana Spencer some ten years later, and one of them in 2011 was troop commander of the Life Guards outride detachment at Prince William's wedding to Catherine Middleton.

The Jersey operation devised a way for UK investors to buy into the offshore fund, which at that time was not possible for exchange control reasons, by creating effectively a 'mirror' fund. This mirror fund reflected exactly the underlying portfolio of the main fund and was priced in pounds sterling rather than US dollars. The currency movements obviously reflected a differentiation in respective fund values, and thus was born the concept of a managed currency fund, which would be launched in a few years' time after exchange controls, introduced in 1947, had been first relaxed and then ultimately removed in 1979.

Slater, Walker had recently also become involved in the affairs of a Jersey commercial bank. It was thought that, having knowledge of marketing funds to professional intermediaries, I should spend some time on the island and assess possibilities in conjunction with the local board. Thus began an interest in offshore funds and international marketing that would develop in years to come.

These enjoyable and happy times continued for a few years. The frequency of my calls on UK agents diminished, but my responsibilities for advertising and the production of new trust deeds and manager's reports increased.

The preparation, proofing, and printing of trust deeds required a highly specialist expertise that involved accurate and overnight type-setting and delivery service. It had traditionally been done by established City printers, and Slaters had used Greenaways near the old Spitalfields market. In the general business depression of 1973 and 1974, I received a surprise call from Willie Welch, with whom I had shared a house in Spa Hill in Upper Norwood from 1965 to 1967. We had moved there together with John Dudbridge: a HYELM refugee group!

Willie had become production director for a family printing business, WB Darley & Son in Burton on Trent that had specialised for decades in printing beer labels; in fact, they were and remain one of the largest beer-label printers in the world! He was desperate to find some … any … print work. With the economy in dire straits, nobody, it seemed, was drinking bottled beer as much as they had!

At some risk to my personal position, I asked him to typeset, proof, and print the trust deed and prospectus for the new Professional Trust. It was quite a challenge for Willie to get the same turnaround of hard copy as we had received from Greenaways. The work was highly specialised and completely unfamiliar to him and his printing staff. No two prospectuses were the same, unfortunately, as trust law (as it affected unit trusts) and regulations were constantly being amended. There was no such thing as a standard trust deed, and before the age of widespread computer use, it was usually a lengthy process. Somehow he managed to get overnight proofs set in hot metal and delivered on time – usually the next day: and although they were never one hundred per cent accurate until final proofs, they were good enough and eventually competitive enough cost-wise to be given every new prospectus needed for funds which were being merged. This gave Willie several years' business income of around £20,000 annually.

Willie has never forgotten this period, which happened at a time when not only was business poor in their traditional business area, but when he had personal difficulties with his managing director within the factory. He says it saved his bacon. In later years he would invite me to Pride Park to watch a home match of Derby County Football Club, where he had an annual season ticket close to the directors' box.

After each trust deed proof had been received, they had to be checked and often amended several times by the City-based trust lawyers (usually Simmons & Simmons but sometimes Clifford Chance, or Linklaters). The trustees also had to see the proofs for checking and amendment. All this activity had to be completed by an already-decided launch date some weeks ahead. Typically, I would invite trade journalists and stockbrokers, a total of about eighty people, to a presentation and lunch at the Howard Hotel near Temple underground station. The menu would be selected by me, as would the wines. The presentation would follow a standard pattern of speakers from within the company and would be followed by questions. It was all very straightforward and always very much appreciated by the guests, However, on one occasion I selected a Vouvray wine which I thought we had ordered before, but this time was far too sweet. (Vouvray can be bone dry or overly sweet.) Did I pay for that error! The directors questioned my sanity and everything else for weeks afterwards, and rather unnecessarily I thought.

Another of my new responsibilities was the production of the unit trust manager's annual and half-yearly reports. As we now managed twenty-two funds, this was a fulltime job in itself, as the dates for their mandatory publication were spread throughout the year. Assembling the accounts and manager's investment reports from those responsible – Alan Maidment, the finance director, DLP (Dave) Hill, and Ron Stone – along with changing statutory information was a responsible role. It involved each trust's lawyers, trustees, and the Association of Unit Trust Managers (AUTM).

These reports and some other service brochures were printed by Billington Press, a small privately owned printing business based in Bow, East London. Les Billington and his son John were the two working directors and joint shareholders of the business, along with Mrs Billington. Our account was immensely important to them, and Les in particular gave us a tremendous service. In the days of hot metal type-setting, the turnaround times would often require overnight resetting for proofs because of last minute changes, but because he was familiar with our requirements and geared up to organise staff to do overtime if necessary, there was never any danger he would lose the business.

A perk was to have lunch with Les pretty frequently. Often we would go to one of several pub restaurants in Smithfield market or Charterhouse Square, or occasionally to Oslo Court in Regent's Park, which was one of his and his wife's favourites. This was a beautiful restaurant with lovely bone china, cut-glass wine glasses, linen napkins and table-cloths, and an interesting menu. We would talk about the business and people within it and occasionally about personal things, frequently about his second home at Frinton-on-Sea to which he planned to retire. Being perhaps thirty years older than I was, he had a fatherly ear. He lived in Loughton.

When he did retire, his son John took over as managing director, and although he was rather more relaxed in his business outlook and management style than his father, he appreciated the large amount of business we gave him, and Billington's continued as our printers.

It was at about this time, in November 1974, that a traditional stone-built, slate-roofed house I had bought in Wales caught fire one Tuesday night. My first wife and I usually travelled down to Rhosgoch, a hamlet just north of Hay-on-Wye, on weekends, covering the 150 miles in three and a half hours, to our property, which had four acres and trout stream. The fire made the house a total loss; three walls were left standing, and everything else lay in a pile of cinders on the ground floor. Charred floor joists were hanging, broken and useless. Forty-one of the forty-two local residents apparently left their homes to see Rose Cottage go up in flames. The outstanding member of the community not to show was a renowned miscreant. The insurers were Sun Alliance & London. In telling them of my impending 'total loss' claim it became apparent that I had not renewed the annual premium, which had been due ten days previously.

Facing the almost certain probability that there was to be no insurance pay-out, I contacted Richard Lawrence, with whom I had been friendly at Bowrings and who was now a loss adjuster. He advised me that normally insurers would allow a grace period for premiums to be paid, typically of fourteen days. I spoke to the insurers again, and they confirmed this but pointed out that the grace period was about to expire. I drove immediately to the London head office in Bartholomew Lane to pay up. Happily and fortunately, they confirmed that the policy could be renewed notwithstanding that there had been a claim in the interim period. Phew!

Eventually, after many months of wrangling over the cover provided by the policy, and after Richard had become involved to represent my interests, and after a meeting with one of the general managers at the company's head office in Bartholomew Lane, the company paid an acceptable ninety-six per cent of the insured value. My acquired knowledge of the insurance market had ultimately been rewarded, and this early experience of dealing with senior executives empowered my approach to future business negotiations. I have advised anyone ever since not to have anything to do with an insurer who tries to settle the claim for less than they were contracted to do. The old city motto 'My word is my bond' had been tested, and I had won.

As previously mentioned, full scale banking crisis was in full swing in 1974. Slater, Walker's banking arm wasn't wholly immune, but in the autumn Jim Slater resigned suddenly. He was replaced by Sir James Goldsmith, a flamboyant and charismatic uber-rich Old Etonian. The announcement was made after a delay of almost an hour, late one afternoon in the basement of Petershill House, where the annual Krug-champagne-fuelled head-office Christmas parties were held. In the shake-up that followed, the investment management business was left largely untouched, but for some reason my star began to wane with Jim Nicholls, Brian Banks, and Eric Farrell, the dealing director, but not with Alan Maidment, the finance director, and Stuart Goldsmith, the senior investment manager and also a director. Quite what stimulated and sustained what became quite unpleasant and personally difficult times, I never knew.

It was almost as if I was being targeted for being error prone, which I wasn't. However, when fund performance dropped in daily figures against a number of measures for our other funds and those of our competitors and against indices, and when I was being picked up on trivial errors (such as spelling 'guilt' for 'gilt' once!) or other inconsequential misdemeanours (in their view), I began to wonder about my career future for the first time. Meanwhile my accusers played office carpet golf the length of the office for most of the day, card games in the dealing room, and darts in the board room whilst the stock market was virtually inactive.

As a consequence of Slater resigning, the company needed to change its name. A few names were bandied about and proposed by the advertising agency and others, and eventually the name Britannia Arrow

Holdings was agreed. After the heady fast-moving days and reputation of Slater, Walker, a more conventional and traditional name was needed. Almost inevitably there was a rumpus with the Britannia Building Society over the use of 'Britannia' in the name. This was eventually settled by an exchange of letters confirming that we wouldn't solicit for deposits and they would not solicit for stock market investment business.

The fund-management business would be known simply as Britannia Fund Management. Choosing a logo and corporate colour again demanded extensive and prolonged thought. It was at this time that I realised that such things as corporate or product names, colours, and logos absorbed more management time than almost anything else they did. Certainly, this was the case when nobody was very busy! Everybody had an opinion, and when it came to colour, not everybody saw or could memorise colour the same way.

In 1976, because my role had become increasingly restricted, I was no longer travelling about the UK, and my company car was not replaced when it came up for replacement. At that time I had a three-year-old daughter Katharine and a one-year-old son William, and a car was vital. Money was pretty tight, but I found a Morris Minor Traveller (XLM 338G) for sale in the *Evening Standard* in East Finchley for £400, which I borrowed from my mother-in law. One Saturday morning I went to see it, thought it looked okay, and drove it home to Putney. I cherished it for nearly twenty years. It was a sad day when I said goodbye to my Trafalgar-blue reliable friend in the early 1990s. She was bought by another Welshman who lived in North Wales.

At some point during this low ebb I was seconded to the life company business. The offices were in the basement of a block adjoining Petershill House. The business, known as Britannia Arrow Life Assurance Ltd., employed about twenty people. Had my Towry Law employment taken me there I wondered? There was also a subsidiary life company based in Guernsey, but I never knew why it existed or who bought its products – if it had any. The managing director of both was Arthur Pierce, a white Bermudan accountant with a combined Bermudan and Scottish accent unique to him.

My role was to work alongside Len Stretfield, a well-known life-long expert on pensions who had, amongst other places and life companies, worked at Noble Lowndes. Len was in his late fifties, a pipe smoker and beer drinker who commuted to Brighton. The role I had was in marketing a money purchase corporate pension plan – more money in the investment management coffers! Having received enquiries, it would then be our job to calculate each member's contribution required from the company and the individual to the scheme to achieve a target benefit based on assumed rates of investment performance and known retirement age. The calculations were complex to me, but they were second nature to Len.

At mid-day sharp, Len would aim for the nearest pub, the Sea Horse, which was just up the road opposite Bracken House in Queen Victoria Street where the *Financial Times* was published. He would usually try and get someone from the office to join him on the pretext that business could be discussed there as well as anywhere else. He was given considerable freedom to 'work' this way.

Amongst my other colleagues were Mike Gordon, who was our company representative or Inspector visiting intermediaries, and John Addis, a number cruncher. Mike was a keen cricketer (a supporter of Essex) and an MCC member. His was a technical and marketing role, and he was clearly very bright. He was always 'taking the piss' and was good company. He came in one day and said that sales for Slater's own endowment policies were rather slow, so we should all take one out! I took out four policies, each for £1,000 sum assured with a monthly premium payable over twenty-five years of £2.50, which in those days attracted tax relief at 17.5 per cent. This meant a total net payment over the period of £637.50 each. I used them later for mortgage collateral purposes. When they eventually matured, having been taken over by Swiss Life, they each paid out over £12,000!

Mike went on to become marketing director at Skandia Life and retired when he was fifty-five. I envied him his retirement greatly, because at that time (the year 2000) my business career was seriously threatening to crumble. He and I would meet up from time to time after the Slater years at international conferences with a colleague of his, Clive Cowdery, who later founded Resolution Life Group Limited, an investment acquisition company with some Slater nuances. This Guernsey-based company became very successful at buying up dormant life company funds and making significantly better returns than they had previously achieved. These people were names to conjure with in years to come.

John Addis was a quasi-actuary announced one day that he had a proven formula for winning the football pools. He and his father regularly picked up winnings, he said. Naturally everyone was sceptical, but he nevertheless persuaded us to chip in, in my case a few unaffordable pounds. In the first week we won about £20 each and in week three over £150 each. We thought we were on a roll, but it never happened again, and after a few weeks no one was participating.

When Chris Neville decided to leave the company in 1978, I was recalled to the investment arm of the business. I had survived my uncomfortable personal crisis and was soon approached with a sponsorship proposal for the restoration of the steam railway locomotive *Britannia* No. 70000 at a cost of £25,000 with a similar sum to acquire the rights to use it for promotional purposes. Having our company name on an iconic steam engine as it travelled the length and breadth of the country held some appeal, but when it became clear that sponsorship didn't include ownership, we backed out.

As part of my resumed brief to generate business through stockbrokers, I had visited those in Douglas and Ramsey on the Isle of Man several times. On one of my visits to the island I visited a brokerage and investment business in Castletown called Mannin International. It was a privately owned investment banking business, and operated from a smart and large Georgian house, approached from a driveway and full of antiques. The majority shareholder was James Gilbey (of the gin family). The other directors were Ronnie Buchanan, the chief investment officer, Graham Reid, a close friend of John Dyson with whom I had worked at Towry Law, and Pieter Kuntz, a South African. As far as I could tell, these were the only male employees. They were interested in my joining their team to offer tax planning and investment advice to wealthy expatriates in a rather similar way as Towry Law had done with its UK-based clientele. For reasons I can't now recall, I didn't accept their offer. It may have been the family disruption, the lack of longevity of the business, or perhaps even the rather difficult characteristics of the people I met – apart from Graham, who was extremely charming, highly knowledgeable on tax mitigation matters and good fun to be with.

Through a connection my mother had made in the 1960s with Clifford Irving, who was then Minister for Tourism for the Manx government and a leading island politician, I was keen to accept his invitation to talk with local civil servants in the Finance Department of the island's government about opening a branch on the island, which my directors had suggested at an out-of-the blue meeting. In retrospect, it shouldn't have been a surprise that the Manx government was very encouraging, as the financial sector of the economy was perceived as a growth sector. Tourism had peaked in the 1950s, agriculture wasn't growing, and competition from other offshore centres, notably the Channel Islands, was increasing. Fishing which had been important economically was also in decline. Manx smoked herrings were no longer exported on a significant scale.

In 2012 I attended my fourth or fifth meeting of the Petershill Reunion Society. It was the thirty-eighth reunion of those who have worked at Slater, Walker, either in the bank, in the property company, or the investment management business. The annual reunions began after SW changed its name in 1974 and become Britannia Arrow Holdings Ltd. As on previous occasions, a motley crew of people tuned up to talk about past times, catch up on what was going on generally and personally, reflect on some who had died since we met last time, and to enjoy stories from the past. I still maintain that, even with most of us now in our late sixties, seventies, and mid-eighties, if we were all put in a room to make a business, we would do so, and it would be more than just successful.

Jim Slater gave a speech in Toronto in 1973, which conveys the way the business was created and run, how employees were motivated, and also something of the man himself who inspired so many to think outside the box, take reasonable chances, and be meticulous about detail. Much of it is as true today as it was at the time. The text of the speech follows this chapter.

Chapter 5

Jim Slater's Perception of His Business

This is transcript of a speech given by Jim Slater at the Empire Club in Toronto on April 12, 1973. It gives a wonderful insight into his modus operandi and his ability to present sometimes complicated ideas simply and logically, and with a not a little sense of humour.

Mr Chairman, Ladies, and Gentlemen, I am honoured to have been invited to speak to you today. Mr Potts, your chairman, has asked me to talk about Slater, Walker, and I hope you are going to find our story an interesting one. As you may know, in some countries the words 'Slater, Walker' are synonymous with the word 'takeover'. Now I would like to make it quite clear at the beginning that we have never taken over another company! We always merge with them. Now it's extremely important to understand the distinction between a takeover and a merger, and to do that I think you have to go back to the parable of the chicken and the pig.

The chicken said to the pig one day, 'I think there is a great future in ham and eggs. I think you and I should get together. We should have a merger.'

And the pig, who was a cautious animal, said, 'I would like to think it over. I'll let you know about your merger proposal in the morning.' The pig thought it over and the next morning said to the chicken, 'I've thought over your merger proposal, and I don't like it. You can go on laying eggs day after day, but to produce the ham, I get carved up.'

And the chicken said, 'I know. That's why I'm calling it a merger.'

To revert to the story of Slater, Walker itself, it all began really in April 1964. At that time I had been working for Leyland Motors for about ten years, having previously qualified as an accountant. I had a fascinating job working as deputy to Lord Stokes, who is now chairman of British Leyland Motor Corporation. In the previous few years though, I had become interested in investment as a hobby. I had found that there were certain shares on the UK Stock Exchange which had well below average price earnings ratios, but in spite of that had very good records of increasing earnings. They were, in fact, due for a status change. These relatively neglected shares often had astonishing increases in share prices, and I evolved a system of investment in them. I started with my savings, which were $5,000, and in the two years 1962 and 1963, with the help of bank borrowings of $20,000, I turned that $5,000 into $125,000. Now at this stage I was still doing my job at Leyland, but there was developing an inevitable conflict of interest. I found that when Donald Stokes said to me, 'I'd like you to go to Finland; we are having trouble with our distributor there. Would you get on a plane and go tomorrow?' I'd think to myself, 'Now, I've got an open position in these eight shares, and the results of two of them are coming out in a few days' time.' It was becoming very difficult for me to leave the country, which meant that I could not do justice to my job. So in fairness to Leyland I left the company on a very amicable basis in April 1964.

Shortly afterwards I met a Conservative MP named Peter Walker at a dinner following a series of articles in the *Evening News* about young businessmen, in which we had both been featured. The meeting was an important one and was the start of a very happy partnership. Peter Walker was an excellent adviser during the formative years of the company, but now, of course, he is very much full time in politics.

A few months after our meeting, Peter Walker and I, together with some bankers, formed a syndicate to buy control of a quoted property company called H. Lotery. Its main asset was the long lease of a property, which we sold at a substantial profit. We were then left with what might best be called a 'cash company'. I injected into that company my investment advisory business. This had grown almost inadvertently, because, in addition to running my own affairs, I had started to advise my friends on a free-of-charge basis, but when I left Leyland I made them business associates! This became a profitable business, and when

I injected it into H. Lotery, we renamed the company Slater Walker, which was subsequently changed to Slater, Walker Securities.

The share price then went up very substantially in anticipation of future growth. I then found a small but very interesting asset situation, which was a company named Thomas Brown, a firm of wholesale grocers in Australia. Using Slater, Walker shares, we acquired Thomas Brown, reorganised it, and redeployed the assets. We then bought another company, and then another, and so on. From 1964 to 1968 Slater, Walker grew enormously. There was a bull market in the UK, and whereas the capitalisation of the company when I bought into H. Lotery was $3.7 million, by 1968 it had risen to about $280 million, and it was by then a vast diverse industrial conglomerate. I denied it at the time, but looking back on it, that was what it was!

However, by 1968, and particularly in America, the word conglomerate was becoming bad news, and rightly so in many ways, because there are very few well-run conglomerates. They are the exception rather than the rule, and it definitely needs a genius to run one well. So we had a good think about the situation, and we decided as a board to divest ourselves of our various industrial interests and to concentrate our activities in five main areas. These areas were banking, investment, insurance, property, and overseas interests. Now banking, investment, insurance, and property all have some very attractive features in common. They all interlink, they are all financial, they are all expanding areas, they are not labour intensive, and they will all benefit substantially from Britain's entry into the Common Market.

As I have said, from 1964 to 1968 we were busy building a diverse conglomerate. From 1968 to 1971 we were divesting ourselves of our industrial interest and, in parallel to that, putting our money and effort into banking, investment, insurance, property, and overseas. Now the sale of 500 different companies is no easy task, and we had to tackle it in several different ways. The main method was the satellite of associated company concept. This was where we sold a firm we owned into a public company, usually a small one, for shares in that public company. We installed as chief executive a very able young man, who in some cases had been trained by us. We kept a substantial stake in that company, and it became an active banking client of ours. This concept was quite new when we first used it, but it is becoming more popular now. It had three great advantages. First of all, it helped us in our programme of divesting ourselves of a subsidiary company by the sale of our interest. Secondly, it created an active banking client, and thirdly, it enabled us to offer excellent positions and exciting opportunities in these client companies to people from our central team. Many of these men are very able and ambitious and would have wanted to leave us to build their own businesses anyway, so it enabled us to have a continuing stake in their talents as opposed to losing them altogether.

One excellent example I can give is a company called Ralli International. One of our most able executives, Malcolm Horsman, wanted to leave Slater, Walker and set up on his own. We therefore helped him to take control of Ralli International, and Slater, Walker took a substantial stake in it. Last year Slater, Walker initiated an agreed merger with Bowater, and Malcolm Horsman is now its deputy chairman and managing director. Bowater-cum-Ralli is now capitalised at over $500 million and is already a very powerful international company in its own right. Needless to say, Slater, Walker has enjoyed excellent capital appreciation on its Ralli International shares, and in their new form they remain an excellent long-term investment.

Another method we adopted was to float off the majority interest in a company to the public, forming in effect a new public company. For example, we had bought three separate listed companies in the rubber manufacturing business which we put together as a group. We improved their profits substantially by rationalisation and streamlining and then, under the name of Allied Polymer Group, we floated them off to the public, again retaining a substantial stake. The shares in this company have since then continued to appreciate in value.

The third method was the straightforward and conventional sale of a company to a willing buyer. A good example of this was Dollond & Aitchison, which was the leading firm of optical retailers and manufacturers in Britain. Here again, we had formed a group, having bought two other companies of a similar nature, put them all together, and considerably improved profits. We then sold the group for cash to a tobacco company which was seeking to diversify outside the tobacco industry.

It was very hard work, selling off all these diverse interests during this three-year period and in parallel building up in the chosen areas of banking, investment, insurance, property and overseas. It is a major challenge for any company to achieve a complete change of direction.

Looking at our position now, we are, in investment banking terms, obtaining a significant share of the corporate finance business available in Britain. We are very well established in investment management, where the outside funds under our control are now in excess of $600 million. As far as property is concerned, we now have, with our stakes in various quoted property companies plus direct investment in certain properties themselves in London and other European centres, an aggregate portfolio of $300 million. In insurance, we have a composite company, a general life company, and an industrial life company. We cover all aspects of insurance, and this sector is going from strength to strength. That sums up the UK story.

We have, of course, also been very busy overseas. In Australia, which was our first overseas venture, we have a company which is now capitalised at $65 million. It was very successful at first, but we ran into management problems about two years ago. The company has now been reorganised and seems well based for future expansion. In South Africa our company has been an unqualified success. From a base market capitalisation of $2 million, with acquisitions and organic growth, the company has now grown to $140 million. Our stake in that company is now just over thirty per cent.

In this country, from a very small base, Robert Smith has done an excellent job in establishing Slater, Walker of Canada, which is now capitalised at over $50 million. In the Far East we have, during the past year, developed substantial companies in both Hong Kong and Singapore, with an aggregate market capitalisation of $270 million. Last year's prime objective was Europe, where we did not have a significant presence. We now have listed companies in Belgium, Holland, France, and Germany, with an aggregate capitalisation of $70 million and an excellent base for future expansion. This year's objectives are the United States and Brazil.

In every country overseas, we welcome local investor participation, and for this reason always obtain a substantial shareholding in a listed company. As a result of acquisitions, our percentage shareholding is gradually diluted, and we usually aim to retain a shareholding of twenty-five to thirty per cent when a company is fully matured. We encourage strong local autonomy, with local management ultimately only consulting us on major policy changes. In this way we hope to blend into the local scene, as opposed to being looked upon as foreign invaders!

Taking into account both its UK and overseas activities, Slater, Walker Securities today can probably best be described as an international investment bank with strong property and insurance interests. Our gross assets are in excess of $1,100 million. The company is now capitalised at over $400 million and is well backed by the fundamentals. Since 1964 shareholders have enjoyed capital appreciation of 1,350 per cent, during which time the stock market as a whole has appreciated only thirty per cent.

A question I am often asked is how it is that Slater, Walker has expanded so fast in so many different countries. What is the secret? I have given a lot of thought to this and whilst there is no 'secret', I think it is fair to say that we have developed a company style and spirit which is common wherever we have been successful. I have tried to identify and define what it is that constitutes our particular approach in the hope that it will be of interest to you. Probably none of the ingredients on its own is peculiar to Slater, Walker, but I believe that all the points taken together constitute the uniqueness of our company style.

First of all we have an outward-looking international approach to business. We are not only interested in what is happening in the UK (which is perhaps just as well at present). We are keenly interested in overseas opportunities. I think I can best illustrate this approach by confirming that we have at present more overseas listed companies in which we have a substantial stake than any other British company, and perhaps any other company in the world.

Secondly, we have in general backed relatively young, professionally qualified people in positions of greater responsibility than they would probably have been given in a more conventional and longer-established company. We have also motivated these young men very highly. We have share option schemes so that they participate in that way, and they also have significant personal stakes, often bought on borrowed money. It helps concentrate their minds! The other advantage of this is, of course, that it gives a complete identity of interest with shareholders. In other words, our managers will only succeed financially themselves if the general investing public profits as well.

An important feature of our corporate philosophy is to cut losses and back winners. A company is often worth a great deal more for its profitable parts if, for example, its only loss-maker is sold for a relatively nominal figure. It is important to have the moral courage to cut a loss-maker, even if it means admitting that a recent purchase was a mistake.

Another thing we regard as very important is administrative speed and precision. I do not like minutes to record at great length the views of each person present at a meeting. Minutes should say who is going to do what by when so that there is no doubt about where responsibility for action lies. We have a tightly-knit central control with well-defined powers delegated to each profit centre and effective lines of communication. We pride ourselves on our speed of decision-making and are always looking for new ways of improving our administrative efficiency.

It is of course essential to have strong financial control. We have monthly figures, and we compare results with monthly budgets and, most important of all, analyse and if necessary do something about major variances. I know this is common and accepted business practice, but I have mentioned it because it is so very important.

One of the most important features is that we have a money-making approach to business. Profitability is after all the measure of efficiency, and it is essential to concentrate on making money as well as on making things. There is no point in making things without making money. A lot of people become so dedicated to their industry and their product that they regard it as a vocation. The fact that they are meant to make money for their shareholders and indeed for their country often escapes them.

I think a good example of unrealistic dedication to an industry emerged at the first board meeting I attended of a company we had just taken over. I will keep the name out of it to protect the guilty! I asked about a subscription of $40,000 to a trade association which was on the agenda.

One of the directors said he was chairman of the association and another was the general manager. I then ascertained that most of our competitors, except our main one, subscribed to the association on a turnover basis.

I asked what our turnover was in relation to the whole, and they told me that we were two-thirds of the industry, that our main competitor was about a sixth, and all the rest together were the other sixth. So here we were paying most of the bill.

'What does it do, this association?' I asked hopefully, 'Does it help control selling prices or something like that?'

'Oh no,' they said, 'the whole idea is to pool research facilities.'

I probed further. 'Well, what have they got that we haven't got?'

'Well, it doesn't work like that,' the directors said. And they told me about a complicated piece of equipment which we had and our competitors were allowed to share by virtue of being members of the association.

Here we were paying $40,000 per annum for the privilege of sharing a unique and costly piece of equipment with the rest of our competitors. When I put it like that to them, they did agree that it needed rethinking! It was a classic example of bad thinking which had not been reasoned through in a money-making way.

Now we come to what I would call stock-market orientation. This really means being aware of one's share price and the underlying fundamental values and appreciating the importance of timing. It means knowing when is the right time to use shares, when to use loan stocks, and when to use cash. It also means having an awareness of the importance of good communications, frank and full disclosure to the press, and ensuring that investors are kept fully informed about the company at all times.

We have always attached great importance to the systematic build-up of assets per share in parallel to the build-up in earnings. Many of our earlier acquisitions were asset-orientated for this reason. With the exception of service businesses, it is the assets which provide the base and the fuel for future earnings, and this is why it is so important for any management to ensure that their company's assets are keeping in step with earnings increases.

We have also always ensured that our cash position is very strong. This is in a sense a form of insurance policy which I have always found to be a great comfort. In the last analysis, if one's company was to run into trouble, a strong cash position would be a great help in getting out of it.

When I was much younger I was fortunate enough to work for a man who had over his mantelpiece a four-word motto, 'It Can Be Done.' Those words stuck in my mind and are now a basic part of the philosophy of the company. My last point, therefore, is that we always approach problems with a positive attitude, and believe that somehow 'it can be done.' These days there are so many regulations and tax laws and reasons why you cannot do what you want to do. We do not accept this. We ask how we are going to do it and believe that there is always a way if one is sufficiently determined.

Quite apart from all these practical considerations, I think it is fair to say that most of our executives really enjoy what they are doing. If I was asked for a list of personal characteristics which executives of ours should have, a good sense of humour would be high up on it. It is vital for business to be fun as opposed to being a chore. For example, two years ago Robert Smith, Roland Rowe, and I were negotiating here in Toronto with Alan Lambert's representatives to acquire control of Unas from the Toronto-Dominion Bank. We wanted to purchase two-thirds of the company and leave Toronto-Dominion Bank and the general public with the remaining third. It was therefore essential to impress them that we were bright fellows and worth backing. We came to the stage of calculating the provisional purchase consideration. The calculation was two-thirds of 283,362 multiplied by $18. I turned to my two colleagues and in clipped tones said, 'Check me.' Each of us worked out the calculation separately, and to my acute embarrassment we came up with three different answers! Fortunately, Alan Lambert's representatives thought this was most amusing and we all burst out laughing. In a sense it helped to cement the deal in human terms, and I am glad to say that since then it has worked out well for all concerned.

I have tried to give you a general picture of Slater, Walker Securities, and of our particular corporate style. Both the company and our way of managing it are of course continuing to change form as we go along. Where we go from here remains to be seen. Our first aim is to build an international investment banking business, and our secondary aim is to make sure that we, and everybody associated with us, will continue to enjoy doing it.

Mr Slater was thanked on behalf of the Empire Club by Mr Hartland M. MacDougall, a vice-president of the club, as follows.

I must say, and I think you will all understand now, that when I first met Jim Slater not so very long ago, almost two years, I was frankly astounded by the quiet, warm personality of this obviously dynamic individual, who may not have admitted it at the time but certainly it could be perceived that he was out to establish at that time the biggest investment bank in the world. His tactics are above reproach as he moved ahead at an incredible pace but somehow, and we've heard today to a large extent how, consolidating his position almost after every step. In this complex age when government and other factors seem to intervene at the most inopportune moments to thwart best laid plans, it is indeed encouraging to see that with well-defined objectives, completed homework, and a very strong will, success in the best way can still be achieved.

Our business community in Toronto and, indeed, in Canada I think has benefited greatly from the presence of Slater, Walker of Canada, and we are happy that Jim Slater saw fit to bring it to our shores. We are even more grateful that he was kind enough to come over himself today and share with us his fascinating background, views, and philosophy that has led to this outstanding success.

Many thanks, Jim, from one and all.

Chapter 6

Isle of Man

So, back to my Isle of Man discussions to open a branch of Britannia Arrow on the island. Quite coincidentally, the PGA (Professional Golfers' Association), was in touch to offer us the sponsorship of the P.G.A. Cup – 'Mini Ryder' Cup to be held in September of 1979 at the Castletown Golf Links on the Isle of Man. It was a biennial event held alternately in the United States or within Great Britain and Ireland and played by teams of golf club professionals many of whom had been full-time tour professionals in their younger days. The sponsorship fee was £25,000 – quite a lot of money even in those days. The tournament would be preceded by a pro-am event which would have four 'personalities' as the 'celebs'. The golf side of things would be managed by the PGA, and Britannia would be free to promote it as we wished. It was an excellent way to launch the new branch office on the island. Most importantly, it would appeal to a significant number of residents of this low-tax haven, which has seven golf courses being the largest participatory sport on the island.

As Brian Banks and Jim Nichols were enthusiastic golfers at Crohamhurst and Addiscombe, near Croydon, it wasn't surprising that they both gave the idea their wholehearted support. Alan Maidment, a non-golfer, on the other hand was much more circumspect. I had never picked up a golf club on a golf course ever, but I liked the idea of playing a part in such an interesting idea.

At about the same time, plans were being made for me and my family to move to the Isle of Man in January of the following year. Initially, I took a suite of rooms in Laureston Manor, a large private house owned by Mr and Mrs Knight, who had taken UK tax exile on the island. I never discovered how they had made their money (typical of many such people on the island), but Laureston, being situated in at least an acre of wooded grounds, was a peaceful place with a long drive up to the house, overlooking Douglas Bay.

Travelling to and from Douglas on the island from Liverpool from under the Liver Building, with the Isle of Man Steam Packet company ferries several times a year became a (usually) pleasant experience. Three hours or so on the boat, having lunch watching the sea and seagulls tracking us before either a four hour drive to our house in London or twenty minute drive to our home in Douglas. One great exception to this was a trip back to Douglas from having stayed for Christmas on 'the adjacent island'.

The Mersey, which was well marked with buoys to show the shipping channel, was in turmoil: high waves and high winds. Having departed on schedule and moving further out to the Irish Sea, and with the north Wales coast and Lancashire coasts becoming more distant and less visible, our ship began to really pitch and roll.

The outgoing tide and a wind from the opposite north easterly direction were making the sea increasingly rough, but we continued albeit at a slow rate of knots. Some while later in the voyage and well out to sea, waves were literally passing the length of the ship, and decks were almost rolling to sea level, or so it seemed. Service of all hot food and drink was suspended and all free standing chairs were lashed to fixtures. Passengers became increasingly unwell. Fortunately for us we had reserved a cabin with bunk beds and so could lie down which alleviated not only our queasiness but avoided watching others be sick on deck.

That particular trip took thirteen hours to complete as the captain had decided to ride out the storm without making forward speed. We literally stayed pointing into the sea. Turning round in such mountainous seas would have threatened the survival of the ship, passengers and crew.

We later met with a fellow passenger who had captained container ships around the world who told us that our experience had been one of the worst he had ever known at sea. It had been caused by the peculiarities of the Irish Sea where tides flow around the island of Ireland combining with opposing high gale-force winds rushing up the narrowing and increasingly shallow Mersey channel.

When my family arrived, the company rented Ballaquayle Cottage, the gate house to the long drive entrance of Laureston Manor. The property was within, or inside, the Isle of Man TT – round the island - motor racing course. This meant that although we couldn't hear the bikes for practice week or for the week of racing in June, it meant that getting to the office or indeed anywhere on the outside for social activities needed plenty of planning. This usually meant getting to the other side before 8 o'clock in the morning or crossing on foot over one of rather few bridge crossing points, or leaving a car on either side. Being on an island, car theft was non-existent as before anyone could take a car away, the police could check all vehicles as they boarded the daily morning ferry to Liverpool, or later Heysham.

One evening Paul Gaskell, previously advertising manager at the *Isle of Man Courier* weekly newspaper and now marketing director at the Palace Hotel Group, and who always had an eye to getting loads of publicity, brought the actors Gareth Hunt and Robert Powell to dinner at the cottage. They were on the island to take part in a pro-am annual golf day at Castletown Golf Links, and the talk drifted towards the PGA Cup, or 'Mini Ryder' Cup, as it was known, and our sponsorship of it. On other occasions Paul introduced me to Frank Carson, a comedian, who was performing for one night at the Villa Marina Theatre, and Alex 'Hurricane' Higgins, then world snooker champion, who was giving an exhibition match and demonstration of trick shots at the Palace Hotel.

In due course Kidborough House on Belmont Hill was bought by the company for £125,000. Maurice Gibb (of the Bee Gees pop group) and Lulu (herself a pop-star) had been the previous owners. The house stood at the end of a short tree-shrouded drive, which I thought would give a good degree of camouflage for visitors on an island noted for its habit of 'spotting' who was seen where and with whom! It was a substantial property of six bedrooms, three bathrooms (one en-suite), three large reception rooms, and a large kitchen with utility rooms, all within about three quarters of an acre of largely shaded garden facing south-east. It needed some redecoration and complete furnishing. Britannia Arrow Holdings Ltd., which was the name of the revamped Slater, Walker Group, sponsored the complete furnishing of the house and some decoration.

Vicky, my then wife, and I visited auction rooms and furnished the house comfortably with a view to residents of the island and visitors being entertained corporately. Having found an office at Number One Athol Street, the principal street for banks, solicitors, and stockbrokers, we opened the business with a dinner at the house attended by Lord and Lady Rippon (deputy chairman of the group), Mr and Mrs Clifford Irving, Mr and Mrs Charles Kerruish (the finance minister), Mr and Mrs Robert Quayle (the Manx government's parliament (or Tynwald) speaker), and two directors from London, Stuart Goldsmith (no relation of Sir James) and Alan Maidment. Catering was provided by a Mr Bishop, who lived in Laxey (some ten miles away) and two ladies who brought fresh food, prepared, cooked, and served it, and then cleared it all away before any guests had left! He and they were wonderful. We used Mr Bishop's services quite frequently thereafter, and always at the company's expense.

Lady Rippon was most concerned that everyone should be placed correctly at the table, which could comfortably seat twelve. She asked if I had prepared a table plan, which fortunately I had, but it wasn't to her satisfaction. The most important lady guest had to be seated to my right as host, and thereafter the seating followed a priority which I can't now remember other than that the most important male guest had to be seated to my wife's right. In the event, it was a most enjoyable and convivial occasion and put Britannia on the map as far as the island's government was concerned.

At our frequent dinners we met many interesting people, one of whom announced that he could make gin. This seemed unlikely until it emerged that Mr Cooper was a pharmacist in Castletown, and very good gin it was. Whenever he and his wife came to the house, which was more frequently than most, green bottles would be exchanged at the door! Gin was quite the drink on the island, and I can remember several parties where gin slings were almost the only drink on offer! (They consisted of two thirds gin, one third lime juice, with a slice of lime – and drunk like wine!)

Organising the golf tournament and pro-am was going to be an interesting and new experience. A preliminary meeting was arranged with one of the PGA's tournament assistants who would meet me on the island. Miss Allison MacDonald was an attractive young no-nonsense Scots girl. After she duly arrived on a flight from Manchester, I drove her to the Palace Hotel on Douglas seafront. My company car was a VW Passat estate with the registration plate MAN456, the Morris was

456 MAN. Manx islanders were keen to have recognisable or personal number plates so that people they knew could see and be seen as they drove the island's small roads. The next day I drove Allison over to the Golf Links Hotel to inspect its accommodation for the visiting teams and officials. There would be sufficient rooms, but there would need to be a good deal of refurbishment and redecoration, which the owners readily agreed to undertake. The captain of the club, Rex Barker, would help liaise and oil the wheels between the hotel and the club's golf pro.

It was agreed that Colin Snape, the PGA Secretary who was based at PGA's headquarters at the Belfry to the south of Birmingham, and I would meet at the Castletown Golf Links Hotel and walk the course a few weeks later. The idea was that he could identify changes needed to the course, any significant hazards for both players and the public, how access would be controlled at the entrance and on the course, where the scoreboard would be situated and how it would be updated, where the hospitality marquees would be placed without interfering with the course or becoming an obstacle for the public, where stands and walkways would be placed, and so on.

Colin was a straight-talking Lancastrian who said things as he saw them. His first comment on coming out of the hotel after breakfast at eight o'clock and looking at the large clock on the hotel tower was, 'Are we running this event on PGA time or Castletown time?' The club house clock was a few minutes slow! This was an indication of how things were going to be and would have to be attended to. Various water points around the course had to be made less likely to influence the bounce of a possible wayward shot, greens had to trimmed and prepared to PGA standards for months in advance, and the rough had to be allowed to grow.

Marquees could be positioned in an agreed area between the first hole and third tee. There would be three marquees, one each for the public, the sub-sponsors, and the press. Entrance to the course could only be controlled at a point about halfway out to the furthest hole, but the hotel car park would only be for the use of players and officials and me! Being on a square-headed peninsula jutting out into the Irish Sea, no protection could be provided against the possibility of anyone falling into the sea some thirty feet below at high tide or onto the beach or rocks some fifty feet below at low tide. It was all new to me.

I recommended to my colleagues that we could offset our tournament sponsorship fee by offering sub-sponsorship packages of each of the eighteen holes to local businesses. As part of their package they would be allowed to put up banners at the green end of their hole (not at the tee, so as not to make the place look untidy) and would have an exclusive area within the hospitality tent to provide guests with lunch and drinks. These costs would be separate from their sponsorship fee. They would be able to advertise in the tournament programme and invite three guests to the tournament dinner on the final day. Colin was very happy with these arrangements.

Our advertising agents, Royds (who had now moved to Mandeville Place, W1) had as their 'meet and greet' a well-known face, Denis (DCS) Compton, the renowned England cricketer and Arsenal footballer. Denis told me to look out for a certain Ian Botham whom he had seen playing cricket as a teenager. 'One day he'll be a good player!' which was his way of saying that Ian would become an exceptionally outstanding player. Denis would try to get Ian to come over for the pro-am, and even mused that he would also try to get Keith Miller, the legendary Australian cricketer, to come over, as he was Denis's greatest and closest friend.

In the event the celebrities were Jimmy Hill (the BBC TV football commentator) who came with Bryony whom he later married, both invited by Denis, John Spencer (reigning world snooker champion) and Cliff Thorburn (a world snooker champion to be) both invited by Paul, and Steve Cauthen (the lead rider for Robert Sangster, who had inherited the Vernons Pools business and become a leading race horse owner and breeder). Steve was a flat-race jockey at the peak of his world-wide success for Vincent O'Brien, Sangster's Irish-based trainer. Robert and his Australian wife Sue lived at the rather inappropriately named house the 'Nunnery', close to our house.

Denis was always easy to get along with and yet would never suffer fools gladly. He told me he was a great admirer of my mother from her BBC television days in the 1960s. He was polite, courteous, and entertaining. He was a true friend, and his passing in 1997 was very sad for me personally. Unfortunately, our contact, dare I say friendship, came in the autumn of his life, when we'd lunch and then go to the Sportsman Club near Gloucester Place, where he would sink a few more bevvies and bet on televised horse racing before going home to Gerrards Cross. It was all too brief and narrow in context.

The sub-sponsorship packages for the golf tournament were sold out within days, including one to Robert Sangster, whose wife Sue arranged a cocktail reception for the teams, officials, and sponsors during the tournament. Sue was a barrel of laughs with her Australian accent, and she never failed to toot her horn if she saw me around the island as she drove her Mercedes sports car. Lunch with them on the terrace of their large almost stately home was always fun, with Robert usually cooking the barbecue while I and other guests sipped large glasses of wine.

We recovered our initial outgoings quickly for the tournament sponsorship. We were now faced with the costs of providing the marquees and paying the costs for our own accommodation and attendance and that of invited guests from the island and the UK. We had to cover our own local advertising, including the publication of the tournament programme and promotion with local press and radio. Media coverage in the golf press would be organised by the PGA. These additional costs amounted to another £25,000, which no one ever suggested was too much.

Paul Gaskell from the Palace Hotel offered his help to get as much publicity on the island and find more 'stars' to participate in the pro-am golf tournament that would precede the Mini Ryder Cup and help with the printing of the tournament programme, as well as arranging editorial coverage with the *Courier*. His contribution was immense in many ways, not least in making introductions to many local residents and golf club members who would be able to direct me to avoid breaking golf etiquette, of which I knew nothing. He even threw a small dinner for a group of us to be entertained by a group of Manx musicians. Amongst the dining guests was John Coghlan, the original long-haired 4 by 4 and vintage military vehicle fan, drummer for the pop group Status Quo. When he replaced the local drummer, he tightened up the rhythm and beat and transformed the whole experience amazingly!

Paul's replacement as advertising manager of the *Courier* was Judy Wood, an attractive, single, and striking auburn-haired girl who enjoyed the company of men. She could sell sand to Arabs. She also proved invaluable in getting editorial material and, of course, advertising into the paper in return for the occasional dinner.

The paper also had a weekly column known as 'Fenella's Diary', written by 'Fenella' (Mrs Eunice Salmond), rather as Betty Kenward, known as, 'Jennifer' wrote in *Tatler*, and later *Harpers & Queen*, where she chronicled the social activities of the upper classes at the time. Fenella's long established column was avidly read by the island's great and the good. She became a staunch ally and was always very helpful and prepared to use her extensive contact list to 'put in a good word' where it mattered. She was not one to cross!

Both Rex and Paul became good friends. Rex showed remarkable friendship to me. One evening during the run up to the tournament, I spent some time with him and Paul in the bar of the Golf Links Hotel drinking several gin and French's. On my way home I ran off the road at a notorious Z-bend leading around Castletown Bay from the hotel to the main road to Douglas. Needing a really good sleep, I had also prematurely taken half a Temazepam sleeping pill. At the bend I had looked briefly across the golf course at a courting couple in the back of a parked car, but suddenly found myself with the car astride a stone wall. There was no way the car could be driven with its wheels either side of the wall. It had a puncture anyway, as I was to discover later.

Rex was soon passing by on his way home and stopped immediately. I was still sitting in the car, unable to open the door. It must have looked a comical sight. Rex realised the potentially serious consequences for me and got me into his car and drove me to the RAF Club on the other side of the bay. He told me to stay put while he went back to the car to clear it of any of my belongings. He duly returned with a few items and took me back to the Palace Hotel.

Next morning, with rather a thick head, I phoned David Mylchreest, someone I knew on nodding terms and a director of the car dealership from which the car had been hired. He said he would arrange for the collection of the car and call me back. Later that morning we spoke again on the phone, and he asked me if the puncture had been the cause or a consequence of leaving the road. I was then able to tell him that I thought the puncture was the cause. As far as I know, no one was ever told about this, and, thankfully, my island reputation was unaffected.

The tournament duly went ahead without a hitch. The Great Britain and Ireland team won handsomely 12½ points to 4½ points! The spectator support was enormous, and the weather was warm and sunny, though not without the island's ever-present sea breeze. I can't remember now who all the players were, apart from Peter Butler and David Jones, both famous golf pros in their time. As the event's principal sponsor, everyone connected with the two teams and the PGA and USPGA were most appreciative and made me feel especially good, even though they must have known I knew next to nothing about the game or its conventions.

This would have shown, unfortunately, at the tournament dinner where, as sponsor, I had to give a toast to something or other – perhaps the event, the teams, or maybe the host club, Castletown. As I have since realised, golf speeches have a tried and tested formula, namely to thank the club, the grounds men, the greens keepers, the public, and the players and, if possible, include a previously unheard golf joke or funny observation or quip. Rex, as captain, did follow this established route, so maybe my amateur contribution wasn't noticed too much, other than the fact that as someone who can never tell a joke, my story fell rather flat. Oh well!

The PGA twice invited me to their annual dinner at the Grosvenor House in Park Lane to announce the Order of Merit winner on the European tour and to sit next to Colin Snape, secretary, at the top table. It was a glamorous occasion in the ballroom. Sandy Lyle was the winner in 1979, the year I went. The room was packed; every big name in golf at the time was there (winners of every European Tour Tournament, and of course the winning PGA Cup, Mini-Ryder Cup team), and many players from the past.

Our local office was duly established at 1 Athol Street in Douglas on the first floor, and opposite the Isle of Man Bank (part of the NatWest banking group), so I was pleased with our prestigious address. It had two rooms and was furnished with chairs for visitors, a receptionist's desk in one room, and a television in my office. We installed two push-button phones with two telephone lines to the office. In those days, long before satellite channels were available, the best I could do was to show stock market pages on Ceefax, which, since I had first demonstrated them some years previously, had become available in return for a fairly hefty subscription. It wasn't much, but it gave visitors some stock market prices and market reports to look at. The office also needed furnishing and decorating. Vicky provided secretarial services between taking and collecting the children from their school (the Buchan) in Castletown, nine miles away.

The information on Ceefax I was able to show was considerably less than the local stockbrokers could do using the Stock Exchange's screen-based data. Buckmaster and Moore were virtually next door, and AL Stott, the island's biggest brokerage, was further along the street, amongst others where casual callers were not really encouraged to visit. They wanted customers to be actively trading.

I was left to my own devices, with only occasional calls to or from head office or from Richard Wilkinson, managing director of the by now well-established Jersey office, and very occasional visits by Stuart Goldsmith, the senior investment director. On reflection, the management of the office was extremely loose: there were no targets or accountability that I recall, and no budget. It was quite a challenge to remain upbeat and enthusiastic, but I remained positive about the outlook for the finance sector on the island. Being one of the first UK fund managers to set up on the island, I thought, would ultimately prove justified, rewarding, and profitable.

The local radio station, Manx Radio, recognised the novelty of us taking a business position on the island by inviting me twice to become a UK budget pundit on the radio, live from the studio overlooking Bradda Head above Douglas Harbour and Bay. This was quite a nerve-wracking experience, as I was expected to offer some deep and cogent comments about UK budget policy being announced on air by the UK's Chancellor of the Exchequer, whilst I and a couple of other Manx business people and a presenter attempted to deliver understandable afternoon's listening for local people. Somehow I managed to pull it off, but in reality the real significance of the programme was almost nothing. Had a mistake or commitment been made, however, it might all have been rather different!

I was offered, and accepted after my London director colleagues' approval, a non-executive local directorship of BCCI (Bank of Credit and Commerce International) by Peter Sydney the local director. He was a gregarious and successful business developer and had worked for several major international banks before coming to the Isle of Man. BCCI, founded in 1972, had become a major international bank. The bank was registered in Luxembourg and had head offices in Karachi and London. Within a decade BCCI touched its peak. It operated in seventy-eight countries, had over 400 branches, and had assets in excess of $20 billion, making it the seventh largest private bank in the world in terms of assets.

By becoming associated with the bank in this way, it was thought that considerable investment monies would flow into my office branch from the bank's international branches. Indeed, some investments were made, but never on the scale anticipated. The concept of association with banking institutions, however, sowed the seeds for my future career development, and a new business development model was identified.

BCCI came under the scrutiny of numerous financial regulators and intelligence agencies in the 1980s due to concerns that it was poorly regulated. Subsequent investigations revealed that it was involved in massive money laundering and other financial crimes, and that it illegally gained controlling interest in a major American bank. BCCI became the focus of a massive regulatory battle in 1991, and on July 5 of that year, customs and bank regulators in seven countries raided and locked down records of its branch offices. Investigators in the United States and the UK revealed that BCCI had been 'set up deliberately to avoid centralised regulatory review, and operated extensively in bank secrecy jurisdictions. Its affairs were extraordinarily complex. Its officers were sophisticated international bankers whose apparent objective was to keep their affairs secret, to commit fraud on a massive scale, and to avoid detection.' Not surprisingly (after I had resigned when leaving the island in 1981, but not because of my decision), the bank began to unravel in the face of regulators' increasing concerns over the bank's management and lack of transparency. The Bank of England had already capped the UK branch network at forty-five, and later bailed out depositors.

Another key island contact was Robin Bigland, who had set up an insurance company, Isle of Man Assurance (IOMA), on the island, which allowed client companies to self-insure their own risks, known as captive insurance companies. Robin had founded the company in 1975. He became a prominent local personality in 1979 on the occasion of the millennium of the local parliament, the oldest democratically elected parliament in the world, the Tynwald. He and others sailed a Viking long ship he had commissioned from Norway to the island. Robin's right-hand man was Robert Randall, who had the eyes and smile of Larry Hagman of *Dallas* fame.

I would meet up with Robert again a few years later in Hong Kong, but IOMA was keen to develop fund management business either as trustees, managers, or agents for their captive insurance company business. The idea was that we would manage their clients' captive insurance reserves. Again, I was too early 'in the game', which has since proved so successful on the island; but at that time it did not prove to be as successful as had been hoped.

I received infrequent visits from London directors to the island, and when they came they stayed in the house. Alan Maidment, who some years later became a personal confidante in my matrimonial difficulties, never advising but always prepared to listen, was finance director. Stuart Goldsmith took the most interest in the development of the embryonic business. Stuart was the director responsible for investment market research with a particular focus on North American markets, and had a keen interest in wine. He told me on one occasion that he would select what to eat from a menu by first selecting the wine. When visiting a local off licence owned by the local Okell's Brewery in Douglas, he spotted some bottles of Chateau Rauzan-Sègla from an early vintage, a fine Margaux Bordeaux claret. The price was well below what Stuart had expected, and so he promptly purchased the entire stock of several bottles.

In between visits from London colleagues, I would visit the City to give reports and talk to fund managers about trends and performance. To minimise costs, because I was aware that the IoM operation had not yet become very profitable, I stayed in rather dingy basement B&B accommodation in Hammersmith. The house my first wife and I owned in Putney was rented out for about £400 per month, and I was reluctant to spend big money in London hotels. The B&B I used most was run by an ex-RAF man, 'Big Bill', who enjoyed a pint in a nearby pub, so that was where I usually finished my evenings after a pizza or a fish-and-chip supper somewhere in the King's Road, Hammersmith.

I tried very hard to engender interest in our business on the island by visiting the local stockbrokers, accountancy firms, and banks, including Mannin in Castletown. Graham Reid, his wife Jules, and their children became close friends. They hosted spectacularly lavish family Sunday lunches whilst throwing themselves fully into island social life. To see them working a room was a sight to behold and would inevitably result in invitations being issued to drinks and dinner parties at a later date, and no doubt new potential client meetings.

John Ormond was another entrepreneur from the City who had come to live on the island with his wife Diane, a vivacious and proudly Scottish lady, and family. He and his family lived in quite a large and cosy farmhouse on the south of the island and were the third leg of our friendship stool on the island. John had founded a unit trust business in the City and sold out very profitably. He developed his own insurance company on the island and found he needed software to run it, so he set up a very successful software company that provides banking software internationally.

I recall writing an article for the *Isle of Man Courier* that recommended that residents sell their Irish gilts and buy UK-managed or offshore funds – hopefully ours. Irish gilts were an extremely popular investment locally. The yield was much higher than on equivalent UK bonds, but were subject to currency variations, since they were denominated in Irish punts. My argument was that the Irish currency would ultimately devalue against sterling and that now was the time to sell!

The furore that swept over me was truly powerful. I had upset all the partners at the largest firm, AL Stott & Co., who had been buyers of our funds, along with a whole host of others. It was quite a while before things settled down again, but it served a purpose in getting the business noticed, and more than a few investors came directly to the office to discuss making investments in our funds. Dursley Stott, the senior partner, had previously had contact with Jim Slater and knew Britannia's history, so he was a natural ally as far as his clients were concerned, so long as he received reciprocal commission (as did every other UK stockbroker who placed more than £25,000 into our funds).

During my time on the island I set up a sub-branch in Arthur Street, Belfast, at the back of an estate agent's office. It was just inside the security zone. Looking for business in Belfast was partly to placate my local Isle of Man director, Stewart Jamieson, a businessman from Northern Ireland. He owned an executive air taxi service that was run out of Ronaldsway, the Isle of Man's airport. He was appointed with a hefty retainer to promote Britannia amongst his connections on the island, and in Belfast, where he would be able to influence locals to invest in our funds via the Isle of Man. The IoM was perceived, wrongly, to be somewhere where money and things close to it could be effectively undisclosed from the tax authorities both north and south of the Irish border.

Flying into and out of Ronaldsway and Belfast City Airport was completely without formalities. Although 'customs' (not border controls) existed, it usually meant the acknowledgement of a single customs officer on the way through the airport building. There were no body scanners, and no examination of luggage was required. Even flying to the main Aldergrove Belfast International Airport was comparatively straightforward, even with the 'troubles' in full swing. Likewise, entry through Jersey Airport had always been distinctly relaxed and informal.

As far as I recall, Jamieson's only business contribution was to introduce me to his lawyer, a Mr Fitch, senior partner of a large solicitors' practice near Belfast City Hall. More usefully, he could nearly always allow me to accompany him, without charge, on one of his weekly flights to the Harbour Airport, which was significantly nearer the city than Aldergrove – the main airport – whenever I made a visit, usually every two weeks. Stuart knew nothing about our business but did invest a modest amount which didn't perform as he had hoped, so he quickly sold out and never took any more interest in anything to do with it.

A small one-room office was found at the back of an estate agent's premises in Arthur Street. It was just inside the city's security zone. The office would be unmanned between my visits and acted as a holding point for literature and for any meetings, though there were never any meetings held there: always at the offices of my connections! The estate agent secretaries would pass on messages or requests when I appeared. It was agreed by my colleagues in London that there would be no signage, even though Arthur Street was well inside central Belfast. To enter the security zone required body and baggage searches at one of a number of checkpoints controlled by local police dressed in black bullet-proof clothing. Intimidating stuff!

Belfast in the late 1970s and early 1980s was, in the light of history, about a quarter of the way through its 'troubles'. The Europa Hotel in Victoria Street, where I had stayed on my initial visits, was surrounded by barbed wire, metal fences, security guards, cameras, and manned sentry boxes. Despite all these measures, it had been bombed numerous times, but it stayed in business, albeit with disruptions from time to time. It was our favoured venue for holding seminars and lunches for the Northern Irish investment community, who all understood the 'drill' should we suddenly find ourselves being bombed by the IRA.

Because of the Europa Hotel's reputation as regular IRA bomb target, I decided to stay at a small pub about twelve miles out of the city. It was situated in a small village, beyond Hollywood on the Bangor Road. It was an away-from-it-all place, and it was also quite a bit less expensive. It had an excellent restaurant with a qualified sommelier, was staffed by very friendly people, and had quiet bedrooms. The breakfasts were truly magnificent; the 'Irish Special' was a regular order. Having tried all the rooms at the back away from the road, over time I came to prefer the Rose room overlooking attractive gardens. I was fortunate that a stockbroker connection from Cunningham & Co. also lived in the village, as did his parents, and he was quite prepared to take me by car in and out of the city every day of my two or three-day visits. On one occasion the *BBC* reporter Brian Hanrahan (famous for his Falklands war TV news report from the aircraft carrier *Ark Royal:* 'I counted them out, and I counted them all in.') stayed whilst I was there.

It turned out that my friend's father was a High Court judge, and I was invited to dinner on one occasion. The house was well set back up a modest drive from a small road and completely hidden from view by trees and evergreen shrubs. As we sat in the comfortable sitting room, I was told that all the windows in the house were double glazed and bullet proof. The house had been attacked in the past, and these were the protections needed. I was very surprised and shocked. It made me appreciate that really nowhere was truly safe.

As with the Europa Hotel, the centre of Belfast was similar to being in a war zone, with barbed-wire barricades, armed military and police constantly peering under cars and scanning buildings, manned sentry boxes, and personal body searches to enter 'security zones'. It wasn't a relaxing place to be. It wasn't unknown for bombs to be set off or for buildings to be evacuated after hoax 'warnings'. I was advised on several occasions either not to go to various places or not to stay too long in others for fear of being identified as a possible military person, because of English accent, dress or sixth sense. The Tudor Inn across the street from my office was, however, a great place for lunch, even though it was close to one of the security entry points, manned by armed military personnel. Lunch was usually steak, salad, and chips on Fridays. Being inside the city centre security zone gave me a considerable feeling of personal safety. Outside it, I always felt that at any time something serious could happen without notice. Certainly, it was always wise to steer clear of groups of people congregating in the streets.

Usually I made my way around the city by taxi or, for short distances, on foot. On one occasion I joined a taxi rank queue and couldn't understand why people around me would get into these black cabs in numbers, while I was never being successful in having one to myself. It turned out that people who lived up the Shankhill Road used cabs from this point. The Shankhill area of Belfast was and still is a predominantly Loyalist area. Residents in this religiously divided city used specific taxis from specific taxi ranks rather than the public buses, which were frequently hijacked and fire-bombed.

On another occasion I took a public taxi from the city out to Aldergrove, now known as the George Best International Airport. The driver explained that, as the normal route was very busy, he'd take me another way, which happened to be up the Shankhill Road. It was a busy commercial road, and we were following a freight lorry which came to a stop at a pedestrian crossing. At once the driver told me to look straight ahead and not look anyone directly in the eye, as there would be a 'raid'. Immediately young men arrived as if from nowhere, mounted the back of the truck in front, and opened its rear doors. They promptly emptied it of its intended delivery of groceries. No one said a word. There was no shouting and, thankfully, no shooting, and the thugs made off into the afternoon shopping crowds with their booty.

My most frightening experience, however, was on another airport taxi trip, this time with Jamieson, out to the city airport. Bobby Sands had been on hunger strike for several weeks, and black flags were draped from houses throughout residential streets which were becoming increasingly choked with traffic. As we had to take off at a particular time, Jamieson told the driver to drive between some metal traffic bollards and to cross an empty car park to save time. The taxi driver said he didn't know where we were now going. Jamieson said he did, and we just squeezed through the bollards. As we reached the other side of the deserted car park, it became apparent that we were about to enter a street where there was a full-blown stand-off between the army and IRA supporters at either end. They stood about two hundred yards apart. It seemed possible that at any moment our appearance would be the distraction for either side to set off a full-blown gun battle.

Jamieson and I were told to lie down on the floor of the taxi as the driver got up speed. We were thrown from side to side as he made his way through nearby narrow streets towards our waiting plane. It really had been quite a frightening experience.

I also visited Dublin and stayed at the Shelbourne Hotel on St. Stephen's Green several times. It had an enormous horseshoe-shaped bar with alcoves of windows that could be moved to shield faces or conversations from other drinkers. It was a luxuriously comfortable place and a watering hole for politicians from both north and south of the border. I once saw John Hume there – later to win the Noble Peace Prize. The Gresham Hotel in O'Connell Street was another favourite hotel, standing opposite the old General Post Office where the Easter uprising of 1916 had been focussed. From this hotel I once went by train to Limerick. On several occasions I flew to Cork, where the airport is five hundred feet above sea level on a plateau above the surrounding farmland. I asked a taxi driver once on the way to my hotel how far above sea level was the airport. He replied that 'it was several miles'! Eventually we got my question understood.

The Isle of Man business and the Belfast office closed when I left the island in 1982. We left because my then wife and I were concerned about the future education of our children. Both appeared reasonably bright at their primary school, the Buchan in Castletown, but we both sensed that secondary education on the island might be lacking and the alternative choice at the local public school, King William's also in Castletown, would be too insular within the island. If either or both of our children were to represent the school, we would face large travel costs for them to travel to other schools in England, which we couldn't afford.

Chapter 7

City Establishment: Cultural Change

From on an advertisement in the *Daily Telegraph*, I applied to join Hill Samuel Unit Trust Managers, based at 55 Bread Street in the Barbican. I was interviewed by Neville Bowen, the chief executive, and I would report to Ron Lewis, a director and lifelong employee within the group. He had a life and pensions background gained through Noble Lowndes, one of the country's largest and most prestigious pension advisory consultancies, and a wholly owned subsidiary of the merchant bank Hill Samuel & Co. He in turn reported to Audrey Head, who, unusually for a woman those days, was a director of City business – an investment management business. Audrey was later to become chairperson of the Unit Trust Association.

She had quite a fearsome reputation, but we got along very well in matters of business. My job was to develop business internationally for both the UK and offshore businesses in Jersey and Switzerland, where the bank had a subsidiary – Bank von Ernst et Cie (BvE) based in Marktgasse, Berne. It was a private bank established in 1869 that became owned by Coutts & Co. and later was part of the Royal Bank of Scotland.

BvE epitomised everything a Swiss bank was imagined to be. Not only was the entrance discretely accessed at first floor level, with only a brass plate notice in the ground floor arcade below of fashionable shops, but on entry no one could be seen. No clients, no staff, no-one behind the bank counter. Within a few moments however someone would appear and ask if I had an appointment and with whom and at what time. I was never ever asked my name. It was all part of exercising discretion and privacy. Ever since, I have cringed in solicitors', doctors', dentists' and other reception areas when my name has been asked for quite unnecessarily.

My secretary in London was a young, single, but attached 'Sloane Ranger' type, Claudia Beale. She was short, attractive, and well-spoken with a very bubbly personality. In addition to being hugely efficient, she was an excellent people manager and became extremely good at protecting me from unnecessary calls and demands. She was an outgoing girl whose family lived in Wiltshire where her father bred Limousin cattle. In fact, he was one of the first to do so in the UK and was chairman of the British Limousin Cattle Society.

It was conventional and tax-advantageous at the time to be offered a company car as part of a remuneration package once one's employment role had reached a certain status, or need. On one of my trips to London for interviews at Hill Samuel, I had called into the Piccadilly showrooms of Rootes Motors (makers of such models as Hillman, Sunbeam, Humber, and Singer). The business had been acquired from Chrysler by Peugeot, who had announced the launch of a new large estate version of the 504, which I liked. 'CGW 704H' was duly collected from a depot in Edgware. It was enormously long, it had three rows of seats (great for two youngsters who could be driven about without irritating each other), but it was so slow to accelerate. It had enormous and noisy wind resistance at any speed above sixty mph. Having been so pleased to have ordered a brand spanking new version of a car, it was the ultimate disappointment!

The investment managers all sat outside the office I shared with Ron. Some went on to great things in the UK. One of them, Paul Manduca, headed up the UK smaller companies analysts team and was notably successful. Quite a bit later, he became chairman of Prudential Assurance after having been a founder of Threadneedle Asset Management and a former chief executive of Rothschild Asset Management and Deutsche Asset Management.

Sometime in 1985 I was summoned to the office of the managing director, Roger Kitson, an ex-naval man. He told me that in 1986 the whole way of city stockbroker dealing would change in a phenomenon known as Big Bang and that simultaneously an EU Directive (Directive 1985/611/EC) would be issued from Brussels allowing the sale 'cross border' of investment funds. It was to become effective in 1988 and was known as the 'UCITS Directive', the first of several directives for Undertakings for Collective Investment in Transferable Securities that would be issued in the following years in an attempt to present a level playing field for the marketing (initially) but later the entire administration, conduct of business, management, and supervisory management of collective investment schemes such as unit trusts across the entire EU no matter where in the EU they were managed. Kitson appeared to think I knew what the UCITS Directive would mean and what its significance would be for the industry. He wanted Hill Samuel to become leaders in this new European market, and my role would be critical for its success. My career was about to take an important and significant new direction.

One of the other directors was Harvey Booth, who commuted from Clifton Hampden in Oxfordshire and who was ostensibly a North American investment analyst but appeared not to do much. He had been heavily involved with the funds managed by BvE. He flew with me on the first of many Sunday afternoon flights I would make in the next few years to Berne to introduce me to the team there. Berne, although it was the Swiss capital, had a small airport with small and intimate buildings. These led out immediately to immaculate flower beds, mostly of bright red geraniums, that surrounded the car park. The Bernese Oberland made for a very attractive backdrop, and the weather there was invariably warmer on arrival than the weather left in the UK. Berne was a very appealing and comfortable place to visit. What wasn't quite so attractive was the sight of bears kept in a circular area some fifteen feet below pavement level near the city centre!

Sunday afternoon flights

BvE had a small range of mostly Swiss franc and some US$ denominated funds. Some had rather odd names. The most oddly named was Crossbow Fund, which invested in European markets. Generally, the overall level of performance of all the funds was average at best. Beat Ungricht effectively headed up the Swiss fund operation, reporting to Fritz Josi, the managing director. Peter Marti was a fund analyst and manager, and George Hemmer was a marketing assistant there.

David Humpleby headed up the Jersey-based funds reporting to managing director Tony Pope, a lifelong Hill Samuel banker who had been parachuted into the Hill Samuel Jersey branch from London. The bank operation was effectively managed by Martin Chambers. Martin was a delightful Jersey man, unflustered, charming, and effective. The Trust Department was run by Peter Watts, a supremely confident, almost over confident individual, but one who knew his business inside out and was utterly professional. I would bring cohesion to the marketing of the funds in European and other overseas markets and in so doing would report directly to both offshore offices, whilst Ron would keep an eye on me in the London office I shared with him.

The Jersey office of Hill Samuel, Hill Samuel (CI) Limited, was a branch of the London-quoted merchant bank (Hill Samuel & Co.) with a local investment arm. The Hill Samuel Jersey funds business had already set out to become a dominant force among expatriates in

Spain by opening a branch near Marbella for banking and investment business. Derek Culshaw claimed to have been part of the pop group Fleetwood Mac before they became 'big'. He had been Watts's assistant in running the Trust Department in Jersey and had moved out to run the Marbella office from his flat near there. Derek had recently separated from his wife, but I was never sure if he was put there to help him recover from his alcoholism. Kill or cure would seem to have been a management motive given that alcohol there was even less expensive than in Jersey! Anyway the concept of selling direct to expatriates effectively killed off the possibility of generating funds in volume through several well-established intermediaries. Because of this half thought through marketing plan and (in my view) because there was no 'office', this Spanish initiative was never successful and after a couple of years it was closed down.

Soon after I arrived, the Jersey office created a Managed Currency Fund ('MCF') with five sub funds denominated in Sterling, US Dollars, Swiss Francs, Deutschmarks and Japanese Yen. An advertising campaign was put together and a prospectus produced using the services of Berkhoff & Co, an advertising and corporate communications agency based in Maddox Street, W1. They produced an extremely clever pictorial device to use as the cover of the prospectus and to incorporate in advertising, showing a chess piece on a chessboard made up of currency symbols. This was to convey the message to a probably wealthy investor audience that managing cash deposits was analogous to a game of chess.

We were the only financial clients Berkhoff's had, which, having always used specialists, was in a way was regarded as a 'positive', as they would be unencumbered with traditional financial marketing concepts. C&A, the high street fashion and department store were their biggest clients, for whom they held the complete corporate design and implementation brief. Despite this and despite their total unfamiliarity with placing financial advertising in the weekend press, the launch campaign for the MCF raised over £160 million. Everyone was astounded and naturally very pleased. My career here had got off to a good start!

Regular meetings were held several times a year in Jersey and Switzerland with Martin Chambers and Peter Watts. In Jersey I generally stayed at L'Horizon Hotel – a five-star hotel right on the beach at St Brelade. On one occasion the Swiss directors also came to stay, and Beat Ungricht complained in the morning about the sound of the sea – only a few feet away throughout the night. He hadn't found it restful at all; in fact he said he would have found the sound of snow falling much more conducive to sleep. Such are the differences in national preferences!

Travelling internationally, on a Sunday afternoon became routine from now on. In Berne, I always stayed at The Bellevue Palace Hotel (at least 5 star!) looking out to the Bernese Oberland and the River Aahr below. It was a very special place, offering what it called 'Bernese hospitality and statesmanlike discretion in an uncomplicated and courteous manner'. Beat, Fritz and I would spend many an evening drinking Swiss wine, Willhelms pear schnapps and other local beverages in the Palace bar, before and after many splendid dinners, with superbly choreographed waiter service. Occasionally we were joined by George Hemmer, a delightful young man, very reserved, highly attentive to his business work and with a wry sense of humour. He was the Administration Manager in the bank. Dining on the Terrasse was especially enjoyable in the summer months.

Belle vue de Bellevue Palace, Berne

'Away days' were a new experience and occurred with every company I worked with from this point on. The first day away with Hill Samuel was to Ashridge College, a management college in Hertfordshire. It was a splendid place. I definitely remember not taking much in or contributing to proceedings very much because I was thoroughly overwhelmed by the size, scale, and beauty of the place and I was feeling rather inferior to the brains around me.

Another corporate outing was to the Boca Raton Resort in Florida. We spent a week there! The expense must have been enormous. It was a huge pink-coloured palace of a place. The most notable session was an address given by the economist J.K. Galbraith, who, although he was a fairly elderly man, gave a most interesting and enlightening paper. Quite what the topic was I can't now remember, but I do recall being very impressed by his delivery and 'presence'.

Working with BvE was always fun especially once a year when a staff day-out was organised for usually an autumn Saturday. Beat would ask different departments to take turns in organising a secret itinerary of events which usually all bank staff would make an effort to attend. One year we met at the main train station and the mystery day began with a two hour trip to Lake Lucerne to visit a the lake-side Chateau de Chillon which Byron had visited and a venue for part of the annual Jazz Festival. We then continued to Cerne which was the site of a nuclear facility (and later the Large Hadron Collider project), and the Bex (*Saline de Bex*) salt mine.

We reached the mine via a trip of several minutes, possibly ten but seemingly longer, in a noisy, miniature underground train similar in size to the Romney, Hythe and Dymchurch railway but with totally enclosed sliding doors similar to a London Underground train. It was the first time I had felt claustrophobia – being enclosed with the tunnel walls passing inches away from the windows and sitting with legs cramped up side by side with other people. Having arrived at a truly cavernous space we found a bar and the train disappeared. Someone made a joke about being left there and having to do some digging.

Train to the salt mines

In due time the train reappeared and we were on our way out to our waiting coaches. The next port of call was at the Clos de la Blonaire situated amongst its own vineyards. We were told that we could have a wine tasting and so everyone began to make the most of the generous hospitality. After a while we were told we'd be staying there for dinner and dancing! I was beginning to sense a Swiss sense of humour! Having also visited Castle Gruyère in Fribourg earlier in the day I was amused to wonder which came first the Counts whose name the castle has, or the cheese.

As usual the dinner was superb. Everyone enjoyed the meal and drinks, accompanied by a small traditional Swiss music group. Later the dancing was to begin, but first, as bank tradition has it, the newest and youngest staff members were introduced, and the longest serving and oldest were presented with small gifts from management. The recruits to the bank were then called up in a line and asked to turn round and bend over. To my amazement they all did so! (Swiss discipline!). Everyone laughed and shouted to loud applause.

It was then announced that the youngest male on the staff would start the evening's dancing with the oldest female! Hilarity! Shouting! Laughter! The young man took hold, rather awkwardly and embarrassingly, with the lady and was poised to start. The band played a march! Impossible to dance to! The young lad tried his damnedest to do at least some sort of dance. The lady played along with the effort, but eventually everyone collapsed in laughter. I then knew I had seen Swiss humour!

After several meetings with my international colleagues, it was decided to develop business directly overseas by visiting areas populated by expatriate workers. Naturally, British expats were likely to be our biggest market, but expats from other countries would not be excluded. We would try to build an international clientele. The concept was that expatriates, from wherever they came, the United States, Europe, India etc., would have their investment savings managed, usually within a wrapper – quite often an offshore discretionary trust administered from Jersey or the Swiss equivalent. Our approach, appealed mostly to professionals and life-long expatriate employees, and would therefore be significantly different to the solutions generally offered, being a good deal more tax effective and totally bespoke.

I was tasked with arranging the international visits – travel, accommodation, appointments, seminar facilities and equipment, and hospitality. I usually did all this either by telephone or fax. During the coming years, I would travel alone within Europe to Spain, France, Germany, Austria, Italy, Cyprus, Malta, Portugal, Ireland, Luxembourg, Sweden, Denmark and Holland. Usually, I would stay for three to four days, depending on business levels and potential.

Further afield, I would travel with Peter Watts as managing director of the Jersey Trust Company, giving tax-based presentations and sometimes also with Peter Marti, an investment manager within BvE, who would give investment-based presentations. I covered corporate background, our investment performance and market outlook. The countries we visited included Saudi Arabia, Kuwait, Bahrain, the UAE, Oman, Hong Kong, Singapore, Indonesia, and Brunei. International 'tours' to several countries in any one region would generally last up to two weeks. These trips took place every twice a year usually in the spring and late autumn.

The Sheraton, Bahrain

Marti was a great follower of charts and various investment wave theories, notably the 'Elliott wave'. The Elliott wave principle is a form of technical analysis that some traders use to analyse financial market cycles and forecast market trends by identifying extremes in investor psychology, highs and lows in prices, and other collective factors. He also followed the Kondratiev wave theory, also called supercycles. These are great surges, long waves, K-waves, or the long economic cycle that are supposedly cycle-like phenomena in the modern world economy. Averaging fifty years but ranging from approximately forty to sixty years, the cycles consist of alternating periods between high economic sector growth and periods of relatively slow growth. Interestingly, although Kondratiev was a Russian, his ideas were not supported by the Soviet government; subsequently he was sent to the gulag and executed in 1938.

We began with visits to Bahrain, Abu Dhabi, Dubai, Kuwait, Qatar, Saudi Arabia, and Oman. Each offered its own challenges, but the meetings, generally held in conference rooms within the five-star hotels we stayed in, were generally well attended. Direct invitations were sent to known expatriates, (because of previous enquiries) in each location, and advertising in local and international expatriate media which announced the programme and timetable of our visits. An attendance of more than two dozen was regarded as acceptable. Of these we would hope to meet later with at least eighty per cent; any more, and we would not have had enough time. At the end of each trip there would be a reckoning of how productive and profitable the trip had been in terms of immediate and future fee income. We never failed to show a profit. Later, business would be developed with institutional investors in these places – bigger in volume and much more profitable. But more on that later.

Meetings were also set up with local banks in each location to promote our international investment management expertise. Not only in the Middle East but throughout my travels discussions were always conducted in English. Middle Eastern banks employed mostly either British or American staff at senior levels. Local Arab men, wearing traditional dress would also occupy senior positions but seemingly in more non-executive roles. Observing local customs was important: such as not showing the soles of your shoes when sitting cross-legged, or raising the palm of your hand which were both regarded as being highly offensive. It was noticeable that all Arab men had the most beautiful, wide, straight feet from normally wearing sandals: not shoes.

This all changed on international flights to Europe when men would disappear in traditional dress to change, as if by magic, into in western dress!

Flying long distances soon became routine. Both Peters would fly to London, and we would all depart from Heathrow, usually by British Airways. Cathay Pacific and Singapore Airlines were very close runners up. A visit to the BA Executive Club lounge was always a necessary prelude, and we usually consumed a bottle of champagne between us. If it wasn't on the counter, Peter Watts would ask for one. Drinking continued pretty much throughout the flights, whilst we were entertained by in-flight audio channels or looked at films displayed on screens placed overhead down the length of the cabin at intervals of about ten seat rows. Within the Middle East and for any overnight sectors to the Far East we flew first class.

On arrival it wasn't unusual for passports to be taken by one official at check-in, to be out of sight for a while, and finally to be returned by another official through another window. This was quite frightening.

The occupation shown in the passport was important information for Customs Officers almost everywhere I travelled to, but especially in the Middle East. 'Marketing manager' created some enquiries and delayed the queue behind me quite often. The occupation which caused most delay was 'Journalist' however, with the passport holder being questioned often for several minutes, even taken to a side room, before being allowed to enter the country. Quite what it was about this profession which caused so much apparent unease mystified me. The only thought I had was that maybe there were things in the country in question which were best left unknown to the outside world.

Bearing in mind that most Gulf States are Islamic and alcohol is banned (at least officially), we found on arrival that all luggage would be routinely opened and everything inspected – literally everything. However, it was widely rumoured that local princes had enormous bars within their palaces, stocked with the very best vintage wines and fine spirits. Magazines, especially colour magazines, showing too much female flesh (underwear advertisements, tampons, let alone fashion shots) were thrown to one side, to be leered at in private, we suspected, by the customs officials later! On one occasion in Bahrain, a fellow passenger had two family size Melton Mowbray pork pies opened from their grease-proof wrapping and was asked what they were. One was broken in half and smelt. The customs officer was told they were cakes. They were not confiscated! We were told that telephone calls were regularly monitored for the use of certain words (undisclosed rather unhelpfully) which could be identified as possible threats to national security.

Our hotels were almost always one of a chain – either InterContinental or Sheraton. We would generally try to keep our costs down by eating in the coffee shops of these places. These provided a good menu of international food. Often they were beautifully decorated with amazing flower displays, and usually they had large and detailed ice sculptures of birds or fish. How they didn't melt within a few hours was always a mystery to me. Other sculptures would sometimes be made of butter.

Flights in the Gulf were pretty routine and uneventful. The airports were by and large brand new, air conditioned, and spacious. Riyadh Airport became one of the most opulent, with wonderful displays of growing flowers and plants and gushing waterfalls. The exception was Qatar airport which was dingy, smoke-filled and cramped. Flying business class meant we were separated from the h*oi polloi* and a good deal of hassle.

Most travellers were not Europeans. Africans, Asians, and Indian sub-continentals made up the majority. They seemed to carry every possession they had with them. Few had anything approaching a suitcase. Possessions were generally parcelled up quite loosely into large cardboard boxes, or large plastic bags and tied up with varying success with string. All of these not only seemed likely to exceed any known baggage allowance but also not survive the inevitable handling treatment they would get before collection at their destination.

Travelling by air between and across these neighbouring countries and looking out of the window whenever possible, I felt great pleasure in seeing such foreign and interesting landscapes. The tracks made by Bedouin camel trains could be seen clearly criss-crossing the deserts which stretched as far as the eye could see. The shapes of moving sand dunes were beautifully curved and sometimes very tall; the rocky escarpments and mountains – especially in the south part of the Arabian peninsula – and the comparatively new green crop circles were all fascinating. These large circles, probably several hundred metres across, of irrigated green crops seemed incongruous in such hostile climatic conditions. The colour contrasted strongly with the surrounding, usually yellow sand. The cost of obtaining the irrigation water, probably from aquifers, or hundreds of miles from the desalination plants, which all these countries relied on for the town and city water supplies, must have been huge.

Visiting the Kingdom of Saudi Arabia ('KSA' or 'Saudi') was a complicated procedure, as every visitor had to be invited by a local person of some standing who as 'sponsor' would vouch for his guests whilst they were in the country. The bank overcame this difficulty by establishing contact through Bank von Ernst with a wealthy sheik, Sheik Yousef, who was a resident of Jeddah on the Red Sea. Documentation and visas had to be obtained through the KSA embassy in London, ideally (but seldom) several weeks ahead of travel. Invariably there would be delays and hold-ups, and because the procedure was lengthy, the bank had someone who did this job and nothing else, not just for Saudi but for other countries in the region and elsewhere.

Jeddah sea front

Arriving in Riyadh on our first trip was stimulating but caused us some apprehension given the procedures and enquires we had to make to get there. We arrived in the late evening after sunset. The airport and the roads leading into the city were mysterious, dusty, rather unkempt, mostly a beige or brown colour, poorly lit, and not particularly inviting. Some thirty minutes later we reached the outskirts of the city. Here the predominantly small shops were more brightly lit, and the occasional rather larger building was floodlit. We carried on for quite some time before arriving at our hotel – a Hilton, I think. It was not especially impressive. It was a sort of sand colour on the outside and rather functional inside, with what we were to discover on later visits was an almost mandatory Bedouin tent arrangement set up in the lobby, complete with colourful carpets, cushions, and traditional Arabian brassware. None of it was for sale, and there was seldom anyone in it, although I suspect the idea was that visitors could sample Bedouin coffee, sweet lemon or herb infused tea and sweet cakes from time to time.

Dress for visiting these Middle Eastern countries meant buying lightweight suits. I had a beige safari suit which I enjoyed wearing, not least because it was very comfortable, cool, and probably rather different from clothes worn by others doing pretty much the same thing as I was. Some of the expats I met in the institutions also wore these. I bought mine in Bahrain. I also soon discovered that, because of the daytime heat, travelling to business meetings necessitated travel by air-conditioned taxi no matter how close to the hotel the offices were, not just here but elsewhere in the Middle East in years to come. Taxis were readily available and would be hailed by the doormen of every hotel I was to stay in.

Only once did it rain in Riyadh on my visits to Saudi Arabia. It caused a surprising event. On my way to one of the banks, my taxi driver decided without any explanation that he didn't want to continue with the journey. Rain was bucketing down, and we were stationary in a traffic jam. Few taxi drivers understood or spoke more than very basic English. Somehow sign language and pointing to maps or business addresses was enough to get from A to B. My driver wound down his window and spoke to the driver of an adjacent taxi in Arabic. I was motioned to change cars in the rain in amongst all the traffic of a multi-lane highway. In retrospect I should have been more circumspect, but a kidnapping wasn't something I had anticipated. In the event, all was well – except for the inability of Arabs to drive on wet roads covered with a dusting of sand. Their skills in these conditions were about the same as Brits driving on ice!

Staying in any hotel in Saudi was quite different to anywhere else, not least because of the sense of isolation I felt. The rules of society were so different. The suspicion that one was being watched every step of the way was quite palpable and intimidating. Going out and strolling around was not something I felt able to do very often in the cooler evenings, so watching TV in my room was the norm. This wasn't easy either, as only local stations were available and none were in English. News reports here, as indeed in most of the Middle Eastern countries I went to, consisted of footage of arriving foreign dignitaries being greeted at the airport, usually by members of the local ruling family, and then being hosted in the local ruler's palace. To boost national moral, news items about naval exercises or air power would be frequently shown. After the local national news, international news would consist of foreign TV companies' footage with Arabic subtitles and over-dubbed in the local guttural language.

Green, being the traditional colour for Islam, and supposedly Mohammed's favourite colour, was the predominant colour for most things, from the national flag, minaret flood lighting, to store signs, to carpets.

We rarely saw our sponsor. However, when we did, he was always most interested in our activities, supportive, and helpful. On one occasion Watts and I were having supper in the hotel coffee shop in Riyadh when we saw him walk through the lobby. We were rather concerned, as one of the rules was that we were not allowed to openly canvas for business. Hence, our presentations were always described as 'receptions', soft drinks and canapés being served before we discreetly closed the doors and curtains and proceeded with the sales pitch! Had we been caught we would have been deported and the Sheik would never have been allowed to invite us again.

Flouting the Rules!

One of our first visits in the Middle East was to the Aramco refinery in Al Khobar in the Eastern Province of Saudi Arabia. It is an immense complex and has the equivalent size and the amenities of a moderately sized town. The whole place is fenced off from the surrounding desert, and although it is within KSA, is obviously an American place with American standards. We made our presentations in a school and were then taken on a tour of the campus where American language could be heard and read everywhere. For Americans it must be home from home. The most memorable thing we saw was a pipe, about nine inches in diameter which, we were told, had been producing oil since 1926 coming out from the ground, and joining other pipes in parallel lines across the site to be refined.

Given the xenophobia Saudi's felt for foreigners (although they would vehemently deny it and always be overly polite and obliging), we were always very concerned that we should not be found out. KSA was unique in my experience in that although everything appeared to be 'normal', the whole place was utterly under the control of the religious and state police and the national army. It was the only place I went to which felt like a closed state. Communication with the outside world was restricted. TV news was reported only on national events or meetings with visiting heads of state. Most expats in Saudi lived in compounds – usually gated housing estates. Generally these provided high quality housing, and their communities would keep alert for any unexpected activity. Obviously, drinking alcohol was strictly forbidden. Occasionally someone would get busted for home brewing beer or wines made from locally purchased ingredients.

On one occasion Watts and I were invited to a client's house in a compound in Riyadh. No sooner had we arrived and the lights had been switched on than the telephone rang. A fellow estate resident wanted to know if our hosts had returned from a visit back to the UK, and would they like to come over for a barbecue. They were told they had guests, but we were all invited and enjoyed excellent food. Somehow they also had gin and whisky, Gordon's and Famous Grouse. We duly imbibed, and it was lovely.

Getting back to the hotel at two o'clock in the morning wasn't a problem, as our hosts knew of and called a chauffeur service that duly rang the buzzer on the gate, and we left. The driver, a Tanzanian, was dressed in uniform with a peaked cap. He opened the door and with a knowing look took us discreetly back to the hotel. We had been extremely foolish, but at the same time we had cocked a snook at the system and had lived to tell the tale. The fear we felt, however, ensured we never transgressed again!

Shopping or just going out to walk in the streets in Saudi wasn't easy. The shopping areas and souks weren't in walking distance in the heat at any time of day or night. The view from the hotel bedrooms was invariably of other tall buildings and minarets. The five daily calls to prayer, here as elsewhere throughout my future years of middle-eastern visits, were evocative, timeless, and to me a wonderful sound which encapsulated regional culture and history. The populace duly prayed, literally wherever they happened to be, if not in one of the many mosques. Shops, large and small, emptied, closed, and were locked up every time only to reopen fifteen or twenty minutes later. Offices seemed to offer some discretion, with some employees going to a prayer room within the building. The inside of all toilet doors, and lifts in hotels and offices showed a sign pointing to Mecca in green Arabic script on a white background.

Marti, Watts trying his hand at salt grading, and me in the Saudi desert

Mad dogs in Saudi.

We all found ourselves in Riyadh one weekend (a Friday), which was a mistake in the planning on my part, as it their weekly holy day and everywhere was closed. However, we made the most of it by asking a taxi to take us out into the desert. So in the heat of the day we set off to be given a guided tour. Eventually we left the city and found ourselves surrounded by the desert that stretched to the horizon sand dunes. Remarkably, we had been taken to a place where the desert was clearly defined between red sand and white sand. We gazed at this phenomenon for quite a while. There seemed to be no explanation for the two sand colours to be so clearly demarcated for miles into the distance. It was here that I collected a desert rose, a hard crystallised sand cluster formed naturally into petals which I have kept as an ornament.

On departure things could be equally eye-popping. Whilst we were waiting for a plane, prayers were called on one occasion and men disappeared into what I found to be the gents. As there was time enough, I too went to use these facilities, only to find as I walked in that the place was full of men with their dish-dashes raised up. They had their feet up on the washbasins while they washed their bums by hand. This was a surprising and unexpected sight to say the least, but I was impressed with this degree of personal cleanliness and adopted the practice thereafter – after first using paper! The WCs were ceramic holes in the floor within open cubicles. The smell was truly horrific.

Flying within Saudi Arabia was always by first class. This ensured a degree of preferential treatment and an expectation that the passengers around us would behave conventionally. This didn't always prove to be the case, as on one occasion I was seated behind a local who had taken a hawk on board, which was chained, hooded, and attached to its owner for the flight. On another occasion it transpired that someone in the economy section had lit an incense burner on the floor to accompany prayers which were announced over the planes PA system before every take off as part of the safety announcements.

Three other separate events in Saudi Arabia come to mind. The first was when at about two o'clock in the morning at Al-Khobar airport while we were waiting for an internal flight to Riyadh and with the departure area almost empty of passengers, an African-looking woman carrying, as many do, a large fabric covered container on her head, was unable to get through the body scanner not only because of her height but her enormous girth. She was told to unload her head load and succumb to a body inspection. This revealed some more possessions – mostly kitchen pots, pans, and utensils. As she released her outer garment, it became caught in a moving luggage carousel. The result was that she had no option but to be stripped to her underclothing as she was rotated by the consuming machinery! She became utterly distraught at her personal humiliation and had to be taken away to be sedated.

The second occasion was one afternoon when I had an appointment with a university professor in Riyadh. This developed into a visit to the university's museum, where I was shown ancient manuscripts and other treasures, including early printings of the Koran with colourful calligraphy, inscriptions and illustrations that are never shown publicly. My Arab host, in traditional dress as was the custom everywhere I was to visit in the Middle East, was most charming and informative and spoke excellent English, but sadly he never became a client.

The third occasion was again at Al-Khobar airport and the final time I left the Kingdom. I was taking a short flight to Bahrain, (the newly opened Causeway linking the two countries had been completed but not yet opened), when I found that after all the normal routine security checks had been made, there was a man sitting and guarding the door leading to the air bridge to the plane. He stopped me and asked me to put my brief case on the floor and promptly groped my testicles. Having had this pleasure he allowed me to board the flight. How I restrained myself I don't know, but quick thinking in the early of hours of a morning brought the prospect of being arrested for grievous bodily harm and put in a Saudi jail being deterrent enough.

Bahrain or Saudi: Causeway choice?

Kuwait was almost as intimidating as Saudi, except that women could work in offices and drive cars. On one occasion I met with a local business consultant who was especially proud of a new Lincoln car he'd bought. (Ford had recently been removed from a black list of importers.) The car was immensely long, black, and angular. In fact, it wasn't very attractive at all. I was collected from my hotel, the Sheraton, and taken to a favourite restaurant of his several times. It was along the Corniche and past the two enormous blue mosaic water towers which are landmarks in the city. I can't remember this man's name, but he said that he had preferred not to buy a Jaguar for himself as it was a 'feminine' car, so he had bought one for his wife. The Lincoln was much more macho.

We usually went to a Lebanese restaurant where the food was truly delicious – usually spiced lamb and beautifully presented vegetables. On another occasion this gentleman hosted a dinner at a Japanese restaurant where we were all required to sit cross-legged on the floor. Various bamboo-caned screens were moved into place, whilst the oriental waitresses prepared the rest of the room's decorations and closed any windows. No sooner had this been done than my friend opened up his business briefcase to reveal that it was full of whisky miniatures. He sprayed these around the low table so that we all had three or four each, and an evening of sushi and whisky was enjoyed by all! It was an amazing and wholly illegal experience, but not a wholly comfortable one.

Of course, everywhere in the Middle East was hot, sometimes very hot at 40 degrees centigrade or more. Kuwait somehow seemed hotter than anywhere else, and I sometimes thought that to fry an egg on a car or on the road would be very easy. I never had the thought anywhere else! For all its imperfections and difficulties to operate in, I quite enjoyed Kuwait. It still retained a subliminal relationship with France, perhaps inherited from some old historic link, and French could sometimes be spoken at my business meetings. I sensed some empathy with things French which I never came across elsewhere, but have never found any concrete reasons for.

The Sheraton Hotel wasn't particularly near the city or the sea, though being surrounded by sand, it felt as if the sea wasn't far away. An Arab wedding took place there during one of my stays. A lot of ululating women, fantastic flower displays everywhere, and mountains of food could be seen for the hundreds of guests. This hotel was taken over by the Iraqis at the time of their invasion of Kuwait in 1991. More than that, the whole place would have been badly damaged and windows blown out – even perhaps of the rooms where I had stayed. It was sad to think that the wonderfully friendly hotel staff might well have lost their lives at that time. The head concierge was always happy to share a joke and be helpful to inexperienced visitors.

Surprisingly, I found that every country was quite distinct in the way they felt to me as a visitor. Bahrain was pretty relaxed and had in the heart of the capital (Manama) a marvellous old working area partly covered with corrugated iron and occupied by metal workers from the Indian sub-continent, stripped to the waist in their hot environment, bashing hot forged metal. I shall never forget the sound of hammers on anvils ringing in a cacophony of un-coordinated sound. This corrugated metal area was situated next door to a modern shopping complex and the InterContinental Hotel, where we usually stayed.

The Holiday Inn however had been our first hotel, but it was rather too far from most of our appointments. The modern architecture here, as elsewhere, was breath-taking. The buildings were built with modern materials, but as the Victorians did with brick in England, it was used in daring, innovative, and imaginative ways. As elsewhere, there was a large expat community who earned and spent their large incomes on having a good time.

It was in Bahrain that I first saw street money changers. They occupied small open-fronted, shack-like premises. I was amazed at the lack of security when stacks of bank notes many inches high, held together with elastic bands, could so easily be accessed without any apparent security. Watching the traders counting piles of notes with dexterous use of forefinger and thumb was an amazing sight. Only later did I become aware that if anyone was caught stealing anything, the routine punishment was hand amputation.

As the city's shop lights began to attract evening shoppers, I recall seeing and hearing huge flocks of starlings covering the evening sky and swirling in great swoops before settling on the roadside plane trees above the noisy traffic. I wondered where they had all come from. England? London? My road in Putney? Possibly. For the most part Middle Eastern women were unseen, until after dusk when they would visit the souks looking for items of gold, and jewellery, and they didn't work. They wore full Arabic dress, being completely covered in black, with faces masked and sometimes veiled as well. They rarely walked alone: usually in small groups of three or four – possibly all married to the same man.

Manama High Street

Dubai, where we first stayed at the Regency which had a grand-prix track in its car park and an indoor skating rink. There was an agent, Ian Young, whose business Young & Co. (later known as Ridgeway Associates) was well established and had built up a significant business using investment products. Contact with him resulted on one occasion in a dinner in the grounds of a sheik's palace on the banks of the Creek. It was a marvellous, noisy occasion in the warmth of a Middle Eastern night. The menu inevitably included barbequed lamb, local, always fresh vegetables, and salads. I managed to avoid the sheep's eyes! Our preferred hotel here was the Sheraton on the Creek, but occasionally opted for the InterContinental, which was closer to the shops and souks, which we visited after sunset when it was comparatively cool.

Dubai had no oil or natural gas wealth. The ruling Al-Maktoum family had recognised that if it were to prosper, the State would have to offer something different from almost all its neighbours who were rich in natural resources. At the time the focus was on building up the port of Jebel Ali as a container hub port for goods being transported east to west and vice-versa. Tourism was rarely mentioned as a likely big-time income earner, and so the developments along Jumeirah Beach, which at the time had only one very swish and expensive hotel, had yet to begin. A sign of changing times ahead however was the building of a new international airport, since replaced by another covering 8% of the country's total area.

Occasionally Watts and I would venture along the coast to two other Emirate states, Ras al Khaimah ('RAK') and Sharjah. The bank had a branch in RAK managed by an Irishman who only ever came to see us in Abu Dhabi once. He never struck me as being particularly 'on side' and it wasn't obvious quite what his contribution was to the business so far away from where the real action was taking place, although he did mention offshore oil drilling rigs, and rather complex financing arrangements. Our return visit to RAK was very fleeting and unproductive. Both it and Sharjah seemed like places which would be ideal for a Wild-West film set apart from the obviously tumble down shacks and buildings. The roads were wide and dusty, nothing looked as if it had ever been tidied up, and derelict cars, buses, and trucks were all around. Tyre shops, battery shops, and dirty shop fronts were everywhere. It all made for an interesting insight into how things might have been not so many years earlier everywhere else in the Gulf.

We usually visited Abu Dhabi after Dubai. We travelled there by taxi for three hours across the desert. We made the trip usually in the late afternoon before nightfall, when camels would like to sleep on the warm road rather than on the sand. The InterContinental was again our preferred stop, or occasionally the Sheraton on the Corniche. This was a beautiful road alongside the sandy coast with wonderful architecture, wide pavements, fountains, and lamps. The Chelsea pub within this hotel could have been lifted straight out of Surrey, with its hunting prints, swirling patterned carpet, Bass beer, and one-armed bandits! It had a beautiful shaded garden on the beach to the rear which compensated for the heavy internal decoration.

Dusk on the Abu Dhabi – Dubai Highway

On one occasion at this Sheraton, Watts and I arrived, as usual rather tired, hot, and sweaty, only to be told that we didn't have the rooms for which we had a confirmation. The room had been taken by members of the local ruling family at a moment's notice. After making a fuss, we were eventually offered a suite on the top floor for the duration of our stay. We tossed a coin to decide which end of the suite we would each sleep in. We were separated by a sitting room/diner overlooking the gardens and the Gulf. We wondered how to make best use of our facilities and decided we would have a butler serve us breakfast in the mornings. This we duly arranged, unable to recognise ourselves with the butler standing by poring juice, coffee and serving our hot English breakfast!

The InterContinental was a larger hotel built on the Mound and quite detached from the rest of the city. It had its own theatre which visiting touring productions from London would use. It also had the most wonderful pool area, again overlooking the sea, and a fabulous palm-fringed al-fresco barbecue and bar. This was a truly lovely place to visit.

Self portrait

Leaving Abu Dhabi on one occasion early in the morning soon after sunrise was rather special. The flight had stopped on its schedule from a destination further east, and I found I was the only passenger boarding. A cantilevered bus collected me from the first-class lounge (I had been upgraded – a very rare occurrence) and delivered me to the aircraft alone. No one else was catching the flight there, and I felt rather as though it might have stopped just to collect me. It caused a bit of a stir in the cabin. Being the only one boarding, I got a lot of 'Who is he?' looks. It was rather enjoyable to be made such a fuss of at the end of a trip!

On one of these flights from Dubai back to London we were held on the ground for quite sometime before the pilot announced that because there was a red light showing on his control panel he would, having checked all the systems, close down all the plane's systems. We were told that the plane needed 'rebooting'. The air conditioning, reading and internal lights, external generators, and so on were switched off. A few minutes later various indicators of returning aircraft life were restored.

'The red light has now vanished', announced the captain. The engines were restarted and we took off, apparently satisfying all 'airworthiness' requirements!

I never felt in all my travels that being delayed on the ground meant that my flight was unsafe. In fact in many ways if an engineer had been called on board to look at a problem, I felt my plane was probably one of the safest possible to be on board.

The relationship between Dubai and Abu Dhabi was a strange and yet familiar one, in so far as, whilst they were and are independent state members of the UAE, Abu Dhabi was the commercial and business capital, whilst Dubai was second in size in most things and considerably less well developed. The commercial relationship between the two was similar to that between London and Edinburgh. Each was fiercely proud and wanted to be seen by the outside world as the better of the two.

When not at meetings we all enjoyed 'down time' by the pool of the hotels we stayed at. On several occasions in different locations we overheard discussions by other visiting guests talking about such things as aviation contracts, or developing infrastructure projects usually civil engineering contracts. Non-UK governments it seemed were keen that one national contractor should bid for a project. If an exporting country had more than one company capable of bidding then it would be pre-determined which one should bid. In this way major contracts could be shared around. The British adopted a different approach by having every company capable of bidding not only competing with foreign bidders but against each other. It didn't seem to make much sense, and a way to spend money uneconomically, but then again it was a different world to mine.

The effective regional airline, on paper at least, was Gulf Air, which had a fleet of ageing planes mostly piloted and crewed by English expats, who we were reassured, had flown with the likes of British Caledonian, Dan Air, Laker, and other defunct carriers. The airline was based in Bahrain the rulers of which, with the governments of Dubai, Qatar and Oman all had a 25% stake. However Dubai thought it could do better via the Al-Maktoum family, who set up the Emirates Airline in 1985 with the latest Boeings and Airbus planes, offering gifts to all business-class and first-class passengers (silver cufflinks, gold plated tie pins, and so on), as well as a chauffeured passenger collection and delivery service if you lived within 200 miles of the departure airport. They started with two routes, one to London Heathrow and the other to Bombay, now Mumbai, also staffed by expats. It wasn't long before Gulf Air responded to the upstart's challenge!

In Qatar, a place I preferred for the Muslim weekend despite it being 'dry', I stayed at the Sheraton. It was quiet and away from the hurly-burly of Dubai's and Abu Dhabi's boisterous expats. Again, the hotel was situated out of the city. It had fantastic guest facilities, all of which were free. On one occasion I was taken by speed boat out to some nearby islands for a lone picnic, prepared with huge quantities of freshly prepared salads and local delicacies by the hotel, while the private boat moored offshore. It was almost surreal. On another occasion I took a small Mirror sailing dinghy out to sea on my own – nobody checked if I had any training or knowledge (which I didn't), or knew what I was doing! On another occasion I went windsurfing – again without supervision, guidance or experience. The sense of freedom was amazing!

Downtown Qatar was undeveloped, with low-rise old buildings and sandy, unmade roads with no driver discipline. This was reinforced by pictorial overhead notices above the main road leading to the city, which advised drivers to drive between the road lane markings, not on them! Shopping for fake watches was usually the excuse to go downtown, but on one visit I bought so many clothes and presents at bargain prices for the family that I had to buy a bigger suitcase.

Buildings were generally no more than three storeys high, rather weather-beaten and dull-looking. We met several expats who explained that while the country is officially 'dry', they could acquire alcohol by exchanging a monthly issue of vouchers with authorised outlets to get their tipple. The voucher system didn't extend to the Sheraton where drink could be bought freely, if expensively.

Oman was different again. Our first stay was at the Gulf Hotel. It was Ramadan time (a moveable annual event determined by the actual sighting of a new moon), which wasn't clever planning on our part. The hotel was built in the early 1960s and showed its age, but its situation on a cliff-top promontory overlooking a long sandy beach which stretched for miles into the distance, was magnificent. It was managed by two married Brits, who cooked the most perfect traditional English breakfast. All the business facilities, however, were somewhat lacking. The pool was small and not in the best condition, and the beach was a long way down the cliff. Although I loved the hotel's position, its location wasn't a practical proposition for doing business.

The fact that it was Ramadan was inconvenient, as eating or drinking anything in public view is unlawful. Marti suggested buying drinks when we could and storing them in the mini-fridges in our rooms to be drunk privately. This we did, and we did it again on one other occasion when my timing for a Gulf visit overlapped with this season, which moves forward eleven to twelve days each year because of the shorter Islamic lunar calendar. The alcoholic enticement worked in so far as it encourgaed expats to come and talk to us, but how much business it generated is doubtful!

Later we stayed at the local InterContinental! This was situated along the beach that was overlooked by the Gulf Hotel. It faced the beach, and at lunchtime when businesses were closed and it would have been sensible to stay indoors out of the heat, I would venture down to the sea for a swim. It was the warmest sea water I have ever known – almost tepid. It was so warm that dogs didn't bother to shake themselves after a swim. I had been warned not to venture too far out because of rays lying on the seabed and also not to make too much splashing. Bathing 'commando' here was truly fantastic. The rays could have me!

One Omani visit coincided with an imminent Gulf Cooperation Council (GCC) meeting. These meetings are attended by all seven of the Gulf States' rulers and senior government ministers. Each country takes it turn to host the annual jamboree. The event stimulates each host country to upgrade its facilities to leave a legacy for the population thereafter. Prior to the event, the whole of the tall airport tower had been festooned in bands of coloured lights of the national flag. Oman had also completed a thirty-five-mile motorway from the airport to Muscat, the capital. The visitors were all going to stay in a brand new twenty-three-storey hotel built on the site of an old fishing village whose population had been moved into new accommodation on a neighbouring inlet. The old traditional fishing village houses were destroyed. The Al-Bustan Palace Hotel was seven-sided so that all visiting rulers from the Gulf Cooperation Council countries could claim a unique outlook. It had a beautiful entrance atrium 165 feet high.

Low rise Muscat

The hotel later came under the management of the InterContinental Group. I never stayed there, as it was miles from my contacts in Muscat, but I did visit it and viewed the 'royal' apartments. Each had servants' quarters and its own kitchen, dining room, sitting room, and so on. Bathrooms were either 'western style' with conventional WC and bidet bowls, hand basins, shower, and bath, or what was called 'national style'. This meant that the WC bowl was replaced with a ceramic hole in the floor. I also heard that visiting government ministers from outside the region would stay here, including Casper Weinberger, the US Foreign Secretary, and other leading government officials.

Oman, being a former British Protectorate, clearly showed and was proud of its British connections. One day I went down to the harbour and found myself close to the Sultan's palace. It overlooked a private bay and was out of direct public sight. In an adjacent small bay was a large naval craft, guns bristling, and next door was the British Embassy. In the clear water below the harbour quay I could see many varieties of colourful fish. However, on the surface I saw lots of small shark-shaped fish. If the babies were here, then the parents couldn't be far away. Now I knew of another reason why I had been advised not to splash too much in the sea when swimming from the hotel!

Sultan's Palace, Oman

Omani Fisherman

One trip included a visit to Salalah, which involved a flight in a small plane along the Indian Ocean coast. The mountains to the north were rugged, brown, and without habitation. I stayed at the Holiday Inn, which was one of only two hotels in the town. It was pretty basic but situated right on the beach. Inside there were pictures and items showing local life, and I was intrigued to see that Salalah was the centre of the world's trade in frankincense, which is found locally. Thoughts of the Three Wise Men passed through my mind. Maybe they travelled from this very spot?

The hotel was separated from the sea by a coconut grove. I was told to keep to the clearly defined paths to avoid (most of) the danger from falling coconuts! The beach had flocks of pink flamingos strutting on the foreshore. The sea and white sandy beach looked very tempting, but having seen some of the sea life in Muscat harbour, I decided to keep to the pool.

Coconut path to Salalah beach

I visited a number of local banks, all rather small and battered places. The chances of a burglary were pretty slim anywhere in the Middle East with the probability of hand or arm removal for anyone caught. Sand and dust were everywhere, and I often wondered how long all the pristine roads and buildings would stay looking new with so much abrasion in the air, not just here but anywhere in the region.

The centre of Salalah was an open, dusty square space. On Friday, tribes people appeared with local farmers for an open air market. This principally involved the sales and purchase of livestock which had been carted to the site in the back of pick-up trucks and open vehicles of all sorts. It appeared to be a convivial gathering with much chatter and laughter. The animals, in varying degrees of immobile discomfort and hot distress from being kept under the baking sun, very much took second place. Braying goats predominated, along with scruffy, underfed poultry.

From visiting the Middle East region fairly regularly, we discovered that demand for investment products existed, not just by expats but by locals also. Discussions with mostly commercial banks and sovereign funds indicated a lack of local investment expertise in almost every international market, and where it did exist was never to very much depth. Typically, local investment managers would be happy to invest in blue chips and household names. Trust in our ability to invest successfully in these markets and to provide security of investment funds and liquidity to all investors all the time was a concept that stretched most of the so-called investment managers we met. In looking at this institutional opportunity, we managed on every occasion to more than cover our costs by holding receptions and giving presentations to expatriates. As a result, considerable thought was put into creating a specific US dollar-denominated product for local investors of all shapes and sizes which would not only satisfy investment needs but also the legal and tax regulations imposed by Sharia Law, which basically forbids the earning and payment of interest – quite a challenge! It would also be ahead of its time.

David Humpleby, in Jersey, set about creating an umbrella fund that would have a number of sub-funds which would exactly mirror the existing range of offshore funds managed from Jersey and Berne. It was to be known as the International Selection Fund. Extensive and protracted discussions took place with the Jersey legal and tax authorities for this innovative fund before it came to fruition. We also identified that such a fund, once established, could be own-labelled by local institutions and thereby marketed as a local product. The advantage of this would be that (we hoped) significant sums would be invested, which would quickly recoup the significant costs of the umbrella fund's creation.

The Jersey managing director, Tony Pope – who actually lived in Chelsea, but had a company-sponsored house on the island – called me one day to say he'd been following up an enquiry from the National Bank of Pakistan to set up a Sharia fund and that he would like me to accompany him to Karachi to meet with some of that bank's board. A flight was arranged and travel plans were made.

We flew directly to Karachi by British Airways. Tony was approaching his early retirement at age sixty and took life pretty much as he found it and not too seriously. I had previously dined with him and his Irish wife Katy at a restaurant in Walton Street in Knightsbridge and found him excellent company, so the thought of being with him for a few days was something I looked forward to. And so it turned out. We happily indulged in the complimentary food and beverages on the flight. At one point we found ourselves in the lift to the floor below the main passenger deck. Quite what provoked this I can't recall, but I do remember we both thought it hilariously funny.

Our base was the Sindh Club, the oldest club in Karachi, built for Europeans in the late nineteenth century and from which locals were barred until 1952, five years after independence in 1947. The story is that until the day after Independence there used to be a sign 'Natives and dogs not allowed' in the hallway! The club still carried all the hallmarks of being a gentleman's club with now slightly faded opulence but high standards of formality. Ladies were admitted as the guest of a member, but could not become members in their own right. Outside were carefully manicured lawns and gardens full of magnificently flowering shrubs. All club staff was immaculately dressed and service was deferential, inconspicuous, and discreetly gracious.

We travelled to our meeting with the bank at their impressive head office building by taxi – one of the most hair raising excursions I have made anywhere. Our yellow cab danced through the variety of scooters, mopeds, rickshaws, buses, and cattle that are the daily norm of Karachi's streets. Traffic police, standing on small, white concrete bollards, blew their whistles and waved their arms frantically. The traffic didn't seem to take any notice, even passing either side of the unconcerned policeman. On arrival at the bank all was calm. We were ushered in total silence up to the air-conditioned main boardroom on the top floor overlooking the bustling, manic city below.

Our meeting with several Mr Singhs and Patels and others was lengthy, polite, and respectful. They said they would seed a new fund, to be own-labelled with several million dollars, when it was ready and approved by all the appropriate authorities. At the conclusion of the meeting, Tony and I were invited to one of the Mr Singh's (the managing director's) house for the evening, an invitation we were pleased to accept. Dress would be lounge suits.

We were collected from the Club by chauffeur and driven out to a select residential district that could have been anywhere in the avenues of tree-lined St John's Wood. As we arrived at our destination, wide gates opened remotely and a short drive took us up the front flood-lit pillared portico. Staff opened the car doors, and we were greeted by our host and his wife and introduced to about a dozen other guests. We were offered several gin and tonics and then shown tables of small cocktail snacks – samosas, curried dips, and fruit. No further alcohol was offered, but soft drinks were.

The Sharia fund never materialised. The various regulatory and administrative requirements were beyond the capabilities of the Jersey authorities. This was a great disappointment given the size of the potential market, but one which was subsequently developed some twenty years later by others!

In due course Watts and I included the Far East as a destination. We visited Hong Kong and Singapore, where Hill Samuel already had bank branches that were able to do a good deal of ground work prior to our arrival. Hong Kong was always interesting; the bank owned a junk which we used for both business and fun at weekends. The local Trust manager was Trevor Batkin, himself a UK expat, who had quite reputation as a lady's man and frequenter of the local hostelries, notably the Mad Dogs pub.

Flying into the old Kai Tak Hong Kong airport never disappointed, but getting there by flying over the Indian sub-continent always interesting even from 35,000 feet. Long before reaching here on one occasion, we had a refuelling stop in Delhi just as the sun was rising over the dusty horizon. We had taken off to continue eastwards, when looking out of my north-facing window I saw the Himalayas and Everest – possibly 200 miles away but absolutely recognisable and distinct in its shape. Looking below I also saw the Ganges snaking its way westwards towards the Bay of Bengal. Seeing both these great geographical features and thinking of their impact on so many millions of people's lives was one of my most remarkable and touching memories.

With a perilous runway that jutted out into the sea and a descent through skyscrapers and craggy mountains, Kai Tak was seen as the ultimate test of a pilot's skills. The arrival was as thrilling and amazing as its reputation. The prevailing conditions required flights to make the final descent through high-rise buildings built on steeply sloping sides of mountains on both sides and, with only seconds to go before touch down, to bank forty-five degrees to the right where the landing strip stretched out into Kowloon harbour. Too much taxiing would inevitably end up with the plane in the harbour! The whole experience probably lasted only a couple of minutes, but it was thrilling and even a little frightening to think how easily things could, and occasionally did, go wrong.

The arrivals hall had an enormously long check-in and arrivals desk. Everything was, as we were to discover would be the case with almost every service activity, handled in an efficient, polite, and courteous manner.

Equally, of course, taking off in the opposite direction was a challenging experience for everyone and for the aeroplane itself. On one occasion in the middle of a tropical rain storm and with only minutes before the airport closed for the night (so as to ensure local residents could sleep in peace), we were transferred from a Cathay Pacific plane to another because of engine problems on the ground. Having been provided with plastic rain covers, we made the trek rapidly and mounted the open stairway in torrential rain. Without much pre-flight preparation and minimal announcements, we took off at full throttle. No sooner had the nose lifted than we were banking left and still in a steep climb up through the clouds, knowing that buildings and mountains were literally yards away. Some crockery went crashing, having not been secured after transfer from the original plane.

Somehow Cathay Pacific resumed their normal excellent service very soon after, as if nothing had happened. The only things missing were the in-flight magazines!

A new airport was being built on Lantau island, which would change that island from a being sleepy fishing area for locals, but I never flew to it.

On another flight, the islands of the Malacca Straights looked like perfectly formed tropical islands – bright turquoise blue water shelving onto islands encompassed white sandy beaches and covered by verdant vegetation inland. One could only speculate what living standards might be like on most of them – basically very poor, I suspect.

The bank-owned junk was moored in Victoria Harbour. It was always piloted by the same jolly local Hong Kong Chinaman, who liked to be called 'Boss'! It was typical of every wooden Chinese junk ever made and fitted with enormously powerful diesel engines. A favourite day trip was to go to Lantau Island, making our way past seemingly miles of identical blocks of tall flats, which were usually festooned with household washing. The sea close to the shore never ever looked clean and was frequently cluttered with garbage of one sort or another. Further out to sea, the view was typical of the Far East, with sharply rising volcanic plug islands rising from the sea floor. Few were inhabited by people, but the vegetation was green, lush, and all-enveloping. The wild life could have been amazing, but we never stopped to find out, unfortunately.

We would be about a dozen on board. The junk was well stocked with beers, and occasionally 'Boss' would serve an excellent buffet. The weather was always warm and usually balmy. Nearer to Lantau, fish farming pens were everywhere. Fish was always a popular choice for most people on the harbour-side restaurants, but it was hard to imagine the waters being clean enough for some pollution not to be present. I became vegetarian on these junk trips!

Our first visit to Singapore alerted Watts and me to the possible pitfalls of this city and possibly elsewhere in the region. Our flight had arrived late at night, and having negotiated our exit from the beautiful cream-coloured, marble-floored, air-conditioned arrivals hall of Changi Airport, we found our taxi. No sooner had the journey to the Hilton Garden Hotel begun than we were asked if we would like to go to a night club. Not once, but several times, and always with slightly alarmingly greater insistence.

'You know, to find a girl each or just one for the two of you!' he said smilingly. 'Or maybe I take you to a bar to relax? You must be very tired. You want to see Singapore?'

'We want to go to the hotel,' we said firmly. He looked surprised and disappointed, but it his offer seemed to be the expected thing after a flight from Europe. We had been warned!

Singapore was altogether different to Hong Kong. Despite our rather shady introduction on arrival, the frenetic daytime way of life was absent. In some ways it reminded me of life in Switzerland – busy, organised, clean, and absolutely no surprises, or not many. We stayed in the garden wing of the Hilton Hotel. The most memorable things about this comfortable hotel were that condensation that formed on the outside of the windows at night and the curtains in my bedroom, which were so huge that they could only be closed electrically. We also saw a mouse scamper along the bedroom corridor! Oh dear!

No visit to Singapore would have been complete without a visit to Raffles Hotel. Watts and I walked through a courtyard to the sound of a string quartet playing typical 1920s and 1930s palm court hotel music. To our amazement (or was it surprise?) all the musicians looked Chinese and were smartly dressed in dinner jackets with slicked down hair! We found the bar and ordered Singapore sling cocktails. Rather disappointingly, they were pre-prepared on the bar counter. Lots of them! The only thing to be added was the gin. The visit hadn't quite lived up to our expectations, and we never returned here.

Not far from Raffles, one of the surprising sights was a cricket ground in the centre of the business district. The Singapore Cricket Club is The Padang. The ground is flanked by City Hall on one side with a view of the Supreme Court and other buildings nearby. The ground itself has short boundaries, but it has a beautiful clubhouse and an immaculate outfield with the centre area roped off for the few pitches that are possible. The SCC has been there since 1852, and it is a real remnant of British colonial rule, rather as the Sindh Club was in Karachi.

Singapore was a very disciplined city. Road traffic was licensed by a system of charging road tax based on engine size. Pedestrians always only crossed the road when a green light showed on the crossing lights and always walked on the left side. Another surprise was to see a large figure of Father Christmas on the outside of a tall office block in

November. Here, at one degree north in humidity of more than ninety degrees, it was all a little incongruous.

On one occasion I had time to find what was the famous PoW camp – Changi. A great friend of mine, a fellow French horn player, and somewhat older, had been a prisoner of war in the camp and I was moved to visit his place of incarceration. I found it now to be part of the Singaporean Ministry of Defence's Changi Airbase Camp. However some remaining buildings could be visited on foot through light jungle along a barely visible path. I passed inhabited corrugated iron shacks with no windows (but televisions in every one!), interspersed throughout quite dense vegetation. In the camp's chapel I found a moving mural painted by one of the inmates, now preserved with four others by the Singaporean government, of The Crucifixion. Rather droll given its location and the artist's personal circumstance. He had included the words 'Father forgive them. They know not what they do.'

Changi Jail wall painting

I noticed a MacDonald's restaurant near our hotel in Orchard Road and was curious to see if one of their burgers would taste the same as at home. Everything about the experience was identical! We also wanted to see some of the traditional Singaporean shop houses where the shop is on the ground floor and living quarters upstairs. They are characteristic of many towns and cities in South-East Asia.

We extended a couple of our trips to Brunei, flying to Bandaseribegawan Airport, a modern airport that was mostly open to the elements. From here we would travel west to Kuala Belait, where expats employed in the oil industry found some of life's creature comforts.

It was immediately obvious that Brunei was wealthy with motorway standard roads leading out from the city. We passed the Sultan's Palace – clearly visible from the road with its gold gilded roof. Nodding donkeys were frequently seen in clusters pumping oil into and along shiny pipelines to refineries which seemed to be spaced at equal distances along the coast hugging road.

Our hotel at Kuala Belait, a surprisingly under-developed town, was small and situated on the corner of a crossroads junction, so, inevitably, there was traffic noise twenty-four hours a day – scooters, mopeds, exhaust-pipe free cars, trucks, and exhaust polluting buses. Our bedrooms being on the ground floor, there was no chance of having a window open. This may have been just as well, as the hotel's sewage ran down an open gutter outside along the side of the road – presumably to go into the river a few hundred yards away. Nothing looked remotely prosperous.

Watts and I went to look around the small town. There was a quayside with small cranes, a few buildings, and oil drums and timber stacked high at a small river harbour. The river was busy with river traffic taking cargoes across possibly half a mile of fast-flowing, murky, rippling water to Sarawak.

Brunei to Sarawak ferry

I remembered a master at school, Dr Gordon van Praagh, who had spent time teaching in Sarawak in the summer holidays. He was an eminent physicist and Department Head of Science. Although he never taught me, he was a kind bachelor who invited young boys to his study on Sunday afternoons to listen to an LP of his choice. I decided one day to do something out of character at the time and listened to Beethoven's Third Symphony. My interest in music was born: and I now had a link with Sarawak!

Breakfast was served in a steam-filled room with every window dripping with condensation. It was full of seated, oriental-looking people. The room was off-white, as was the food and the clothing of the people, who were all slouched over their food, some wearing traditional Chinese woven straw conical hats. There was nothing on the menu that was remotely recognisable as breakfast food. Instead we were offered, from hot steaming trolleys brought to our table by waiting staff, a selection of steamed delicacies – all grey in colour and most unappetising. We made do with a couple of dry rolls and tasteless tea, and we repeated this for the next few days of our stay.

We held several successful seminars at The Shell Club, which was even smarter inside than it looked from the outside. It was an expensive-looking sports club, with no doubt complimentary membership to Shell employees and their families, with tennis courts, swimming pools, lounge areas, beautifully manicured lawns and gardens, as well as full health club facilities indoors. The restaurant and bars were on the first floor, overlooking a perfect white sandy beach fringed with tropical trees. Clearly the budget for maintaining and running this place was significant, and it gave the impression that as the country's biggest foreign-currency-earning company, everything had to be of the highest standard. Nowhere could have been more different from our hotel!

We returned by road to Banda to stay one night before flying on to Bali. We again saw the Sultan's large and impressive golden palace roof across what seemed to be a large, possibly defensive, lake. We stayed at the National Hotel, which, on paper, looked to be a reasonable place. It wasn't. Our bedroom doors showed signs of forced entry, which didn't make us feel that we or our belongings were safe. The decoration throughout was in a dreadful condition, and there was no air conditioning. We also happened to arrive on Thanksgiving Day, which meant that, although we were residents of the hotel, we couldn't use the restaurant. The expat Americans had taken it over.

Watts and I booked a restaurant to have dinner, and the plan was to go by taxi, which we did. However, while waiting outside the hotel to enjoy the warm balmy air, we realised that we were being surrounded by hookers and almost every passing car hooted their horns, thinking we might be looking for a pick-up. What a place of contrasts!

Bali was quite different. The hotel we were staying in, the Tanjung Sari Resort Hotel had been booked by the Singapore office. We arrived in the evening and were collected by a hotel chauffeur and driven on comparatively rough roads to the hotel. The roads seemed to pass through both flat and flooded paddy fields and forests of tall trees. The airport taxi driver also drove deliberately over and killed a scampering scorpion.

On reaching the hotel, we noticed that the reception area, surrounded by the foliage of trees and shrubs, was outside. As we got nearer, two great gongs were struck thunderously by uniformed bell boys; apparently all new arrivals get this welcoming treatment. Having signed in, we were shown to our rooms. These consisted of straw-roofed, one-room en-suite bungalows set within bougainvillea filled gardens. Almost every bungalow's garden had a small Buddhist figure, often dressed in coloured check material, put there to keep evil spirits away from the guests. It seemed as if everything we did would have some accompanying local custom.

Life on Bali seemed to be run in a way completely opposite to ours in the West. Daily life is normally conducted outside – eating, drinking, socialising, and so on. Buildings are only used for sleeping or for getting out of the rain, which can be very heavy. Sleeping in our 'rooms' should have been very peaceful, but unfortunately the straw roofs were home to gecko lizards. These are harmless, shy creatures up to about eight inches in length. They are silent as long as they sense movement in the room, but as soon as you lie quietly and are about to drop off to sleep, they start their movements in and on the dry straw above.

The hotel was situated on Kuta Beach. It was separated from adjoining properties by a patrolled fence to stop beach vendors approaching hotel guests on the hotel's private, gently sloping beach. On the shoreline typical Balinese sailing boats could be hired. These were single-hull craft with a long float on one side. They were very colourful, and fishermen would go out in the evenings with lanterns alight, reflecting on the water.

Outside the hotel, life was also colourful. We didn't see any normally constructed shops, but instead there were rows of corrugated shanty huts. The shopkeepers would ply for trade by calling from their open shop fronts. Their counters were covered with their goods for sale. Watts and I were keen to by some traditional Bali batik shirts and perhaps a desk plaque – a carved wooden, usually made of teak, name plate. These were carved on the spot, and the lettering gilded in a couple of hours, and all for the equivalent of a few pounds. I still have mine.

Further out, I wandered off the road to explore a fire which I had noticed burning. I was hoping to find some indigenous, perhaps tribal people! Having walked several hundred yards carefully – not to disturb snakes, scorpions, or worse – I came across a tree trunk which had been carved out. The shavings from that day's work were being burned and would probably continue into the evening. It had obviously been gouged out by hand and not by machine, and I felt fortunate to have seen it, even if I hadn't seen anyone nearby. Perhaps they had seen me!

Lighting fires at dusk was obviously a daily ritual for the islanders. I was told that to do this would drive away the evil spirits (again). When we finally left the island on an evening flight back to Singapore, I counted more than twenty fires' smoke columns rising to the sky.

On one occasion I visited Bangkok (the airport only) en route from Hong Kong to Madrid. To say I was disappointed would be an understatement. I had to make a connection there and visited the British Airways Executive Club lounge and took the opportunity to browse the rather dismal airport shops. I was interested in looking at silks but found nothing appealing. The lounge was a dump, with inadequate seats and limited bar facilities, and it was full of over-weight Thai men who wouldn't have looked out of place as Olympic wrestlers, weight lifters, or sumo freaks.

Hill Samuel and Bank von Ernst had put me firmly into the international marketing and sales arena, and I was enjoying it. What I wasn't enjoying, however, was working from the NLA Tower, where Hill Samuel had its large administration offices for its life and pensions business, in East Croydon – known locally as the Threepenny Bit Building. This was due to its resemblance to a number of the old three pence coins stacked on top of each other. It was close to the railway station.

I had been relocated there from the City when Ron Lewis retired, and the business was looking to save costs by using its City building more intensively. I wasn't happy being away from the centre of things in the City, although I enjoyed the small compensation of the occasional drive in my Morris Minor Traveller across south-west London or the train journey from Putney to East Croydon. My problem was that although I thoroughly enjoyed the job, I didn't enjoy the location or the predominantly administrative environment. My office colleagues were all engaged with UK pensions business: far removed from what I was trying to develop. This, together with a burgeoning credit card debt of several thousand pounds, often caused me to become rather depressed. I would often wonder how I could get out of these ruts and move my career along.

The usual occasion for these thoughts to come to me, for some reason, was when I was walking from East Croydon railway station over the railway bridge the short distance to my office. In fact, prior to purchasing the Morris Traveller, at the time when the financial pinch seemed at its greatest, I hadn't felt so low and possibly not far from full depression. Dark days!

Chapter 8

The Fidelity Years:
Eastern Promise

When the opportunity arose for me to move back to the City in April 1986, I jumped at the chance. I had met Richard Timberlake on my travels when he was managing director and a founder of Schlesinger, a small fund management group. Richard contacted me soon after he had begun to establish Fidelity International as a sister company to Fidelity Investments, the biggest fund management business in the world. Richard reported to Glen Moreno, an American polymath and long-time Fidelity figure who was close to Ed Johnson III whose family owned the business from its beginnings in 1946. The worldwide head office was in in Boston, Massachusetts. Fidelity International was Fidelity's non-US business, and its City offices were in two buildings opposite each other in Lovat Lane, an attractive pedestrianised cobbled street just off Eastcheap, and close to The Monument. It was in this locality that the Great Fire of London had begun in 1666.

Fidelity occupied two buildings, conveniently opposite each other. The east side building was full of investment managers and analysts, while the west side was occupied by us, the International Division, and some institutional sales people headed up by Hilary Smith, a no-nonsense unmarried lady in her early thirties who lived in Roehampton. Billingsgate Fish market was at the bottom of the street, and when the wind was in the right direction the outside air was 'fishy' to say the least! Inside our buildings the air was air-conditioned, and all were all furnished with the same design of pale wooden furniture and carpet.

Computers were becoming commonplace for all but the most junior staff.

In my introductory period I met with investment colleagues across the street to learn something of the Fidelity investment philosophy. I was intrigued by seeing electronic messages being exchanged between the various worldwide offices – not by fax but on computer screens. I discovered that Fidelity had one of the first intranet systems anywhere, which connected all the company's offices around the world and it gave them the immense advantage of being 'in the know' about everything that was being reported locally on a daily basis – sometimes several times a day. It allowed messages to be transmitted on screen almost instantaneously. I had never seen or heard anything like it, but it was obviously an early forerunner of such facilities and email in years to come.

Richard, along with his extremely bright assistant Paul Forsyth, wanted me and two others, Martin and Caroline, to bring in funds for management from outside the UK, primarily through international investment banks, as well as through other institutions that would be managing significant sums either for themselves or for third parties. Martin had been a commodity broker, and Caroline had had a career in some high-powered job in New York which I never understood. Both were of a similar age to me, single and intellectually intelligent. Forsyth was a number cruncher. He was an unsmiling and mostly serious guy who had been with Fidelity for several years and well-connected within it.

For a brief period we all reported to Peter Rees, who was almost invisible as sales director. He had, prior to recently coming to Fidelity, been a director of Rothschild Asset Management, but he always appeared to be out of his depth and never, as far as I knew, had an original thought. He was, however, very keen on having his pencils very sharp and pointed and carefully arranged on a carefully managed desk each morning.

To support us all we enjoyed the company of Nicola, who was rather studious and lived in Kennington, Richard's attractive secretary Nikki Weeks, a recent divorcee who lived in South Kensington, and Polly Kaminski, very much a single woman enjoying fun and with strong interests in the arts and music, who lived in Islington. All of us – especially Nikki and Polly – were up for at least one glass of wine after work with our workmates at the end of the week. We were a good group.

I well remember meeting up with my immediate colleagues and thinking, 'I have made it!' The air of calm professionalism pervaded everyone, everywhere. Being part of the largest fund management group in the world, one that had an unsurpassed reputation for excellence and resources to back its ambitions, was all immensely reassuring. My title was 'International Marketing Director'. In reality, it didn't amount to much in terms of executive responsibility, but it looked good on my business card.

Visits from Fidelity's head office personnel in Boston were reasonably frequent and generally relaxed affairs – after all, the business was successful and growing. The Boston connection, however, had an undercurrent of which I wasn't but should have been aware.

After I had been with the company for several months, I was asked at the end of a late afternoon meeting with Richard that was attended by Ed Burns if I would like to join him alone for dinner. Ed Burns was one of a few key right-hand men Ned Johnson had, and was head of the US equity investment team. He had been with the company since the late 1940s, looked like a senior statesman, and was always immaculately mannered and dressed. I felt honoured to be asked, but knew that Martin and Caroline had been invited previously, which gave me confidence. After all, I wasn't an investment professional and he was an eminent one! The two of us were to dine in Lowndes Square at a favourite restaurant of Ed's and would travel there in his chauffeured car.

The restaurant was discreet, calm, and dignified as one would expect and we took a table in the basement. Everything was going fine when the conversation turned to Northern Ireland and what I thought about the situation and troubles there. I don't know if I was fortunate or not, but after I mentioned my business experiences there, it became perfectly obvious that Ed was an IRA sympathiser and became uncharacteristically vitriolic and almost angry with me, and I hadn't a clue why. I have little doubt he, and possibly Fidelity, would be contributors to IRA funds. I was quite shaken by the experience, and of course I have never mentioned it since to anyone until now.

Another visitor was David Saul from Fidelity's Bermuda office, whom I was to meet up with later in Hong Kong to play tennis at a house owned by a client. He was a delightfully charming (white) man, and spoke without a hint of West Indian or American accent. He was slim, slightly under six feet tall, and, like all Fidelity executives, immaculately dressed. I had no idea at the time that he was the Bermudan finance minister and was later to become prime minister. Wikipedia says:

> Dr David J. Saul was elected in Bermuda Parliament in 1989 and soon became the Minister of Finance. The next few years he focussed on navigating Bermuda through the trying times of early 1990s recession. He had taken several measures including introduction of National Pension Scheme, initiating Trust Business, putting down legislation for Government Borrowing and more. During his tenure as the Premier of Bermuda, he had led the negotiation with Britain's Prime Minister that resulted in Bermudians getting rights to full British citizenship and also to hold UK/ European Passport so that they can work and live anywhere in Europe. Dr. David Saul surprised many by announcing his retirement while being at the helm and also choosing to limit his directorships in business, and deciding to spend much of his time in local charities.

I would never have guessed at his political prowess from his mild unassuming, and charming manner.

As for Ed Johnson, you just would never know that he was the owner of a worldwide business that managed then some US$2.5 billion at the time (now many times that amount). He was quietly spoken, polite, courteous and even respectful of his quite obviously highly valued and appreciated work force.

The administrative offices were in purpose-built building at Hildenborough, near Tonbridge. The building was set in several acres and was home to several large outdoor sculptures, all owned by the Johnson family.

Martin focussed his business development efforts on European institutions in France, Switzerland, and Italy. I focussed my efforts in the Middle East, Spain, and Scandinavia. Finding the appropriate personal contact within banks overseas was done through a thorough vetting of information within various almanacs which listed individuals and their responsibilities and in some cases the clients they managed funds for, and, most importantly, their full contact details. I would then telephone these identified contacts, make an introduction, and seek an invitation to visit. Usually this approach worked, and thus began a sequence of regular face-to-face meetings at which I would try to establish how we could best provide our expertise within the institution or investment service which they had no capability to provide.

The initial plan I developed was to promote and expand on the fairly simple concept which Hill Samuel had begun. However, we would not have an umbrella fund. Instead we would have a range of investment options that included promotion of individual funds, portfolios of selected funds, and discretionary managed portfolios, all of which, if the potential volume was large enough and the commitment strong enough, could be own-labelled and promoted within individual countries by the promoting local institution.

In addition to this own-labelling concept, I began to promote the idea of businesses setting up employee savings schemes into which both employer and employee would save a percentage of individuals' salaries each month. Most of the banks I met said they would be happy to push this idea to their corporate clients. In addition, I started to make appointments directly with local businesses.

One such was Al-Gashobhi Trading, a large Saudi family-owned general agency with subsidiaries throughout the Middle East. In addition to being a major contracting company, they also acted as import agents for every conceivable type of consumer product imaginable – from cars to freezers, from furniture to earth-moving equipment. It was a fantastic business, and their main office outside Saudi Arabia was in Bahrain. They were intrigued with the concept, and although local wages were low, they began to install employee savings schemes in a number of businesses. They'd accumulate a large monthly payment from numerous small savers, accounting for how much each had contributed and how much they as employers had, and then remit this monthly sum to us for investment. We were so far ahead of the game, it was ridiculous!

To assist in developing regional credibility, we decided to open a branch office in the Middle East. We began with a branch in Bahrain, which was managed by a Fidelity Jersey employee, Craig, an ex-army captain who talked well but not effectively. In due course, however, it was decided that the regulatory environment for the Middle East was better in Dubai, and the decision was taken to close the Bahrain office and say goodbye to Craig. The Dubai office was then managed by Paul

Forsyth, who had acted as go-between in establishing the company's credentials with the licensing authorities.

Nevertheless, whilst employed, Craig developed some connections in Bahrain and elsewhere in the Gulf. He also serviced Cyprus agents from here – convenient for him, as he owned a derelict cottage on the island that he was planning to restore. His apartment in Bahrain was convenient for Manama City and was in a residential district. He built up a good social life, which made for more relaxed evenings than I had enjoyed on previous visits. He told me, however, of some local customs and the difficulties that sometimes occur between the Shia and Sunni residents. In particular, he told me of self-flagellation, which the Sunni community engage in at particular times of the year. It wasn't unknown for people to die from their self-inflicted wounds and then to be regarded almost as martyrs to their beliefs.

On one occasion I met Craig in a hotel near Limassol, on Cyprus to discuss progress. After a good dinner in a local restaurant, we returned to the hotel I was staying in for a few night caps. Our discussions went on into the late evening, and at some point we were challenged by some men at the end of the bar to confirm whether we were military people, as they thought we were ear-wigging their conversations. We weren't, but Craig and I had both remarked on hearing their Irish accents. Craig decided the best way to mollify these men world be to buy them some drinks. However, it then became apparent that they had already made up their minds that we were military personnel. They had also made the deduction that we were there to pick up on their conversations as part of an intelligence-gathering operation, all of which was utterly contrived and without any truth. It was only by visiting the gents loo and then going directly to my room that I escaped the uncomfortable experience. Craig carried on and had the mother of all hangovers the next day.

I often used Cyprus as a stop-over after making my middle-eastern sorties. Despite having contact with westerners and living in westernised environments in most hotels, I found the way of life in the Middle East restrictive and somewhat alien, and it made my adjustment to the full liberal freedoms of western life difficult. So a couple of days visiting intermediaries on the island, allowing time to enjoy the sights and pleasures of the beach became quite important to me and my transition to coming home.

It was on one of these occasions that I heard of the IRA bombing of the Grand Hotel in Brighton in an attempt to murder Mrs Thatcher's cabinet. From the eastern Mediterranean, the UK looked as if it was descending into unbelievable violence. The thought briefly crossed my mind to suggest, when I got home, that my young family should up sticks and move out to this delightful island. At least the south of the island was calm, English was widely spoken, driving was on the left, and there was good local wine and beer. The list of attractions was beginning to look rather tempting, but not sufficiently for me to consider suggesting it!

One afternoon I had been visiting agents in Nicosia. I had driven north from Limassol and decided to explore some of the island away from the main road. The Troodos Mountains looked interesting away to the north. They appeared rugged and high and offered a good vantage point to view the island. As I climbed up the narrowing and twisty road, I saw what looked like a look-out point with a Turkish flag flying nearby. After continuing for a few more minutes, I decided to retreat. Obviously the mountains did give a good view of things below!

Nicosia was a busy and bustling place. I recall having an excellent meal there in a typical English pub, but also finding the metal wire fence running through the city rather sad in that regardless of what the Cypriot islanders wanted, it had been divided by the Turks who now occupied the north-eastern part of it.

On the way to Cyprus I stopped off in Cairo three or four times visiting bankers who showed interest in my story. Here I did spend some time visiting some of the better known sites from the InterContinental Hotel which over looked a truly Nile green river. I visited the Pyramids on a February evening for a Son et Lumière presentation. I took a local bus through the dusty rundown outskirts of the city, which threaded a way through ass or donkey drawn carts, in the gathering dusk. Sometime before actually reaching the visitor area some miles away, I saw the largest of the three pyramids through gaps between the ramshackle buildings we were passing through, standing up so high, I couldn't believe my eyes. On arrival a local man in traditional dress raced past on horse back, galloping at high speed with loose fitting garb flapping behind him, horse's mane swept back, and dust flying, into the night. It seemed a typical 'Arab scene': and not done for my benefit!

On another occasion, I had three hours to spare and went to the National Museum, found a guide near the entrance and, having the limited amount of time, was given a fantastic tour. He took me to see exhibits on a number of different floors, a lot of early medical implements I recall, which I would not have appreciated without him shining a small pocket torch on to them in the mostly gloomy exhibition rooms. One of the highlights was seeing the death mask and mummified body of Tutankhamun – surprisingly small but every bit as beautiful as I had imagined.

Another Mediterranean island I visited was Mallorca at the invitation of a broker, TFL, whose head office was in Godalming. The senior partner was Hywel Thomas a thrusting, purposeful former Special Services officer. Amongst many army roles, he had served as a ski trainer for Arctic operations and had been seconded to the marines. Hywel's outlook on life was to work hard and play hard. Life with him was focussed on being professional on everything he did; his presentations were rehearsed until he was word perfect. The fact that I was employed by Fidelity and accompanied him on his 'road shows' gave him some kudos, and attendances to his invitation-only presentations reflected this.

On Mallorca I stayed at the Sheraton, a delightful hotel with its own tournament golf course some way out of Palma. It was memorable for being the first hotel I had stayed at where it was possible to have champagne from the buffet at breakfast. At the end of several days, which had been organised by Hywel's local office secretary Hillary, a dinner was organised at a restaurant up in the hills that was renowned for its local cuisine. To get there three taxis were required, but only Hillary, knew how to get there.

The idea was that she would lead the other two taxis, but her driver failed to wait and was out of sight before anyone else was ready. By using newly available and large mobile phones we all duly arrived, and arrangements were made for us to be collected several hours later. The meal was excellent and the wine flowed. Gradually the place emptied of other diners and we were left alone with the staff as we made more and more noise.

Hywel declared he could build a stack of chairs on a table in the middle of the room and stand on his head on top of them. He said that he had never fallen off his skis and nor had he ever fallen while doing this stunt however much he'd drunk. Sure enough, he built the stack of chairs and did his head stand, which he held for several minutes. More drinks and hilarity followed, before the taxis were called to take us back.

Inevitably there was a disagreement about how much we should pay. Hywel's point was that the service we had received in getting to the restaurant was appalling, and he point blank refused to pay the full price being asked. The ensuing row, mostly in Spanish, with the three drivers raising their fingers and threatening to call the police would have been good viewing for *Fawlty Towers*! In the end one of the drivers tugged at Hywel's leather jacket collar. Before he knew it the driver was out for the count on the ground. Hywel had used a body manoeuvre from his army training, and the Spaniard had no chance. It was spectacular in its speed of execution and effectiveness. The other drivers moved away, and the adjusted bill was rapidly agreed and paid.

The fun of the evening hadn't finished, however, as Hilary announced that she had just moved into a new flat, and her bed hadn't been constructed. Several TFL guys and I went to help sort her out, built the bed, unwrapped the mattress, and then decided we were all too tired to go back to our various hotels and so stayed the night. Quite a day!

Assisting intermediaries in gaining business by accompanying them on foreign trips was a minor part of my role as international director. In many ways what we were developing was way ahead of its time. International bankers and sovereign funds with whom we had contact acknowledged that they had little investment expertise in many markets, including the US markets. Typically, local investment managers would follow the herd and invest in blue chips – IBM, Coca-Cola, Boeing, and the like, which amounted to no more than index tracking. Our position was to offer greater depth of analysis and constant monitoring to achieve better performance.

In both Abu Dhabi and Kuwait we had established a number of connections with Sovereign funds. These connections began with Graham Nutter, a colleague responsible for the American desk, who had joined Fidelity from Scudder & Co., a large New York stockbroking firm. His connections with the Abu Dhabi Investment Authority (ADIA), and the Kuwait Investment Office (KIO), amongst several others, formed the basis of making contact and obtaining investment mandates with a number of similar institutions in those countries. But none of this was for individual investors.

My plan for creating investment products based on our existing fund range for retail investors with the local institution fronting the product and its marketing was first taken up by two banks in Qatar, the Qatar National Bank and the Commercial Bank of Qatar. They translated our fund portfolio management brochure and application forms, and I held training sessions with a handful of staff in each bank. I had expected only one bank to show interest, but they both felt the competitive pressure and decided there was a risk that clients could migrate from one bank to the other if they didn't offer a 'me-too' service. No other foreign institution was then prepared to follow our lead.

The result was that I developed similar relationships with banks in Bahrain (Gulf Bank being the largest), Dubai, and Oman. Business growth was slow with all of them, partly through lack of local investment marketing expertise, but also because most local investors were happy to keep their money under the carpet in US dollars. Gradually and after my time, with the development of computerised communications, peoples' awareness grew and the concept became significantly more widespread.

Dubai in the early 1980's was just beginning to build itself up as an *entrepôt* for world trade. It had few natural resources, and one day these would run dry. Recognising this, the ruling Al Maktoum family began developing industry and tourism on a grand scale, building a vast new airport (reputed to be the same area as the cities of Birmingham or Cardiff) and developing container port facilities and industrial activities that would see it emerge as a regional if not worldwide economic power. I would stay either at the Sheraton or InterContinental Hotel. From here I would watch the view across the Creek and the traditional commerce conducted on the quayside. Dhows criss-crossed the water, frequently embarking on a hazardous journey across the gulf to Iran or further afield to India with crates of white goods and kitchen cleaning materials, typically piled high on deck with the crew members left pretty much out in the open.

Sunset over Dubai Creek

Already urban development had destroyed many of the traditional 'chimney' houses. The well manicured and verdant grass alongside the road from the airport was a sure sign of wealth, as it needed watering throughout the day either by Indian immigrant attendants manhandling large hoses or large automatic sprayers. The road was also separated now from the sandy desert beyond by the graduated vegetation on both sides and the various outside buildings. At the time the tallest building in the Middle East was in Dubai. It was used exclusively by commercial business and was surrounded by grass on which stood a large sign that read, 'Green grass – the gift of God'.

Dubai traditional wind towers

The country's first golf course was under construction with only the greens being grass. The tees were known as 'browns' being areas of compacted tar.

Dubai's first golf course under construction

In Oman I happened to meet the son of my school doctor. John Scott was general business manager for the Oman General Bank, and I had high hopes that he would regard my Fidelity proposition as favourably as other banks had in Qatar, Bahrain, and Kuwait, but sadly he didn't bite. It was another case of the expats he knew having their affairs dealt with by UK-based advisers and the bank not offering anything other than pure bank products to its clients, either individual or corporate.

Doing business in Scandinavia, mostly in Sweden where opportunities seemed greatest of the Nordic countries, was completely different to visiting the Orient. The major retail banks were all well versed in equity investment through funds, so my predominant focus was centred on getting ours accepted as one of what was usually a small range of foreign-managed internationally invested offerings. Of the major Swedish banks, Handelsbanken, Swedbank, and Sparbanken were the leaders, and meeting their investment directors, all of whom travelled internationally, always led to an excellent conversation. On one occasion I met with a Mr Wallenberg, who seemed exceptionally well informed, extremely charming, and influential. I later came to know that his family was and still is one of the most powerful both in business and politics in Sweden.

Occasionally, I indulged in the cultural life of the places I visited. On one visit to Stockholm I took the boat out to The Drottningholm Palace Theatre which is an opera house located at Drottningholm Palace, located on an island a short distance from the mainland in the Stockholm archipelago. I was told it was the Swedish royal family's summer home and very beautiful it and its gardens were. I attended an opera, which one I can't recall, other than the son of Jussi Björling, also a tenor and a very fine one, was a lead singer. Generally the theatre focuses works by Haydn, Handel, Gluck and Mozart and with an emphasis on authentic performance. It made for a very pleasant interlude.

It was in Sweden that I mislaid my passport for the first and only time. I discovered this when I arrived at the Arlanda airport at the end of a visit. The problem was that the airport is about forty kilometres outside the city it serves, and it was Friday afternoon. This meant that getting back into Stockholm and finding the British Embassy open would be a challenge if I was to make my flight. In all the time I had made my travel plans I had always allowed myself the full check-in time the airlines requested. My colleagues had frequently criticised me for doing this, but on this occasion I had not only allowed myself this amount of time but had arrived even earlier, as no one had wanted to see me on a Friday afternoon. In desperation I taxied back to Stockholm to the British Embassy to find that they had not yet closed for the weekend. After the inevitable questioning about my identity, I was issued with what was effectively a one-day pass to get me out of Sweden and into the UK. I was supposed to have surrendered it at UK passport control, but they didn't ask for it.

I also visited Amsterdam and The Hague in the Netherlands. Business people there were considerably less pressured than almost anywhere else I went. The Dutch way of living had a lot to be said for it – easy-going, well dressed, professional, and polite. This was all rather different to Copenhagen, which I found scruffy and less caring.

Investment marketing conferences generally lasted two to three days. They were opportunities to network with other people who were doing pretty much the same job as I was and also an opportunity to learn of new ideas and hear the latest gossip. The venues for these events were usually smart hotels. It became my habit to collect a sheet of hotel letter paper and envelope as a cheap souvenir, and these have been filed. One of the most memorable was the Loews Hotel in Monaco. Getting to it involved a flight to Nice and then a ten-minute or so helicopter flight along the coast. It was a fantastic experience. Loews Hotel is the famous hotel right on the very sharp left-hand corner of the Grand Prix track, standing on a hill before the racing cars enter the tunnel approaching the harbour. My room overlooked the track, and I walked the length of the curving tunnel trying to appreciate the sheer noise of Formula 1 cars racing through at well over 100 mph with the exit out of sight! The noise of ordinary traffic was pretty big as it was. I also walked around the extensive shopping area of the hotel on the ground floor. Everything had prices beyond my imagination!

Whilst attending a conference in Monaco, I visited the Monte Carlo Casino which was quite an event. It was extremely opulent, if not elegant, featuring lots of red velvet and gold curtains, deeply carpeted with high ceilings and gold-leaf adornments on the walls and painted ceilings. I ate dinner there one evening for nothing after paying a modest entry fee. I think the idea was that they'd recoup the cost of the meal pretty quickly afterwards at the gaming tables. I didn't play but watched other conference attendees trying to break the bank!

Flying long-haul to and from Middle Eastern and Far Eastern destinations meant we got to know different airlines quite well. I also particularly liked flying Cathay Pacific to Hong Kong. I once purchased a Glycine watch for £36 on board because its face looked like a Rolex Oyster and had a classic Rolex style stainless steel and gold strap. It has kept immaculate time ever since. I even returned it for a service and it came back with an additional but as yet unneeded strap for only a few pounds. Cathay food was always excellent as it was on Singapore Airlines, who, it was generally thought, had the most modern fleet of planes. Both airlines produced very beautiful printed menus.

Emirates also had brand new planes. Being a new airline owned by the ruling family of Dubai meant that it inevitably attracted a good deal of Arab custom. On one occasion I had settled into my preferred window seat at Heathrow with a good deal of curiosity about what to expect, when an Arab gentleman arrived rather out of breath and flustered to sit beside me. I made polite conversation and asked him if he had had trouble getting to the flight.

'No,' he explained, 'Emirates picked me and my wives up from Holland Park in a mini-bus. They managed to get our entire luggage in, but we had to leave the snooker table behind. They can only bring it to Dubai tomorrow!'

'Do you know how big and how heavy a full-size snooker table is?' I asked him.

'Yes, of course,' he replied, 'but the airline said they would take my entire luggage!'

He wasn't a happy man, but he showed something of the temperament I found amongst certain Arabs: they were obviously wealthy and used to being able to have things their own way.

Emirates also gave business-class passengers and (no doubt) first-class passengers small gifts. I still have a pair of gold cuff links, and a Cross pen given to me on flights. I have greatly appreciated these over time.

On one occasion I flew Saudi from KSA to London. It was the only available and convenient flight, and I followed the company rule, 'When in Saudi, fly first.' I had thought that although it would be 'dry', the experience would be a good one with plenty of seat and leg room on the top deck of a 747. There certainly was, but what I hadn't expected was that an Arab family had taken most of the other seats. The husband sat away from his wives, who would usually have been booked in business class downstairs along with accompanying nannies, known as 'yamas' (pronounced *'yarmars'*). The toddler youngsters roamed freely all around and between the seats to see their father, look out of the windows, and cause general disruption, making the possibility of a quiet and dignified night flight totally out of the question.

Thai Airways was quite the opposite. Flying with them was a delight; the very attentive stewardesses would do anything to make the flight comfortable. Meals could be taken at your convenience and not with everyone else. If you wanted to sleep they would note what time you wanted to be awakened and what drink you'd like at the time.

On another occasion when I was flying from Jeddah to Zurich for a meeting with be colleagues the next day in Berne, on a Korean Air flight (not recommended) one Sunday, the flight was diverted to Geneva because, so the pilot told us, of a thunderstorm at Zurich (which is surrounded by mountains). Arriving at short notice and for an unscheduled stop while the weather cleared we were parked well away from the terminal buildings, and surrounded by both French and Swiss police. Passenger frustration grew despite cold drinks being served when suddenly a passenger who lived in Geneva, and had only hand luggage decided he'd had enough and would escape from the plane down the stairs which had been positioned near one of the front doors. These had been opened to allow some natural air into the cabin. The two police forces couldn't decide on whether to reload the escapee, who quite vehemently indicated his desire to stay where he was, or not. The plane took off for Zurich without him some two hours later. Beat Ungricht from BvE told me later that he and his girl friend had been in Zurich all the weekend and enjoyed beautiful warm, sunny weather. It was a strange and intriguing experience which lends itself to all sorts of conspiracy theories!

My hotel stays in Switzerland were always exceptionally good. The Hotel Penta in Geneva was beautifully situated up in the Old Town with cobbled streets all around and a pleasant stroll down to the commercial area or to the lake. It was too expensive to eat in, even on expenses, but there were plenty of good restaurants nearby serving rosti and fondues. In Zurich I stayed for one night in the Dolder Grand, which was hugely expensive. It too was situated in an elevated position with views out to the lake. The whole place was really smart and had an elegant dining room. Here I noticed a young couple enjoy a splendid dinner with wine and then complain about it and demand a refund. I thought they seemed very practised at the process and that they may well have performed this act before.

Our business focus was developing within Europe – again aiming to target domestic investors with own-label products. Rules and regulations varied widely between countries. Procedures for allowing foreign funds to be marketed from outside foreign jurisdictions were almost impossible to unravel – most notably in Switzerland and Germany. France, Spain, and Italy were less restrictive, and so it was here that the most intensive efforts were made.

My trips to Spain became monthly, not least because of the Hispano-British Chamber of Commerce and British Embassy, who proved to be most enthusiastic that we should be successful. I first met Anna Ni Clerig, who worked at the British Council, at an investment conference at the Hotel Continental in Madrid. She was unhappily married to Louis with three late teenage boys. In her early forties, she had mixed Irish and Scandinavian roots and a strong Irish accent. She had lived in Madrid and had taught English at the British Council for more than twenty years.

It turned out that she knew of Fidelity and could make business to business introductions. It seemed too good to be true! She was so enthusiastic that it appeared as if she might be on some sort of commission deal with the Spanish financial community. In fact, it turned out that she was on a retainer for a London-based financial public relations and advertising company called Moorgate, which allowed her occasional trips to London. Through Anna contacts were made with senior directors of all the major Spanish banks, firms of lawyers, and stockbrokers. Fidelity paid her no introduction fees, but we did ensure she had plenty of dinners and opportunities to develop her personal relationships as a social/business climber.

Moorgate was a relatively small specialist business founded by Jeremy Bond who had become frustrated working for an insurance company. It provided bespoke public relations and marketing expertise to financial service institutions. Every year they sponsored a six-a-side cricket competition at the HAC ground, which they overlooked from their offices in Bunfield Row. Six teams of six players played, including several current and former professional cricketers along with clients of Moorgate. The first year I played with John Emburey and Derek Randall and won the event, during which I bowled out Mike Gatting, the England captain. David Gower and Alan Lamb were other players. The second and last time I wasn't so successful.

Such was Anna's commitment that she became almost identified as a Fidelity employee by the business community, with the result that occasionally we would both find ourselves invited to private dinner parties or musical soirées, which all helped get the business off the ground. Madrid was without doubt the most stylishly dressed of all the cities I visited for both men and women. The people I met professionally were, with one exception, all extremely smart: shoes, suits, shirts, tie – the lot. Business lunches could be heavy-duty affairs and always took place at superb restaurants. Casa Botin, reputedly the oldest restaurant in the world, Jockey, and El Zacain (both Michelin starred restaurants) come to mind, and there were many more of equal standing.

I particularly enjoyed meetings with Banco Popular, Banif (a private investment bank), and Beta Capital, a firm of stockbrokers who employed the economist Dr Pedro Schwarz, whom I later heard several times being interviewed about Spanish economic affairs on BBC Radio 4 as a Madrid University economics professor. Having lunch with him, and from time to time with others, in the various excellent business lunch haunts of Madrid was always enjoyable. We always drank Marqués de Cáceres red or white wine. Memorable and delicious! I also had many good times with a local partner of Theodore Goddard, a London firm of lawyers, who was an Englishman married to a Spanish lady. He was a very cultured man and was always full of helpful and perceptive thoughts about how the business could be successful in Spain.

I regularly stayed at the InterContinental Hotel in Madrid. The Madrid hotel got to know my favourite rooms overlooking the quiet interior courtyard, waterfall, and gardens, away from the front of the building facing the busy Paseo de la Castellana thoroughfare. The occasional exception in Madrid was to stay at the Palace Hotel, a really elegant hotel close to the Spanish Parliament (Cortes Generales) and the Museo National del Prado and backstreets where wine merchants, in room-sized, tile-fronted premises had the most wonderful stocks of old wines in dusty bottles, stacked high in seemingly chaotic fashion and sold inexpensively. The Palace Hotel has a beautiful atrium lounge where sipping late night drinks to the accompaniment of two traditional singer guitarists made staying here *perfecto,* if expensive!

The exception to the high standard of dress amongst the business community here was a Señor Gomez Acebo, the senior partner of a large firm of financial and corporate lawyers Gomez-Acebo & Pombo. He was always slightly scruffy, with grey-streaked hair curling over his lightly scurf-covered shoulders, and wore a crumpled three-piece blue pin-stripe suit. He never met me at the appointed time but always made me feel most welcome. He had travelled to the States frequently, and knew London well. His voice was that of a well lived-in man, and one morning he admitted he had been up rather late the night before. This isn't difficult in Madrid, where to start dinner much before eleven o'clock at night is not regarded as good form.

One day he invited me to his firm's box at the Plaza de Toros in March or April, early in the Madrid bull-fighting season. I had never been to a bullfight and had never really thought about it much, but without any knowledge or misgivings I thought that I should go. After all, my father, who had visited Spain in his twenties, had spoken of the bravery of the animals and of the toreadors. The box was situated high up in the circular stands, on the shady side not far from the President's box and the trumpeters. The whole place was buzzing with talk, shouting, and laughter. Everyone was smartly dressed, except for Señor Gomez, who was his usual crumple suited and scruffy self.

For all this he was excellent company, very helpful and understood English ways. At the *Corrida de toros* he introduced me to several extremely smart, beautifully dressed and attractive young women with dynastic family names like Domecq and Gonzales. Not having a clue about the procedures or etiquette of the occasion, I constantly asked for explanations and commentary on what was going on far below. It didn't seem to me that many of the thirty or so people in the box were taking much notice anyway. They were far too busy socialising, talking, and drinking cold dry sherry, and looking forward to dinner. The whole occasion was a social event first and foremost. I later learned that Señor Gomez was a brother-in-law of the King, Juan Carlos of Spain.

My regular visits to Madrid were often extended to include Barcelona, which I also enjoyed. Business life there was a little calmer than in Madrid, but no less intense. I used to stay in a large hotel on the Diagonal and walk in the evenings down the Ramblas and generally explore alleyways and markets. I was never that struck on what I saw of Gaudi's architecture and preferred the grand style of Madrid's classic buildings and fountains. By comparison, the centre of Barcelona seemed dowdy, dusty, and in need of more style. It seemed overhung by its past and the constant fight to establish itself as the capital of Cataluña, and importantly separate from the rest of Spain. Several years later in 2012 I was to visit Barcelona with my second wife, Diane. We couldn't have been more enraptured with everything we saw of Gaudi's, and we loved our time there!

I stayed on for several weekends in Madrid, exploring mostly La Mancha on the advice of Anna. The places I visited included Segovia, Avila, Gredos, Toledo, Salamanca, Escorial, Burgos, and many villages in between. It was in one tiny hamlet of a few buildings and a bar, way into the country on a hot summer's afternoon, that I saw José Carreras return to Spain from the United States, where he had been treated for leukaemia. His return was shown live on Spanish TV, and all the men in the dusty bar cheered and raised their glasses and voices when he descended the aircraft steps. Outside in a small circular brick-walled ring, a donkey was pulling a flat piece of wood over wheat to separate the chaff. It was a picture and experience that went back centuries. All was peace: birds fluttered and tweeted to and fro in nearby farm buildings, and men drank wine from clay flagons in the shade of an old farm cart.

Old town Madrid

Castillian Castillo

Goya's Toledo

Siesta peace

Anna and I were invited to visit Christopher Neville, my former colleague from Slater, Walker, who also knew her and who had emigrated to live in an apartment in Andorra. Anna had somehow got to know Christopher, so it was a happy reunion. Christopher had studied music at Aberystwyth University at the same time Prince Charles was studying agriculture there, and he had music composition skills. He decided he would make his fortune writing a song for the Barcelona Olympics in 1992. He had begun to write a few chords and verses, but he also mentioned that he had heard that Freddie Mercury and Montserrat Caballé had collaborated in singing a song called 'Barcelona', which, as we now know, became a huge hit. Christopher's song obviously didn't get far.

On another occasion, travelling by car from Andorra on a Sunday morning to return home from Madrid, I came across a monastery, the Monasterio de Henāres. It was a beautiful old building set back from the main road. Having entered, I heard the monks singing Gregorian plain chant, and although staying there while a service was in progress was not allowed, I decided to try to hide and lay down on a stone bench in an alcove in the cloisters opposite the chapel. Birds sang springtime songs, the monks sang their Gregorian Chants, and the world seemed a wonderful place to be. Herons were roosting in the chimneys above the refectory, and the large, cloistered courtyard was full of springtime perfumes. I hadn't known an experience of calm like that even though I knew I shouldn't be there and even though my heartbeat was racing. After a while I was discovered by a smiling monk in full brown coloured habit who ushered me smilingly out through the tall, wide, weathered wooden door I had used to enter a piece of heaven on earth a couple of hours earlier.

Much of what I enjoyed about the Spain I saw was that it was steeped in tradition and old values. People had a genuine fondness for each other regardless of age, be it in the workplace, at public occasions, or in every day places – even nightclubs. Good manners and decorum could be observed everywhere and anytime. I loved it. One of my favourite villages was Chinchón, famous for its clear, herby, aniseed liqueur which turns cloudy with added ice – no water! The circular, cobbled main square was surrounded by a dark, old timber-framed gallery above restaurants and bars with verandas. The square was used occasionally for *Corridas de torros*. It all seemed very medieval, and yet it was somehow attractive, evocative, and acceptable.

Chinchon – a favourite place

It was often possible in the peace and tranquillity of such places to saunter around in the hot afternoon sun, just looking and exploring. The fountains, the cobbled streets and squares, Mediterranean trees and shrubs, the old buildings in various states of weathered condition but invariably still used for their original purpose, and the local folk engaged in conversation and invariably smoking, all created a heady experience. Private courtyards could often be seen brimming with colourful displays of potted flowers. It was all truly rewarding and delightful.

Business at Fidelity was a real eye-opener. The sheer scale of this worldwide business was a remarkable experience, all controlled by Ed Johnson lll, son of Ed Johnson ll, who founded it in 1946. When I joined in 1986 there were offices in Boston, the Bahamas, Australia, Canada, and Hong Kong. All the offices outside the United States and the Bahamas were managed by Richard Timberlake who had established them. The new Montreal office was especially contentious, as the United States parent company regarded the London office as trespassers on its backyard – the more so since it had grown the Canadian business immensely. It had been set up with the assistance of Martin, Caroline, and Richard's new secretary, Jenny who had replaced Nikki Weeks. Jenny was a pretty Sloane Ranger type of girl with bundles of energy but light-headed. They all stayed in an all-expenses-paid house and by all accounts worked exceptionally hard at making the launch of the business successful.

The international team of Nicola and Polly had been transferred to Hildenborough from the Fetter Lane offices. As both lived in London, it made sense for me to take them back to London after my weekly visits from the London office which I continued to use to allow me to contact my Middle Eastern connections on Saturdays and Sundays when they would be working.

Sometime in early 1987 Fidelity decided to launch an investment trust called European Values as a follow-up to an earlier launch of American Values. Nomura Securities were the underwriters. A road show was put together, and we made visits to all Fidelity's office locations to drum up business. As a throwback to my earlier experience of launching underwritten funds, it was fun and successful. We managed to get the fund oversubscribed at launch with in excess of £28 million. Nobody said 'well done' or 'thank you'. Success and achievement of this scale was expected. The connection with Nomura was obviously helpful and allowed us to make meetings with a wider group of potential investors than had been known previously. My liaison with Hildenborough personnel became frequent.

The Hildenborough office was a purpose-built administration office set in several acres of parkland near Tonbridge. Its design was personally approved by Ned Johnson in every detail. The grounds contained statues and the building, paintings and artefacts which he had personally selected. The gardens and lawns were always beautifully maintained. The building was literally bomb-proof (supposedly, nuclear-proof!) with its basement surrounded by several feet of concrete, its ability to keep computer systems running for seven days, and dual energy supplies from either end of the building.

Later in 1987 I was asked if I would go out to the Hong Kong office for three months. Meanwhile the local management led by Alan Mearns, went to Taiwan, where after several months of negotiation, they received all the relevant licences to open an office and offer investment products. I jumped at the chance on the proviso that my wife and family could come out for a few days and I could continue to service my Spanish connection each month. Richard agreed.

I arrived in August and stayed in the Victoria Hotel in Central District. It was about a twenty-minute walk from the office along a pedestrian walkway that ran alongside and above the main road leading from Causeway Bay. The Victoria had twin towers of about thirty storeys each: one was full of apartments while the other was mostly a hotel but also had offices on the upper floors. The two towers were linked some way up with a health club and outdoor swimming pool. My room overlooked Hong Kong's Victoria Harbour with Kowloon opposite – a spectacular location. Sadly, it lacked opening windows or a balcony, which I would have appreciated instead of the constant noises of the air-conditioning system.

The only way to enjoy being outside was to go to an outdoor pool several stories above street level between the towers. The pool was okay, but using any of the sun-loungers wasn't particularly pleasant, as smut from the traffic and air pollution generally meant being covered in dirt quite quickly: the atmosphere was also very unpleasantly humid.

Hong Kong was an eye-opening place. It is built on a small island, subject in season to storms of such severity that at the highest rating businesses close down. The dense, interweaving dual carriageway roads in Central Hong Kong are designed to cope with these storms, with many earth banks concreted over to ensure there are no landslides. The weather at the best and worst of times is warm and humid, which doesn't make land-based activities much fun at sea level.

Not only did the roads interweave but so did the pedestrians in the crowded pedestrian walkways, elevated pavements, and shopping malls. The locals had an amazing knack of being able to avoid even the slightest of nudges as they passed by, usually at some speed. In fact I discovered more about what locals think and feel about human interaction when I had drinks one evening with a waitress from my hotel. She confirmed that physical contact with another person, other than someone you knew intimately, was definitely to be avoided. She also said, while talking about bigger things, that the people of Hong Kong regarded Europe as 'old, historic, and not a place to visit'. There was nothing she felt the West could pass on to the emerging East!

Inevitably, I took advantage of being able to have clothes and several pairs of bespoke shoes made, and all of these have lasted and are all still comfortably wearable. The shoemaker Meyer was near the top floor of the Mandarin Hotel, known locally as the hotel with a thousand arseholes because all the windows looked like large portholes. This was all rather unflattering for one of the very best hotels on the island. The Captain's Bar was a place to go on Friday evenings to see and be seen. The hotel had an excellent and reasonably priced restaurant on the ground floor and a very expensive and exclusive one on the top floor. It was there that I saw a bottle of wine priced at over US$1,000. I asked how much a second one would be before settling for a bottle of the house wine! No answer was given.

Robert Randall, an acquaintance from the Isle of Man, his wife Deidre, and their young sons had moved to Hong Kong and were living in a sprawling and prestigious house with a live-in maid high up on the Peak overlooking Hong Kong and its harbour. The Peak was the area where most of Hong Kong's wealthy and influential people lived. Robert had taken a position Hong Kong & Shanghai Bank and was really living the high life in every sense, albeit with long hours but nonetheless oiled by the use of a chauffeured car. They made me extremely welcome and provided an opportunity to socialise with other local businessmen and expatriates from around the world.

Kowloon was a cheap 'Star Ferry' ride away across Hong Kong's astonishingly busy harbour. It was less glitzy than Central where I was staying and working. Its streets were closely packed, rather smelly, and very brightly lit with neon signs for every type of business and entertainment. Robert took me there one evening to a night club where we talked to several girls – all obviously on the game – in rather gloomy reddish light. He seemed to enjoy it all. I was rather bored with their rather simpleton conversation.

One weekend I took the opportunity to visit mainland China. I went with a small group into Guangdong, now Guangzhou Province. The border crossing involved being made to queue up and hand in or have noted any valuables such as watches and cameras and to have the passport stamped and numbered. We were told it was not permissible to bring out any local currency when we returned (but I did). Once across the border, our group was shepherded around a bustling town, with possibly thousands of cyclists and chaotic driving. We were shown something of the countryside – oxen in paddy fields and the sight in the distance of hundreds of labourers building what looked like a steep bank for a railway or road. We were encouraged to photograph the scene from the bus and not to take too long, as the traditionally dressed land worker wasn't to be humbled by us western visitors.

Lunch in the Bamboo Hotel was carefully orchestrated. Our group was taken to a designated dining room away from the locals, whom we could see in rooms with packed tables, all talking in the rather high pitched and excited way they do. The food and presentation in our room was presumably prepared to show something of the best of Cantonese cooking. It was disgusting and tasteless.

The highlight of the afternoon was a visit to a small museum, where some exhibits from the Terracotta Army were displayed. Photography was strictly not allowed, but I was anxious to get some pictures so I held back from the group. I noticed some closed-circuit TV cameras, so I restrained myself, only to be invited by a beckoning finger to peer through a creaking doorway. There I was given a scruffy cardboard-wrapped parcel. I had no idea what was inside, but I took it anyway. Was I being foolish? Anyway, I caught up with the group as they passed the terracotta horses and soldiers displayed behind glass, which really were wonderful to see.

On the way back to the bus I again separated from the group and was attracted to a man at a stall in a large square selling black and white photographs of (local Chinese?) people. I had deliberately 'dressed down' by wearing a white shirt and grey lightweight trousers, but the stallholder, a local man, insisted he wanted to take my picture. He positioned me with a large, rather bland white building behind me and took my photograph. He immediately burst out laughing, and I hadn't a clue why. I later discovered from the guide that he had put me in front of the local Communist Party regional headquarters. Simple humour!

Returning to Hong Kong meant queuing in the same order as we had entered the country. Due note was taken to see that everything we had taken in had come out, just to check that none of us had sold any personal possessions to anyone. My mystery parcel attracted no attention, but when I got back to the hotel, I discovered I had been given three miniature models of terracotta figures all smothered in a powdery dust. I had to wash this away in case it was something I shouldn't have. This I did immediately, hoping the figures wouldn't be disfigured or dissolve like clay. They didn't, and I have enjoyed having them ever since.

Holding the fort while the manager and another local colleague were in Taiwan involved management duties within the office, visiting intermediaries locally wasn't stressful, and I had little contact with senior management from London. During my time, an annual investment industry conference was held, which meant the arrival of several international marketing directors and press to attend. Being reunited with so many familiar faces from London was extremely enjoyable and interesting, and it gave me the opportunity to spend some time getting publicity for Fidelity from a local perspective.

The conference also coincided with a particularly bleak time on the world's stock markets, and with the announcement, which I heard on the BBC World Service on a small transistor radio, that Hong Kong was to become part of the Republic of China in a few years' time.

On one of my visits to the Hong Kong office of a major London firm of stockbrokers (James Capel & Co.), I witnessed something which to this day I find hard to believe. I was taken through various security doors to what appeared to be a general office. Television trading screens were everywhere, and local employees were busy with calls. In the corner, however, there was literally a scrum of people climbing over each other, all trying to give dealing requests and instructions to unseen people beyond. It was a mad house, and it confirmed an impression I had formed and still hold that Chinese investors, at least the 'Joe Public' investors, are gamblers. Market movements are more extremely driven there by the herd instinct than anywhere else I know.

Another memorable experience was when I witnessed a punch-up caused by a disgruntled local investor, who arrived in the office to harangue the receptionist and then a local employee over what he considered the dismal short-term performance of his investments. Another UK fund company, Gartmore, had had a similar event in their offices with another individual a few days before. As a result, we and they recruited some external security people to ensure that the trouble did not reoccur.

Living in Hong Kong for a short while made me aware of a significant cultural difference in the way people handle money there. The basic rule was that if you couldn't pay in cash for something, you couldn't buy it. Credit was virtually unknown. Being overdrawn at the bank was impossible. It made me realise then what a strong discipline the Chinese had towards money. This would account for their ability to weather western economic storms without apparent or significant problems.

At the end of my thoroughly enjoyable stay, during which I maintained monthly visits to Madrid, I returned to London via Madrid and Paris where Fidelity was about to launch another new office with a party up the Eiffel Tower on the public viewing platform. After such a long period in Hong Kong I had bought clothing, shoes and electrical items and the inevitable fake watches. I had made a list of my purchases to show Customs in London, just in case they wanted import duties paid. I went through the red channel to declare my purchases and discovered that it was just as well. Had I gone through the alternative green 'nothing to declare' channel and been searched I would have been charged the full duty for the full retail price of original, not fake, watches. Why? It was explained to me that in bringing in fake watches I had hoped to dupe the system.

Richard Timberlake was particularly keen to enlarge Fidelity International's worldwide presence. For the Paris office he had recruited a bi-lingual Englishman who had managed a US brokerage there and developed a range of funds for the French market which he hoped would be attractive and successful with French institutions.

There then followed regular visits to Paris hold meetings with intermediaries which had been set up by the new local office. We never really achieved a significant breakthrough, despite offering a loyalty commission based on the half-yearly collective value of investors' accounts. Meetings were always cordial, but the information flow seemed always to consist more of them asking me about my business development feedback locally. Much more significant business was placed by specialist fund agents, which I had researched, in Lille.

Throughout my time at Fidelity I travelled abroad at least twice a month for several days at a time. Standing at Putney Bridge station waiting for a District Line tube train to the City and looking skywards at the Heathrow-bound planes made me appreciate how lucky I was not to be a regular commuter with a mind-boggling, boring work routine. I was doing something I really enjoyed. I also realised that without any tertiary education or professional qualifications, I was lucky to be doing what I was doing. I knew I was part of a generation that would be the last to achieve responsibilities of the sort I had without these qualifications.

All this came to a fairly abrupt end in 1989 following a severe stock market downward correction. Glen Moreno was parachuted into London from Boston. He headed Fidelity's audit committee as chairman of its Boston head office, having previously been at Citigroup in Europe and Asia, where he ran the investment banking and trading divisions and became a group executive. (Moreno later became permanently resident in London whilst still retaining a farm in Virginia, and was a leading adviser to the UK government through the financial crises of 2008 and onwards.) He was a big corporate beast! He oversaw the rapid growth of Fidelity worldwide in the mid-1980s to become the biggest fund management group in the world. How many billions of dollars I can't recall, but a lot! Nevertheless, with the market and prospects looking for a while uncertain at best, overheads had to be reviewed, and both Richard and I, amongst a few others, were asked to leave.

Typically of Richard, after leaving Fidelity he set up another fund management group, 'Portfolio', whose approach to fund management was to pool several external fund managers within a fund range as 'funds of funds', a throwback to the days of IOS (International Overseas Services) and Bernie Cornfeld in the mid-1960s. Richard recruited Tim Miller as marketing director (ex Mitfords and Royds). In addition Richard made a name for himself by aggressively analysing fund management costs known as total expense ratios (TER). They are now used extensively as a key analytical tool by investors and advisers of funds and their management.

I was now seen as someone whose international days were numbered as interest in the products was diminishing because of the weak stock market. I was offered a redundancy payment of just over £23,000, which I had no choice but to accept. Unfortunately, the internally appointed replacement managing director, Barry Bateman, hadn't seen the offer prior to being asked to sign it off, and he promptly refused to do so.

Reluctantly, I accepted a lower payment and left the company rather despondently, but not before I had had a chance meeting with Clive Williams (formerly of Towry Law) who invited me to meet him for lunch 'to chew the cud'.

Chapter 9

European Creativity

Clive invited me to join him for lunch in one of the City's better restaurants, the Baron of Beef just off Cheapside. Over what I was to come to know as a typical 'Clive experience', we enjoyed an almost unrestricted lunch in terms of cost: the best of every course with wines to match. Clive had become Managing Director of Sun Life International after being Chief Executive of an industry consultancy, LIMRA International, in Watford. The brief was to develop products and services using the considerable existing strengths of Sun Life Assurance Group Limited and its principal shareholder, Union Assurances de Paris (UAP). Most of Sun Life's personnel were based in Bristol, whilst Clive was based in head office in Cheapside, where he reported to John Reeves, the CEO of Sun Life Group. There was also an offshore fund management company based in the Isle of Man – with delegated fund managers at the Cheapside office but full of administrators.

Clive was interested in my joining him to develop international fund marketing and sales function, which if justified, would establish offices within Europe. The dominant shareholder (29.9%) of Sun Life was UAP, a French state-owned multi-faceted *banc-assurance* business with representation throughout the world. It was a huge business partner, and Clive had already established that UAP would support his plans for development of Sun Life Europe as part of Sun Life International.

In October 1989 I moved into my own office on the sixth (the Executive) floor of Sun Life's eight-storey head office overlooking Cheapside. My secretary was Jane Hutchinson, who although not the brightest of people, was efficient and had a very happy disposition. I soon discovered that the company had a deep corporate culture that had grown from its establishment in 1810. This culture manifested itself in various ways, of which only an insider would become aware. Being on the executive sixth floor with only board directors above me on the seventh, for example, meant that I was entitled to have my own coat hanger, enjoy a circular (rather than square) waste bin, and be served morning coffee and afternoon tea and biscuits served by waitresses in black dresses and white aprons from the board and managers' dining room, which was on the top, eighth floor. By such things your status could be judged!

Clive, a rather loquacious north Walian, had already identified the development route for the company and the UAP connections that would be needed. Every day, lunches in the eighth floor dining room provided Clive with an audience to whom he could regale his latest thoughts and the development of his baby. Resources were made available to analyse and scrutinise every detail of his business development plans.

Eventually the Chief Executive, John Reeve, decided that the dining arrangements were out of line with modern expectations. Daily lunches in this dining room were scrapped, and we were all told to eat in the self-service ground-floor staff canteen. Certain fellow diners mumbled and grumbled about not being able to have discreet business conversations and the additional cost this would cause by having to go out. But the change worked for most people, apart from the board members who rarely made an appearance and, when they did, were shunned by the *hoi polloi* staff members.

Key amongst Clive's resources were John Riley, an actuary and my first working colleague to regularly use a computer (still comparatively uncommon), Richard Clarke a salesman/technician, and Geoff, a business and systems analyst. All three were based in Bristol and were long-term servants of Sun Life with over twenty years of service each. John was to become Clive's right-hand man thanks to his colossal ability to attend to detail and forecast business profitability with his actuarial skills. He was also of great help to me, in providing immediate authority with other employees of equal standing within the organisation but who had, like John, Richard, and Geoff, never been employed anywhere else.

Our appreciation of our mutual strengths and business capabilities was very apparent, and as a team we worked extremely well. I felt I had total support in looking to achieve success, and after considerable market analysis, I decided that despite widespread market awareness for developing business amongst expat communities in Europe, which we could do anyway, it would be better to focus on creating a brand new indigenous business in Germany. This was based on identifying the size of the existing, predominantly locally invested funds market there and the potential to offer internationally invested diversification. Only four other foreign, all US, investment houses had operations there.

Germany was a new market to me, however, and it was imperative that we should find a consultant who was familiar with the German investment and savings market and able to communicate and understand the English business mind. It was my great good fortune to become aware of Axel Schmidke, who was based in Munich. He fulfilled these criteria and for an acceptable fee prepared a marketing dossier for Germany with market analysis, product recommendations, and specifications.

He suggested 'mixing and matching' a number of existing Isle of Man-based funds into 'Lifestyle' products, as well as developing investment services which would appeal to German pension funds and which would attract tax breaks to the investing institutions. Axel's comprehensively analysed and budgeted recommendations, contained in two 100-page documents, were accepted by the Sun Life Europe board of which I was International Marketing Director.

The German financial regulator (BAKred – *Bundesaufsichtsamt für das Kreditwesen*: The Federal Banking Supervisory Office) required all fund management companies wishing to operate within the country to be 'sponsored' by a local bank. Finding one willing to cooperate with a foreign institution was extremely difficult, not least because the local banks perceived a marketing threat if not the threat of an actual take-over! I was fortunate in identifying a private bank in Frankfurt which, after due diligence of Sun Life on their part, was willing to join in with our venture for a small fee of one quarter of one per cent of net sales per annum. Bankhaus Gerbruder Bethman (founded in 1746) in Bethmanstrasse was the essence of private banking, highly professional, courteous, and discreet. It was also part of a much bigger banking group – Bayerische-Vereinsbank AG, and they and other banking subsidiaries had clients who might even be persuaded to invest in these foreign products. For a time I had exclusive access and use of an office within their Bethman building.

The building was an unimpressive flat-fronted fairly modern grey-coloured building about four storeys high. Immediately inside was a traditional banking hall with a marble floor and a curving staircase with elegant ironwork banisters leading to the floors above. A couple of lifts were also available. The cream-toned walls were dotted with large portraits of eminent people who had been connected with the bank over the centuries. My office was along a carpeted silent corridor with paintings of rural scenes, and through a heavy wooden door. The decoration here was again mostly shades of grey – a colour which seemed then and still seems to dominate corporate Germany.

The bank was controlled at one stage by Prince Johannes Erbprinz Thurn und Taxis, who was said to have been the richest man in Europe in the early 20th Century, controlling Bayerische Vereinsbank, the fourth largest bank in Germany, with four subsidiaries in Frankfurt, including Bankhaus Gebruder Bethmann. Bethmann-Hollweg of this family had been Chancellor under Kaiser Wilhelm. He was a cousin of the Frankfurt Rothschilds. Bayerische Vereinsbank also owned a controlling interest in Banque de Paris et de Payes and Banque de l'Europeène Paris. Thurn und Taxis was a direct descendant of William of Orange, who chartered the Bank of England.

Whilst I was working in the building I learned something of the way Germans behave in business, and in general it wasn't impressive. Getting a telephone socket installed took months; negotiating with unavoidable and usually invisible layers of authority or management through more layers of apparently interested or possibly affected parties took forever; and getting a decision about anything remotely significant felt having won the war! Axel by comparison had been a revelation in his outlook and positively optimistic approach and willingness to support our entry into the German market. Equally, it proved invaluable to have Berndt Wallacek on board as the local manager. Having had experience of working in the funds business in the States and wanting to be part of a cutting-edge opportunity, his approach to and understanding of the national psyche was hugely beneficial. And both were truly lovely men to spend time with, both in and out of the office. Berndt reported to me in London.

In due time, we found an office of our own in Beethovenstrasse near the centre of Frankfurt. The office was within a building that was originally built as a block of flats. It was on the second floor and had three rooms and a kitchenette. Berndt and Axel got along well, and the launch programme for Sun Life Deutschland Gmbh. was planned. Approval for the marketing of funds in Germany was obtained after a good deal of hard work by a London based colleague Peter Conrad, with the lawyers and BAKred– the German regulatory authority. We were one of the first companies outside Germany wishing to market funds there to obtain approval. Many companies had tried and failed, but Peter Conrad's obstinate streak and determination could not have been more focussed.

Conrad was a qualified lawyer and accountant, and he had been in the funds business, including Save and Prosper, for many years. His role was to oversee everything to do with the legal aspects of the funds' structures in a compliance role. We used a prestigious firm of Frankfurt lawyers Bruckhaus who were magnificent with their help and assistance, dealing with German banking and financial services bureaucracy. At the time there was no such thing as a compliance officer, but that was Conrad's role in effect. He was immensely accurate. He enjoyed his work and a glass or two of *Fleurie* in a wine bar not far from his office in Cannon Street most lunch times. We got along famously, and I visited him at his home in Tunbridge Wells from time to time at weekends, where he was a *bon viveur*, and lover of Saab cars. He had some delicious recipes for sloe gin and for salmon in pancake rolls *hors d'oevres*, and he cooked delicious game and meat pies. Sadly, he died quite suddenly in the mid1990s. Peter Conrad was a true pal whom I always respected. I have missed him and thought about him frequently

Together we packaged a number of existing offshore Isle of Man-based Sun Life funds into Lifestyle products designed to meet investment needs and requirements at different stages in life: young families, pre-retirement, retirement, and so on. They were relatively complex in structure but easy to sell to an unsophisticated and in some ways naive audience. All the marketing material was designed, translated, and produced in Germany. It was an innovative product range, and depending on its degree of success, it could be developed further given Sun Life's insurance wrapper expertise.

Axel's accepted suggestion was that the Lifestyle products should be launched at a series of presentations to be held in six major cities, Hamburg, Frankfurt, Berlin, Munich, Hanover, and Dortmund. It happened that all had enormously tall television towers with public restaurants – some revolving – at a high level. The usual cast of guests from the local and regional financial community was invited to each, and the remarkable fact that emerged was that a large proportion had never visited their local tower. So there was a double attraction in being invited.

The trade press just loved the story of a long-established City institution becoming a front runner to open up business opportunities, with a Frankfurt office in a newly liberalised Europe. The Frankfurter Allegemeine Zeitung wrote an article in June 1992 stating 'the advantage to German investors is obvious: they benefit from a range of specially designed products previously unknown to German investors … in a market which is recognised as the world's most competitive and innovative'. As, 'Portfolio' noted, also in 1992, 'all German independent financial advisers are going to be free to shop around …. and so are those in France, Italy, Spain and the rest.' It was exciting times, and we were ahead.

The Berlin *Messe-Funkturm*, and Munich *Olympiaturm* towers were the most memorable for the views they provided. Looking out over Berlin over Alexanderplatz, and the as then unreconstructed (from World War ll), enormous cathedral, was interesting for showing so clearly the difference between the smart boulevards of West Berlin and the narrower, concrete streets lined with grey slab-sided high rise flats of East Berlin. The Munich tower was very memorable for overlooking a visually beautiful city and for being close to the Olympic park where there had been the terrorist Israeli hostage crises at the 1972 Olympics. Also for the view above the white BMW head office tower. The tower's design mimics the shape of four cylinders in a car engine, with a museum representing a cylinder head. Consequently it has several local names: *BMW-Vierzylinder* "BMW four-cylinder", or simply BMW Tower.

Generally the reception to our launch presentations was good. Over 550 people representing almost 400 companies participated, but there would be a big learning curve for intermediaries first and clients second for Berndt to overcome. Despite this background, many agents knew of a few other companies who had, at that time registered their funds with the German authorities, including Pioneer from the United States, who had developed a range of indigenous *fonds* which had performed unsatisfactorily. There was a desire to see specialist fund companies such as Fidelity create awareness by entering the market. We, Sun Life, somehow might fall between two stools, being seen as a life insurer first and/or investment manager second!

My usual hotels in Frankfurt were the InterContinental (no surprises) and my preferred small family-run hotel, the Hotel Villa Diana Westend, in Westendstraße, a little further out of the city but within walking distance through parks from the bright lights in a residential street. The small hotel had no en-suite rooms, but it was generally possible to have a bath in a room next door to my preferred room, which was at the back and overlooked the garden. The procedure to follow to have an early morning bath was that I would call the lobby and say I'd like a bath run. A maid would then come and run the bath, all very discretely and politely. The reason for all this performance just to run a bath was so that the staff could ensure that the bathroom was clean every time before it was used. It wasn't possible to use the bath without this attendance, as the plug was taken away!

The hotel was always a cosy place – great in cold weather. It had wooden floors covered with oriental rugs, there were some antique furnishings, and everything was very calm and quiet. Opposite or at least nearby were some restaurants. I'd frequently go to a Polish restaurant which was very good and inexpensive with friendly staff who, after a few visits, remembered me. There was also an excellent Italian restaurant which was also quite lively and fun.

When the weather was warm, I would stay out in the Taunus mountain foothills in a hotel, near Bad Homburg surrounded by its own farmyard. To reach it off the road to Wiesbaden, there was a drive through a forest which opened up onto wide open farmland. Final access to the hotel was around and through farm buildings with free-range chickens and ducks enjoying an untroubled existence. There were no hedges, but the land was peppered with small towers used by farmers as hides from which to shoot wildlife. The hotel was ultra-smart but not excessively pricey, except the restaurant, which only provided an à la carte menu. It's situation and facilities were first class. Nearby there was a village which had a selection of good restaurants at economical prices. I enjoyed staying there and the drive to and from Frankfurt.

Lufthansa provided me with the worst flying experience of my career one afternoon when flying from Frankfurt to Munich. Soon after take off an announcement was made that because of storms ahead we'd make a diversion and would be landing later than scheduled. Whatever action the pilot took was clearly insufficient as we were soon within a major hailstorm and being thrown violently about: fortunately with seat belts on. The noise of hailstones on the fuselage roof was deafening. It was truly scary! In due course we landed safely, but the damage to the plane was clearly visible. The nose cone covering the forward radar dish was severely indented, and the fuselage and wing surfaces' paintwork was pot marked. The plane had to be withdrawn from service.

I visited Munich to see Axel quite frequently and usually stayed at the Englischer Garten Hotel on the fringe of Englischer Garten public park. Again, this was a small family-run hotel, but it had en-suites and continental breakfasts to die for. Although fairly central, it really was a breath of fresh air in this city which could become really hot in summer. The park had many pathways through woodland and across and around a lake with swans and geese. It was a good spot.

Axel was keen to take me one evening to the *Oktoberfest in Munchen* where we sat on long trestle benches shared with total strangers drinking enormous glasses of beer. There was quite a good noise of people enjoying themselves, locals and visitors alike. The weather was warm, and it was comfortable to be sitting outside. I always preferred drinking from a glass rather than the traditional stoneware stein drinking mugs. The evening was going well, when Axel sensed a change in the weather and said we should drink up and be leaving straight away. Other people were also beginning to leave before finishing their drinks.

We made our way to Axel's car through the tables and benches as the wind picked up strength. Marquees began to flap, and more and more people made for the numerous exits. No sooner had we reached the car than there was a huge clap of thunder with lightning. The wind became violent. In no time tree branches and leaves were falling and swirling across and down the road. Axel's senses had been right. Apparently these instant storms are not unknown at Beer Festival time!

On another occasion Axel and I went out on the beer to a large bar in a Munich suburb with outside and tented seating, which was absolutely thronged with joyous Germans. People stood three or four deep at the bar exchanging stories and experiences about their newly found freedom to move between East and West Germany. Freedom of movement between East and West Germany was officially allowed from November 1989, and families that had been split were being reunited and stories told of how life had been behind the Wall in the East, and sadly also, stories of valiant but failed attempts to escape to the West. Everyone was so happy to be there and unwind with family and friends.

I visited Berlin shortly after the Wall had been breached in 1989, but before German reunification, to visit the man in charge of the city's (ultimately unsuccessful) decision to bid to host the 2000 Olympics. This had been announced within a week of the reunification of Germany in October 1990. He gave me a number of souvenirs, including a tie with the Berlin Olympics logo – a rather bright yellow tie! In the event, the 2000 Olympics were held in Sydney, so the souvenirs took on a different and somewhat historic significance of a country yearning to be seen as united and strong.

I took the opportunity to visit East Berlin by taking a taxi and asking to go into East Germany and be shown the sights. The driver's English was minimal, but we negotiated Checkpoint Charlie, a US-manned entry point, and I was driven around. Checkpoint Charlie required me to hand over my passport and be given a ticket that had to be returned when I came back. I was hoping to keep this ticket as a perhaps rare memento of this transition period, but I wasn't allowed to. The streets were pretty much as I expected: rather cold, grey, and treeless, and without much in the way of 'life'. Most of the Wall, which in the city was two parallel walls with 'no mans land' in between, was still standing – covered in graffiti on the western side but just grey and weathered concrete on the eastern side about fifty yards apart.

Nevertheless I saw some memorable sights the most powerful being that of street vendors standing behind steaming trolleys rather like the ones I had seen in Indonesia. Here, though, they were keeping frankfurters warm. I bought one of these in dry bread roll priced at three Ostmark, I was told by the gesticulating taxi driver raising three fingers. This was equivalent then, to one Deutschemark. The drably dressed lady behind the steaming trolley said she had no change for my proffered ten Deutschemark note. The taste of a traditional East Berlin roll had cost three times more than it should have done! Capitalism had arrived quickly in formerly communist East Germany!

When currency conversion was introduced, prior to the Euro, the Bonn government (to be moved later to Berlin) offered between two and five Deutschemarks for each Ostmark, depending on a number of 'wealth factors' in an overly generous deal for which the West Germans were to pay economically for several decades as a unified nation. This has made me forever question the Germans' ability to manage grand European economics.

Whilst Germany was still divided as East and West Germany, I visited Leipzig to promote Sun Life. I arrived at the small airport determined to go to an evening concert – hopefully with the Leipzig Gewandhaus Orchestra with which I had fallen in love while at school. (A recording of theirs of Beethoven's Seventh Symphony became a favourite and still is.) The orchestra was away, I discovered at the City Information Desk in the airport, so instead I bought a ticket for a one-off performance of Puccini's opera *Madame Butterfly* at the Oper Leipzig that evening and was told of a concert to be held at the St Thomas Kirche, the next day.

The drive to the hotel (by taxi) on straight autobahns built originally for wartime direct and speedy access to the enemy (even to be used as aircraft landing strips), across flat uninteresting countryside populated by ramshackle farm buildings and occasional cattle, readily conjured up ideas of former impoverished communist rule. I arrived at my hotel, quite a grand place; the Hotel Astoria. It had light-coloured, highly polished wood panelling everywhere. The carpets, curtains, and wall coverings were well past their best. The dining room had chandeliers and silent loudspeakers mounted high up on the tall walls. It was all very redolent of a place where the communist party faithful could meet, smoke, drink, and plan. Maybe the Stasi had used this place? My room was basic. The television was bulky but in colour, so I was surprisingly able to watch the FA Cup Final. I was amazed that British TV could already be seen in the former East Germany just a few months after the Wall had come down.

My ticket to the opera had cost about seven pounds (about a tenth of the cheapest London prices). On my arrival at the opera house (a truly grand building but in need of decoration and new carpets), I found it had bought me a seat a few rows back from the orchestra pit and stage, as well as a thick programme with libretto! The quality of the performance was terrific. It was hard to believe this was a one-night-only performance. Interval drinks were served in a large room. The choice was red or white wine, Martini, beer, or soft drinks. They were all free!

What was evident on looking around the room, which was mostly full of women aged fifty-plus, was that there was an air of excitement at having the opportunity and freedom to go out in the evening. The ladies had made every effort to dress for the occasion, but the mix of brightly coloured handbags and matching shoes (lime green and pink!), so obviously new and worn with pride, clashed awkwardly with the sombre colours of their everyday clothing. My impression again was that the availability of western items in the shops was new and that for these people to show off was an important part of feeling and demonstrating that life had changed.

The next day I visited the St Thomas Kirche and marvelled at the history and beauty of this comparatively modest but beautiful church where J.S. Bach had been organist and choirmaster. I tried to picture him there, creating all the magical music of his time. Richard Wagner, who was born in Leipzig, had also been a musician in the church. Interestingly, there was no memorial or statue or even street name to Wagner, whose recognition by Hitler in World War ll had not found favour with the local burghers!

Reminders of the recent past were everywhere. Across the square from the hotel was an enormous relief sculpture on the side of a long building that showed workers symbolically pulling together. Other statues around town all showed former Soviet influence. Cars and motor bikes were all old and noisy. It was very apparent that a generation of young men had already left the East to find work in the West. This made for a strange imbalance when looking at everyday street scenes and shops. These were mostly not fully stocked and offered limited choices. Some items, such as toothpaste, had sold out. By contrast, the spanking new trolley buses were an outward sign from the authorities to the people that investment from the West was coming.

Life in West Berlin was showing sometimes surprising consequences of reunification. It wasn't unusual for poor East Germans to travel to the western side and try and steal food from supermarkets. The traffic lights system in the different parts of the city worked in different sequences. The underground railway had not yet been reconnected because of system differences. Generally, West Berliners didn't want to have much to do with the easterners or to go as tourists out of curiosity to see the East. They were, however, proud that they would be reunited.

Sun Life's German project initially spluttered along with frequent and usually unhelpful contributions from the Isle of Man administration office. Berndt continued to work hard and had occasional good results.

He negotiated over sixty distribution agreements. One of these was his success in UAP's Strasbourg broker office, which although based in France covered a large area of south Germany, to promote the Sun Life Lifestyle products. This began to show encouraging sales quite quickly.

UAP soon pressed the button on a pan-European product that would be offered through its Luxembourg office. The planning meetings for developing the life products linked to Sun Life funds were coordinated under Pierre Labardie, a director of UAP (L'Union des assurances de Paris). UAP's elegant head office was in Place Vendôme and it wasn't unusual for twenty people to attend the meetings, which were conducted in French, with two or three representatives from several of UAP's European offices. The sessions would break every few minutes for Riley, Clarke, and me to be updated on the discussions. When we spoke in English, it appeared that everyone around the large table understood us. It was a mistake when, after a period of French talking, I asked a question which referred to something which hadn't been mentioned in the briefing to us. I had heard the word *elasticité* and wondered what its significance was to the detail of our discussions! The frequency of briefing updates within meetings diminished from there on, but we got by!

The meetings lasted all day with an elegant four-course lunch, with cheese served before desert, served in-house in a suite of dining rooms across a small street nearby.

Relations with UAP, out masters, developed well. On one occasion I was sent to Paris to a conference arranged by Lafferty, a publications company, to give a speech which had been billed as being given by Lord Gaunt, a non-executive director of Sun Life in London on behalf of the Sun Life chairman. I felt comfortable and confident about my role and the contribution I was making to the European project and, because of the company's investment in Sun Life Europe, in the contribution to the future of the business as a whole.

The Euro-project was launched at a seminar up the Eiffel Tower. I had flown from Madrid and met up with Clive, John Riley, and Michael Clarke at the Hilton just a short distance away. Clive had made all the accommodation arrangements, and true to style he had ensured we all had superior rooms and balconies. Clive held reception in his suite in the evening, followed by dinner for us and other Sun Life personnel flown in from London. Later we went to the bar for a night cap, only to find the place being set up for a live New Orleans jazz night. Clive decided we should all stay for this, and it was terrific fun. It turned out to be a late and 'heavy' night!

Not long after this, there were profound changes within Sun Life head office. Clive had left, probably pushed, and Richard Surface, an American who had previously been MD at Pearl Assurance, had taken over the reins of Sun Life International. He was an abrasive individual who had precious little understanding of either the life business or the investment business. His style was appreciated, however, by John Reeves, and it soon became apparent that Surface, all calm and smoothness on the outside, felt my role was superfluous and that he would do his best to make sure I left. He accompanied me on a two-day trip to Spain, arranged at short notice to fit in with his diary, which went well. But he had already made his mind up: I was going.

I was offered redundancy and left after four weeks with no immediate employment in prospect. I kept my car (a Fiat Croma 2-litre turbo), my Waring & Gillows leather-tooled desk, and two chests of drawers. Sun Life also provided unlimited 'job counselling' with Coutts Agency. This provided rather unsophisticated one-to-one counselling in how to think about the future (bleak), how to search for employment, and how to prepare the CV. They were very keen on psychometric testing using the Myers-Briggs papers. One of the personality traits I had, possibly still have, is a tendency to over-analyse situations and problems. Whilst analysis is obviously a good thing, over-analysis can be detrimental, as it can mean that decisions aren't made when sufficient information is known to come to a good decision. Drilling down into situations or problems can ultimately prove destructive. I found that hard to accept, but that was the experts' conclusion.

Their offices were in New Street, just off Bishopsgate, and it was a mental and peaceful sanctuary: apart from when the IRA attempted to blow up two Christopher Wren City churches a stone's throw away. However, continuing to go there meant that I could maintain the discipline of 'going to work', be amongst others to share the experience of self-doubt and job seeking, and get the occasional morale boost from my counsellor. It was a low point, and despite their best efforts over several months, the agency did not directly contribute anything towards my next appointment.

In addition, I spent days in the library at the Institute of Directors which I had joined soon after beginning with Sun Life. I found their research facilities for the fund and investment business better than those at Coutts. I also used their Members' rooms for meetings in response to job applications. It was a venue many people had never previously visited, and I thought it might also give a good impression.

I toyed with the idea of launching an investment fund investing in second hand 'traded' endowment life policies due to mature within ten years or so, including some with much shorter maturity terms. The concept obviously combined various strands of my career work to date, and it was at the time a novel idea, but because of a variety of contributing factors, in particular lack of confidence but also lack of finance, I was unable to get the idea off the ground. My secretarial needs were met by Putney Business Services in the Lower Richmond Road. Some months after I had decided not to proceed with it, Barclays and one other institution launched exactly the product I had formulated, and in due time I did invest some money in one of them and made a reasonable profit.

Another distasteful aspect of leaving Sun Life concerned the Discretionary Executive Incentive Scheme, which was a Jersey-based trust arrangement into which I had been enrolled, without invitation or warning, by management. This scheme was designed to incentivise and reward executives with the payment of a bonus, which at the time of my leaving entitled me, according to a printed statement, to £66,000. When I left, I was told that I would not be receiving this. The reason given was because the scheme was 'discretionary' and operated as a trust by independent trustees in Jersey. The company remuneration committee had no influence on the trustees' actions, and no-one knew who the trustees were, or so I was told! None of this made any sense to me. In fact it seemed very unlikely that some mysterious, possibly mythical figures in Jersey could take this decision without having input from my London senior colleagues – probably board directors, who had put me in the scheme. Others of a similar seniority were being given their bonuses. I engaged my brother John's firm of City solicitors, Simmons & Simmons, to help me fight my cause.

I made vigorous representations to John Read, the assistant general manager at Sun Life's Cheapside head office, who was the interface with the remuneration committee and the Jersey trustees, with what I thought were cogent arguments for me to be included in the scheme for payment, not least because in their wisdom the remuneration committee had put me into the scheme in the first place. Despite all the obvious and not so obvious and vigorous arguments we made and the conclusions to be drawn, the company refused to support my case with the trustees, and this money was never paid. The only possible, but inconsistent justification could be that I had not been employed by the company for very long. It was a great disappointment, having been made aware of the potential payment.

As part of seeking for work I continued to 'front up' and look confident, but I was mentally losing it. I attended many interviews which lead nowhere, but out of the blue I received an invitation to an evening reception in Arlington Street in St James's, just round the corner from the Ritz. The hosts were a couple of American guys I had met in Zurich who had presented a new concept in fund marketing which involved 'hub and spoke'. This combined different elements of the Hill Samuel ISF model with the portfolio management service concept I had devised some years ago. There were a number of guests I knew, including Roger Cornick, whom I had heard about but had never met. He had been employed at both Abbey Life and Hambros Life but was now deputy chairman and marketing director at Perpetual, a young and successful fund management company based in Henley-on-Thames. He told me he was working on a project to expand into Europe and asked if I would be interested in working with him on it. However, he couldn't tell me if or when he would get the go ahead.

Several increasingly anxious weeks and then months went by until one day, after making some carefully worded telephone calls which would not expose my true desperation, I was invited to meet him again in Henley to discuss his ideas and my 'availability'. He was keen for me to join but wanted me to submit my remuneration package. This was where Coutts did play a part, and with their help I submitted what I thought was a good package, which I sent off. Roger soon invited me down to a formal interview one hot July day in 1989. I thought the interview went well – in fact, well enough for me to buy a celebration present for myself to hang in the house I was living in, and now separated from my first wife, in Reading – a limited edition print by Russell Flint. Roger duly confirmed that I would start work in September.

Chapter 10

Perpetual, but not for long

Perpetual had been founded in 1973 by Martyn Arbib, himself a highly successful fund manager, who thought that developing his skills into a business and employing other proven managers in areas where he was not strong would make a good business. As he lived near Henley, he also thought this would be an attractive location to lure key staff. On the back of a very successful and young fund management business, Martyn developed his interest in flat racing and owned at least one horse. His success on the race track wasn't, however, ever very significant. 'Horses for courses' as the saying goes!

The head office was an attractive Queen Anne house on the River Thames in Henley, close to Henley Bridge, which Martyn had totally restored and refurbished. Within this elegant riverside mansion worked the investment managers. Neil Woodford was already an outstanding fund manager of UK income funds. Kathryn Langridge was an outstanding Far East and Emerging Markets specialist. Others, including Bob Yerbury, were all to go on to become significant industry figures. They were a stimulating group of people to be working with.

Perpetual had several other offices scattered about the town, all in line of sight, which enabled radio links to be established for management information transmissions directly to computer resources. As the business flourished, it built a new head office opposite Henley's railway station. Later still, it also took on a disused hospital on the Fairmile Road out to Wallingford, which it converted into an elegant office complex situated in the midst of park land.

My office was in a converted Elizabethan house behind Hart Street. Access from the road was through an electronically operated large wooden double-door gate that opened onto a delightful garden in which up to six cars could be parked. I was provided with a VW Corrado 6 cylinder coupe. Roger had a Porsche Carerra. I was given the title of European Sales Director, and my role was to advise the board on developing their business in Europe. The building was shared with several regional consultants who covered the UK intermediary market.

The company had established an outstanding performance record for all its funds and was beginning to look for corporate and pension fund accounts. Whilst I was employed there, the company took a small stake in an investment company based in Georgia in the United States. After I had left, Invesco ultimately bought the Perpetual business and changed its UK name to Invesco Perpetual. Invesco had become a significant fund management group in the US.

Monthly investment meetings were held at Leander, the UK's (some would say the world's) preeminent rowing club. These meetings were attended by all fund managers, and I was invited as an observer. Guest speakers would make presentations on particular investment markets, and a discussion would follow. Gavin Davies, who later became Chairman of the BBC, was one speaker while he was a partner at Goldman Sachs.

One such discussion was about whether the emergence of computers was a 'good thing' for output, employment, and economies. A few managers believed that computers would be able to do the work of several people and therefore unemployment would rise and therefore computers were a threat to worldwide employment. Others took the view that productivity per worker would increase and that therefore they would be a good thing for output, employment, and world growth. I can't remember now which side won that argument, but it was an issue at the time! The design of computers hadn't changed much since becoming commonplace in the 1970's. They were still large grey metal boxes sitting on their hard disc towers on, or near to the user's desk.

My secretary, Alison, an attractive girl in her twenties was not the brightest, but she was a keen worker and an excellent PC operator. Floppy discs which she used for some data storage had become popular add-ons for computer use. She was keen to arrange my trips back into Europe; my days of travelling any further afield were now over. The reception I had with contacts I had made over the years remained good in the European markets I now concentrated on. However because of the investment potential identified in Germany, my efforts were now primarily focussed there and also in Austria.

A small specialist firm of Viennese lawyers, called Grohmann as I recall, was found with excellent English skills who had previously undertaken similar foreign business registration work. I found a representative bank, Schiller & Co., a similar bank in many ways to Gerbruder Bethman in Frankfurt which would fulfil a similar role. It was privately owned with a wealthy clientele. They would act as our Austrian representative bank as required by Austrian Law, and through them all financial payments would be made and received. The hope was that they would also invest client monies with us, but they didn't do so to any significant degree.

Austrian business worked in a peculiar, rather remote and long-fingered but cosy way. There were a few large banks with their own fund departments and a few middle-sized banks and specialist fund management brokers. Banking secrecy seemed somewhere close to the Swiss model, so the idea of investing in British unit trusts, even though they weren't particularly tax-efficient, had some appeal as they were seen as being protected from local disclosure, provided the charges, which had been significantly reduced from their normal levels, could be accepted. All transactions which we undertook were all accepted on a full disclosure basis.

Roger took little regular interest, it seemed to me, in what I was doing, although he received written reports after every overseas trip. A discipline I had maintained ever since beginning my meetings with intermediaries on all my UK and foreign travels. I had begun to feel that Roger was disinterested in overseas expansion; the volumes of business to which he was accustomed from within the UK just weren't immediately forthcoming from Europe. Organising the necessary procedures and protocols were distractions to him.

Perpetual was unwilling to go to the expense of setting up mirror funds, which could have been managed from their Jersey offices, in foreign currency denominations, and neither were they willing to offer different types of units for different categories of investor. Such offerings were beginning to become available, and to do so would have been a clear statement of their seriousness about expanding internationally.

Nevertheless, volume business was taken through Raffeisen Bank and two brokerages, one opposite St Stephen's Cathedral and another near my regular hotel, the Malbergerhof in the city centre in a courtyard off a pedestrianised street. Both of these brokerages had an excellent grasp of international fund managers and funds.

In France Roger had recruited prior to my arrival an agent named Craig, a bilingual Brit, who was on a Perpetual part time retainer and commuted from Dallington, East Sussex to Paris each week. His role was to obtain meetings with French intermediaries for me to meet. The arrangement worked well, if expensively. Olympia, an intermediary broker, and Rothschilds were our biggest customers, but business could have been so much greater with more detailed commitment to the project. Occasionally I wondered how 'clean' the money was that was being put into UK-authorised unit trusts. It was just a feeling or suspicion I had without any substantive proof that, due to some quirk in French regulations, putting monies into UK funds gave French investors an element of secrecy from French disclosure. In addition, I wasn't entirely sure if Craig wasn't possibly acting for other parties and would only bat for Perpetual when he knew I was wanting to visit, which was about every four or five weeks.

We had some good times together in Paris and enjoyed each other's company, although he was a seriously heavy Gauloises smoker – or worse, Camel. On one occasion he took me to a soufflé restaurant where the entire menu comprised different soufflés – starters, main courses, and afters. It was all far too much egg with uncomfortable consequences for my digestion! Most mornings we'd have several café crèmes, and in the evenings he'd love to visit some bar or an Irish pub next to my hotel in Rue St Honoré. He would invariably know *le patron* in each of these establishments.

Some progress was made in getting European interest in the funds. We offered the novelty of 'loyalty commission' based on the half-yearly value of investors' accounts: but the company needed to invest in designing more suitable products for the European market, rather than just expecting European Investment Directive UCITS funds to be sufficiently attractive to that market. They needed to become as committed to the idea as Hill Samuel, Fidelity, and Sun Life had been, and more so, as most fund managers were now seeking to grow into Europe and beyond. I wrote a paper suggesting the creation of sub-classes of units denominated in Euros for the sterling-priced funds that had appealed to investors so far. This idea was way ahead of its time and was not implemented.

My by now clear conclusion was that the company didn't want to over-expand into foreign markets it didn't understand and potentially put its excellent UK name on the line. In retrospect, it may also have been that Invesco were already planning their eventual takeover of the business and indicated their unwillingness for Perpetual to expand internationally before they had majority control. Thus there may have been an unknown political dimension to my appointment – something that would again raise its head in a few years' time!

For the time I was with Perpetual I was extremely grateful. To be plucked out from unemployment at forty-seven years of age was extremely fortunate. That period of redundancy had probably been at that point in my life the gloomiest of times. The frustration at Perpetual was that I really believed they could have been successful in expanding the business internationally. But I wasn't to know what international undercurrents there were.

Chapter 11

Greece: Surprise Posting

From time to time, at Perpetual, I would receive phone calls from head hunters in the industry asking for names to contact to assist with job searches. One such was from Korn Ferry International, who one day asked if I knew anyone who might be interested in being marketing director for a large financial institution in a southern European country. I thought this might be Italy, Spain, or Portugal, where I already had established contacts, any one of which I would have been happy to live in and rebuild my personal life, in which a divorce had been agreed but not completed. After a few moments thought, I said I might be interested, and in no time an appointment had been made for a few days later. I arrived at their Regent Street offices, and the interview began with the question, 'Do you speak Greek, George?'

Obviously the answer was "No!", but the follow up comment to the effect that this was "Excellent" rather threw me. The client, I was told, was looking to appoint someone who could develop the investment fund business within the Greek market and would be working for the investment company, Intertrust, within the largest domestic financial services company in the country, InterAmerican. Despite its name, the business had no American connections at all. Instead, it had been founded by the chairman almost ten years ago on the back of his being a successful life assurance salesman. He was now ranked seventh wealthiest of all Greeks – quite something, considering the legendary wealth of Greek ship owners. I was told Intertrust needed someone who could knock the heads together of the marketing and sales directors and report to the MD, a Mr Theodopolous Bounterakis – 'Mr B.'.

Mr B. duly interviewed me some weeks later at the Landmark Hotel near Marylebone Station. He had a French look about him, short and dapper with close-cropped dark hair and narrow facial features with a hint of stubble. He was obviously comfortable to be in London, and he 'knew his funds'. Quite coincidentally, a few days later I was advised by Roger that Perpetual would not be continuing with the European experiment. They were reluctant to be diverted from developing in the UK. I wasn't altogether surprised, and when I was offered redundancy, I accepted. How different my circumstances this time round (my third redundancy) were compared to the last! Shortly afterwards, Mr B. confirmed my appointment, and terms for a two-year contract were agreed. I would be paid a monthly salary with a quarterly bonus and would have a house, utilities, and car provided, which would be fully expensed, and I would have four return flights to the UK each year. It was effectively a six-figure remuneration package.

The package would be sufficient for me to regularly save considerable sums. The temptation to live up to the limit and to enjoy some big extravagances had to be avoided. I had met too many expats around the world over the years who had earned substantial incomes throughout their careers, only to find that when contracts or working life came to an end, they had virtually nothing on which to retire. The worst case was of a man engaged in the oil industry for thirty-five years in the Middle East, who, when he found he and his wife had to return to the UK, had virtually no savings or pension provision. The only area they could afford to buy a house was in the far west of Wales. I asked them what their priorities were on getting back to the UK. He said, 'A ride-on lawn mower.' His wife said, 'A fur coat, because it going to be cold!' Dreamers!

In a way my unexpected career development fulfilled a desire I had begun to feel, which was to know what it was like to be an expatriate myself and see things from the other side of the fence. By now I had seen and met many expatriates in a variety of countries, and hopefully I had learned of some of the benefits and disadvantages, as well as some of the difficulties that can arise. Benefits generally could be summarised as being primarily financial. Disadvantages would include being away from immediate family. Dangers would be squandering a high income and finding that on returning to the UK there wasn't much to show for having lived an interesting life for what would now be for me possibly only a few years.

Before I started in November 1995, a number of big things had to be done. My terraced house in Reading had to be sold, a house in Athens found, and my household possessions and belongings sent out. I would also have to do something about not being computer literate! I bought a Toshiba 486 laptop computer that stayed in its box until I arrived in Greece. It intimidated me enormously!

The house in Reading, 36 York Road, was a two-up, two-down Victorian terraced house less than a mile from the station. It was also close to the river, just downstream from Caversham Bridge. My journey to Perpetual's offices in Henley took less than twenty minutes. I thought briefly about renting it out, but in view of the fact that the plaster on the staircase seemed highly suspect and would need replacing if the wallpaper was removed, possibly opening other unknown cans of worms, I decided to sell up. Within a few weeks a young couple who had been renting a house a few doors away, made an offer and the deal was duly completed.

In the meantime Intertrust had been in contact, inviting me out to Greece to meet my new colleagues and to view five residences on a Saturday. I felt a mixture of excitement, even amazement at where I had found myself and the pride my parents, both now dead, would have had. I also had a degree of concern about how the future would go. I realised that the motivation or incentive for me was to see things from the other side of the fence – being abroad rather than going abroad. I anticipated that working with foreigners, any foreigners, first hand would help my CV when the time came to return to the UK.

I knew a place, Farnham Castle, in Surrey where people who were about to work overseas could go and learn about the ways of that country. Intertrust readily agreed to pay the cost for me and my future wife, Diane, who would be coming to Athens with me, to attend a two-day residential course. Farnham Castle is used by multinational companies and the UK government for staff and employees to be made aware of the benefits and pitfalls of overseas employment. The course covered every aspect of living and working in, in my case, Greece. We were told, for example, about the November 17 underground terrorist movement who emerge from time to time to pick off individuals. We learned about local customs, the weather, the health service, tax implications (both there and the UK), dress codes, and religion. You name it, and it was covered. Not least, we received information about a group based in Athens called New Comers.

This group was effectively a club for people new to the country, which could make introductions to other expats as well as offer guidance about local doctors, dentists, shopping, restaurants, and so on, while also organising trips to various places of interest, sometimes with overnight stays. It had a membership of about one hundred, ostensibly set up for Brits and by Brits, but it also included English-speaking members from the United States and the Commonwealth. Diane attended monthly meetings for several months without making much headway in meeting people who wanted to do more than just that – meet at the meetings. People in the group, who in some cases had lived for many years in Greece had formed friendships and had little need to invite others to join. It wasn't exactly cliquey, but we had a difficult time being in a new place without local friends. Eventually we made a breakthrough and formed several friendships which have continued ever since.

We had some great times both with the group and with our developing number of friends, revisiting places we had first gone to with New Comers and exploring, mostly in the Peloponnese and some nearby islands. In due course we seemed to climb the acceptability list and were invited to the bigger social occasions. These included black-tie musical events ('Mini-Glyndebourne') in the gardens of the South African Embassy, an annual evening garden party in the grounds of the local area representative for Martini Bacardi which had multiple stalls of international cuisine and copious amounts of drinks served by formally dressed waiters, and ultimately membership of the Athens Whisky Society.

We were invited to join by the President of the Whisky Society whose wife Diane had met at New Comers. Membership was limited to twenty-four members who took turns to host quarterly whisky-tasting evenings on a theme selected by the host. The evening's dinner would be hosted by the member's wife. Most of the members were Scots whose employment covered all aspects of business, civil engineering, banking, travel, and so on. It was an entertaining group. On one occasion I hosted an evening of whiskies all from the Spey, and the idea was to provide some clues about each one of six whiskies and for the guests to identify the distillery. It wasn't competitive, but it was fun. Some of the members were often one hundred per cent right even when unusual or rare whiskies were occasionally tasted – sometimes flown in diplomatic bags from the Scotch Malt Whisky Society of Edinburgh. After the tasting had been completed, the opportunity to drink more of the evening's preferred choice would follow!

Attendance at the annual St Andrew's Ball was socially mandatory. This was *the* social occasion for expats and for an increasing number of locals who knew it would be a great evening. Several hundred people would attend, and many would stay overnight at the InterContinental Hotel. Raffle prizes would include European holidays, trips to New York, and cases of wine. It was a sumptuous occasion with a piper and band flown in from Scotland. Burns Night was another 'full on' evening on a slightly smaller scale but conducted with the utmost attention to tradition and detail. On a lighter note, we also became involved with Scottish country dancing. Meeting monthly in the British School of St Catherine's we learnt many tricky steps and thoroughly enjoyed the friendship and good humour of the people who came.

But back to my reason for being in Athens. In the past I had had to acknowledge that different cultures, even in the 'new Europe', demanded that products had to be 'made local' or at least look as if they were. A local presence was compulsory and product literature also had to be available in the local language. So experiencing 'being foreign' seemed a good idea to me, and it would reinforce my awareness of these needs in the likely event that I returned to marketing internationally but based from the UK, as I hoped I would.

Flying to Athens for the first time and looking out at the Adriatic, and then Aegean Seas and Mediterranean landscape below with the thought that this was going to be my life's new base was a rather surreal experience. No longer would I have the bustle of UK life, but instead I would face the stimulation of a foreign culture surrounding me morning, noon, and night. Looking down at the landscape surrounded by blue sea and just imagining the pleasures that would lie in store was an amazing feeling. I would be living permanently in a holiday destination. It couldn't get much better!

The company arranged accommodation at the Pentelikon Hotel in Kifissia in the northern suburbs of Athens and about an hour's drive from the airport. I was met at the airport by Costas Demitricopoulos. Costas would become a good friend as well as being a Mr Fixit, not just for me as it turned out, but for a number of other expats working within the InterAmercan Group. I was the only Brit. Costas had been employed by the Group for years in the Property Department looking after all the group's branches throughout the country, of which there could easily have been a hundred, possibly more. He seemed to know everybody and was a thoroughly decent and pleasant guy. He had previously lived and worked in the United States, which gave him an international perspective – something I would find lacking generally amongst Greeks.

Looking at five potential residences in a day and having to make a choice there and then was quite challenging. Diane, who many years later became my dear wife, accompanied me, and we found it hard to choose between four large houses and an apartment, each one of which had negatives to put against positives, all being clearly 'up market' spacious places. Some would need redecoration and some garden clearance and maintenance, all of which would be undertaken by InterAmerican staff. We settled on a house in Orfeus Street, Ekali, to the north of Kifissia, about six miles to the offices in Maroussi, about half way to downtown Athens and about 400 feet above sea level, which would make it slightly cooler than the centre of Athens. It had easy access to the countryside and the coast about five miles away to the east, through pine covered hills to Nea Makri. The house was part of a larger three-armed property set within a large triangular corner plot where two roads converged to join another. The owners, a fairly elderly couple, Mr and Mrs Perdikes, lived in one of the arms, and the other was empty but ready for a sibling to move into. We rarely spoke to either of the Perdikes, but we saw him most evenings in the summer watering the rose garden and shrubs which surrounded us.

Our house, whilst substantial, was modest compared to others around us. Each one was detached, individually styled, and palatial. Many would be floodlit at night, and many would be guarded by sentries in sentry huts on the corners of the plot they were protecting. Others lived in gated houses with closed-circuit cameras along boundary walls. Several politicians, including the then prime minister, lived in the neighbourhood, as did several big ship owners. Just along the road was Yiannis Latsis, then one of the world's richest people, who invited Prince Charles to use his yacht for both of Charles's honeymoons with Princess Diana and later the Duchess of Cornwall. He also owned the local water company, and it was said that if ever there was a drought, our area would be the last to feel its effects – a power play Greek style!

Costas arranged the payment of rent, the heating oil bill, the telephone account, the terms of the contract, and the payment for all the household furnishings we needed. The biggest expense was lighting fixtures throughout the house. Most of the rest of the house was furnished by my possessions and some of Diane's which had been shipped out by road. The journey had taken three days by Chapman & Sons, a removal company from Oxford, who had charged the company about £3,000.

The whole process of becoming an employee in Greece was very bureaucratic. Before beginning any work, I spent several days with Costas taking me from one government office building to another. I was registered for tax, and my papers had to be doubly rubber stamped by the authorities. I had to produce my passport endless times, I had x-rays taken before being accepted within the medical system, and details of my bank account were recorded, amongst other requirements. It was helpful to have a Greek taking me from place to place, because the fact that someone couldn't process my papers before someone else had done so set up a civil service merry-go-round that I wouldn't have been able to handle alone. For me, it was an early exposure to the Greeks' inability to take individual responsibility for even the smallest process or decision.

In due course I also became aware that the black economy was enormous at about thirty per cent of the GDP. It wasn't difficult to see why. For example, the rent agreed by the house owners and the company was officially declared to be half of what had been agreed. The other half was paid 'under the table' and was not declared for tax purposes. Again, I was told and nobody denied it that cheques were rarely presented to a bank. Goods for which payment was required would be passed from supplier to consumer in the usual way, but only the last recipient in need of cash would actually bank the money due. The government threatened to take shops to court if secret inspectors who challenged shoppers for sight of a receipt were unable to provide one. We were never challenged and never knew anyone who was. Occasionally there would be a clampdown on vehicles with foreign registrations showing more than six months after they had been imported. This too could easily be circumvented by going to Italy for the weekend from Patras. And cash was king!

Within a week or two of arrival I was invited to a corporate jamboree on a Sunday afternoon to celebrate the twenty-fifth anniversary of the company. It was held at the huge basketball stadium of Pathenaniakos, a large sports club with an internationally known soccer team, near Piraeus. In many ways it was a good way to understand the significance of the business within Greece. The business had been founded by a Mr Kontominas, who had been a successful door-to-door life assurance salesman. From this he had built up a network of clients and connections to the point where he thought he could build a real business! Several hundreds, if not thousands, of employees from throughout the country attended this event. The scale of the presentations, hospitality, and professional management of the day was truly impressive.

Throughout my period in the country I would see advertising hoardings promoting the name 'InterAmerican' alongside all the major roads throughout the country. It was a company that every Greek would know, because its tentacles touched almost every Greek's life. The group was the largest motor insurer, offered the biggest road-side recovery service nationwide, was the biggest private medical insurer, owned fifty per cent of the largest mobile phone business, promoted the Visa credit card, and had a shareholding in Eurobank and no doubt other interests. I felt proud to have been engaged by InterAmerican within Intertrust, a subsidiary investment management company offering a modest range of unitised funds with above average performances.

Intertrust's offices in Maroussi were within the Head Office building of InterAmerican. It was situated just off Kifissias Avenue, a dual carriageway arterial road from the centre of Athens. It was a smart, comparatively modern, well-maintained white building, five stories high, with manicured gardens to the front, which included fountains and fish-filled ponds. Inside all the floors were white marble, and everywhere was air-conditioned.

My office was on the first floor looking across the street to a small shopping centre that included a small supermarket, a photographic shop, a barber's shop that could have been lifted from 1950s New York with its bright scarlet plastic-covered furnishings, various other shops for ladies' goods, an optician, a pharmacy, and a couple of reasonable restaurants and cafés. It was the biggest building in the immediate vicinity, which was a predominantly residential area. Also across the street was InterAmerican's car park, all at road level but likely to become multi-storey. To the side and in a deep depression were two stone-built, almost dilapidated but occupied cottages of considerable age which time had passed by.

My colleagues were Mr Theodossis Bountourakis, 'Mr B' or 'Theo', who had interviewed me in London, George Smirlis, General Manager, Kyriakos Apostilidis, Sales Director and Markos Fragoulopoulos, Marketing Director. There was about a dozen staff of which Marco's secretary, a lovely, bright, slightly seductive girl Tina Koutsogiammi, Spyros Simotas who had obtained an MBA in Sydney, turned graphic designer, and Markos' assistant Fotis Katsaitis a willing helper if ever there was, were the people I had most daily dealings with. Kyriacos had a sales team of six who were based in different parts of the country. Markos developed marketing strategy strategy with Spyros. My role was to co-ordinate Sales with Marketing. Having observed the business for a few weeks I put forward my Marketing Report.

The plan, if executed fully, would increase sales, make sales more profitable, and increase retention. Some of the ideas, such as a call-centre operation and the establishment of 'money shops', were a concept far ahead of anything offered even in the UK, and all were relatively easy to introduce whilst not requiring much in the way of capital expenditure. The InterAmerican business had plenty of underutilised office space in a number of towns throughout Greece.

My proposals were fully accepted, and weekly Monday morning meetings were planned at ten o'clock with Kyriakos and Marcos and others by invitation. They would be held in my office. The first few meetings were rather patchy affairs with one or other of the key participants not attending. Punctuality seemed alien to InterAmerican culture. Prioritising this meeting over others was another apparent difficulty. In due course people began to attend on time. Minutes were taken and action points agreed, along with accountability. In quite short order it became apparent that all these basic requirements were all alien to the way things were normally conducted. In fact, I began to wonder how anything progressed at all and whether what I was experiencing was in any way unusual either within the company or more generally.

Banking my quarterly bonus in a branch of Eurobank next door to the office and transferring this sum to my personal account with a London merchant bank (Leopold Joseph, where a former colleague at Hill Samuel now worked) was always a very happy experience. As I was being paid in Greek drachma (GRD) I was always interested in the exchange rate, which for most of the time stayed at around 420 to the pound. I was, however, very determined that all of these payments and some additional monthly salary savings would be invested and begin to provide for my future and ultimate retirement. In later years I would attempt to obtain a state pension from Greece, having paid in substantial contributions. This was agreed to be paid in 2013 but not yet received at the time of writing!

To say that I was busy in the office all day every day would not be true. After all I was a hired consultant motivating others! Quite some time early on was spent familiarising myself with a Toshiba 468 laptop computer I had brought out with me and which Theo helped me understand. Every day I would spend time self-learning Word and Excel, gradually building up my abilities, taking them home and in the evenings most days getting connected to the Internet and developing skills I have never regretted having. There had been a time while I was unemployed from Sun Life when I had wondered whether I would get on the computer conveyor belt, as I saw it with its constant change and 'upgrades', and be part of this new world! I needed to get up to speed as everyone else seemed hugely computer literate, and this concerned me quite a lot.

I planned a visit to New York, ostensibly to attend a global investment marketing conference, but which was more about me testing my marketing ideas with mutual fund businesses there. I stayed at the Meridian, a marvellous hotel quite close to Central Park, 5th Avenue, and the Rockefeller Center. Breakfast was always poached eggs done in a way I have never seen before or since – perfectly cooked but in the shape of a large tadpole. I did the city bus tour, stopping off at various spots. I went as high as you can up the Empire State Building, walked the length of downtown Broadway (avoiding the rather dubious 'parlours' of one kind or another), caught a Staten Island ferry to view the Statue of Liberty after admiring some jugglers who entertained the waiting crowd, and later, on a Sunday, went to see St Patrick's cathedral, where I found people throwing up outside whilst Mass was being celebrated. I could not believe my eyes!

After this New York trip, which confirmed my ideas for Greek business development, I grasped the opportunity to introduce a number of investment marketing ideas which would almost certainly revolutionise the business. The marketing plan would unavoidably include changes to the administrative systems and other parts of the business, not least IT. I calculated that it would be possible to introduce some state-of-the-art ideas that were working well in the United States and some that were not even yet used in the UK. It was as if we could move the business from the Middle Ages to the late twentieth century in one leap, ignoring almost any legacy within current systems built up over the company's short lifetime.

As time passed, I began to realise that personal non-accountability was a well-recognised national trait. No one, in or out of the business, would make or take a decision without reference to countless other people. In effect that meant that there was a corporate sharing of the decision so that no one could be fingered as being ultimately responsible. As an example, Greeks paid for their telephone account through the electricity company via the bank so as to ensure the money is paid and received. Asking a bank clerk for the first time how to pay this bill, which is universal, could not be answered by any one clerk, but was referred around several bank personnel before the suggestion (only) was confirmed as to how it was done.

It generally followed that whatever had been discussed at my meetings in English would then be reported and dissected at a meeting the following morning attended by my Greek colleagues without me, with George Smirlis and his board colleagues. Mr B. generally kept a very low profile, and although he did not seem to contribute much, he always knew what was going on. However, he rarely saw me to discuss anything of much importance. Within quite a short time I had a call to meet the chairman, founder, and owner of the business, Mr Kontominas. His office doors, both heavy and engraved metal, possibly bronze, double doors, were only opened remotely after one's arrival was announced by speaker-phone at his office suite's entrance.

The first office space was occupied by three secretaries, and on arrival a cold drink would be offered. Kontominas's voice could invariably be heard on one of several phones on his enormous desk. One entered his inner sanctum through two further huge, thick wooden doors that led into a capacious room in which there were many personal possessions. On cabinets surrounding his desk were signed photographs of Kontominas with US Presidents and international sports stars, and of course the inevitable Greek business accessory, a cruising yacht – not a sailing boat, but a multi-cabined floating gin palace. He was utterly charming and most interested to know what my plans and ideas were and how they were progressing. He had 'presence' and clearly enjoyed his wealth. He told me that he'd recently bought a second house in Athens which would need complete restoration but that his new wife would choose everything!

My office was next to that of Markos Fragoulopoulos, the Marketing Director. He was bright and open to new ideas and took a surprising interest in the funds industry outside Greece. The staff were all highly educated, and I was surprised to find that almost a quarter had MBAs, mostly from the United States and Britain, with a couple from Australia. I would have thought that with this amount of trained business acumen they would have been self-sufficient. What I discovered was that here, as in Greek life generally, it didn't really matter what foreign education or business experience you had. It was generally not used. Qualified people such as these seemed loathe to use their skills at home.

Soon after my arrival I became aware of the Commonwealth Management Group (CMG). It had been founded by UK expats who had all been in Athens for over twenty years. Most prominent was Gordon Ball, a congenial man whose business was in advising expats and their businesses, if required, on how to become statutorily and fiscally established in Greece without becoming mired in too much in bureaucracy. (He was sadly to die intestate some years later.) This was an informal club with an unwritten constitution. Its members were all chief executives of companies operating in Greece whose head offices were in Commonwealth countries. Quite how I managed to infiltrate into this august group I can't recall. Suffice it to say that rubbing shoulders on a monthly basis at convivial lunches, usually at the InterContinental Hotel, with British Airways, Abbot Laboratories, Ove Arup, United Distillers, bankers, and so on – in fact the entire spectrum of industries – was extremely stimulating. I was the only member working in the investment management field.

General activity in the office stopped one day when we were subjected to an earthquake. My desk and chair shook, or more accurately, wobbled disconcertingly. Window frames creaked and doors swung open. I had been very aware of something happening, but my colleagues outside my private office in the general office hardly showed any reaction. They knew there had been an earthquake, but were able to accept that this wasn't a big one. It was, however, big enough to knock down a school near to our house!

After a few months some discernible progress could be seen as the result of my work. A money shop was opened in Thessaloniki, attended by the chairman and my director colleagues. A ground floor office within the head office building was redesigned to showcase the money shop concept, and external signage was installed. This office would also be used to house the embryonic call centre. This call centre and its equipment were developed in house, despite several visits with Markos to London to look at proven international call-centre support systems for call-centre development. This approach to develop systems and software locally would obviously be much cheaper, but it would be a Greek solution to building the appropriate business solution. This call-centre management decision would inevitably fall short of being world class with long-term future support and development. Taking my ideas and adapting them rather than keeping the tailor-made solutions was a difficult thing for me to accept. I began to wonder if this way of doing things would continue.

With a retail shop established in Thessaloniki and Patras, in addition to head office, and a call centre in place, progress was being made on all fronts. I then began to develop a structured product which would be geared to the performance of the Athens stock exchange, Wall Street Dow Jones, and the FT 30 indices. Initially the directors showed some enthusiasm for this, as it was perceived to be not only good for Intertrust but for the wider InterAmerican business. It would attract bigger investors than those who had traditionally bought the group's products. However, when it became apparent that there would be a need to provide the guarantee at some cost via an external bank, internal attentiveness to the idea diminished, at least amongst those who had taken any interest in it. It was a step too far ahead.

Greek investors typically invested in a Greek Bond fund named Stathero which performed reasonably well. There was growing awareness and interest, however, in equity funds, and a series of fund packages was put together to meet different investor profiles. This concept was also promoted through the InterAmerican Visa credit card company, who, it was thought, would have access to a target audience with access to capital of £25,000 or more. 'Visa George' ran this enterprise with enthusiasm and with imagination.

In addition, approaches were made to all the national retail banks. These didn't lead anywhere until an alliance with the General Bank began to be discussed. This bank handled the accounts of the national army, the police force, and state health employees and appeared to offer a number of unparalleled marketing opportunities. The discussions, handled exclusively by Intertrust's management, were protracted but were making slow progress for the remainder of my time in Greece. Whenever I asked how the discussions were progressing, I was told that the generals and civil servants would make a decision quite soon! Bureaucracy ruled.

There was some talk of developing the business into nearby Balkan states, where InterAmerican had identified opportunities for some of its businesses. This had obvious attractions for me, having developed businesses in foreign countries before, but this time with the full corporate backing of the whole company. However, talk never materialised into concrete action during my time.

Throughout my time at Intertrust, I never once had a social invitation to any of my colleagues' homes. I found this strange but put it down to the fact that most of my colleagues' families would be non-English speaking, and Greek families are large, very close, and somewhat xenophobic. Costas, however, did ask us to his house to celebrate his father's eightieth birthday. This was a delightful occasion in the garden of Costa's home. We were also asked to a Greek wedding for the daughter of one of the directors. Whilst we thought this was a special invitation, it turned out that frequently invitations to Greek weddings can be issued to everyone the families have ever known. Apart from the principal guests, dress was very informal as was the ceremony. People came and went and held conversations throughout the service, which lasted several hours. Meanwhile the bride and groom exchange vows with the priest, are locked in crowns of olive leaves, and become married. Informality extended to the choir who, far from being on show within the main body of the church, could be viewed in T-shirts, shorts, and trainers behind the organ from where they would occasionally sing chants. Most guests were not asked to the family celebrations that followed the church service.

After a few months, in the late summer of 1996 Diane and I attended a cocktail party at the seaside home of Gordon Ball, at Porto Rafti, a sleepy, rural, seaside idyll on the Aegean coast south of Athens. We were so taken with the position overlooking the sea and small islands nearby we asked if a neighbouring small cottage, with oleander and bougainvillea filled garden which appeared to be available for rent, was still on the market. It was, and for most following weekends that autumn until we left some eighteen months later we spent quiet times on the nearby beach thoroughly enjoying our Greek lifestyle.

By April 1997 I had begun to ask for reassurance that my contract would be extended from the end of October when my two years would be up. Mr B. and George Smirlis could not or would not give me any firm indication that it would be. Sometimes there would be more positive signs than others, but by the end of August I had concluded that it wouldn't be renewed. I then began looking for work with other Greek financial institutions, banks, stockbrokers, and intermediaries in Athens, doing pretty much what I had been doing with Intertrust. I had encouraging meetings with several banks and some stockbroking firms, but in the end I concluded that all they (and for that matter Intertrust by this time) wanted to do was to pick my brains. I also considered becoming a consultant but not before I had proposed that Intertrust should become a fund supermarket and offer a platform for a whole range of domestic funds – a concept not yet established in the UK but beginning to take hold in the US.

I completed a research study for Lombard International Assurance S.A. entitled 'The Ordinance of Greek Taxation & its Application to Personal Financial Product Development', but in the end I again concluded that consulting would be too difficult, not least because of the language, let alone the feeling that what I had found within Intertrust would be replicated again and again. Importantly the number of financial services companies looking to develop business indigenously within Greece was almost non-existent when so many other European countries already participating in the Euro-zone, had greater immediate potential.

Quite late in the day it became apparent that my appointment in the first place had been at the insistence of the Chairman, Mr Kontominas. Mr B., despite his involvement in my enrolment, had never genuinely felt the need for external or imported marketing advice. Thus the contract was not renewed, but I was given a retainer for a further twelve months payable to me in the UK on my return.

Another part of the reluctance to extend the contract was probably a subliminal Greek characteristic – xenophobia. It was perfectly apparent at the time that there were comparatively few foreigners in Greece, as evidenced for example by the lack of foreign restaurants of any kind. Albanians, who seemed a significant minority, in particular were given a hard time. They would clean windscreens in no time at all whilst traffic lights went through a single sequence, or sell traditional flatbread rolls at road junctions, or try and sell huge bunches of roses during the day or night in restaurants in the evenings. Newspaper reports frequently referred to crimes across the country being attributed to Albanians.

By and large it wasn't a place to which African, West Indian, or Asian people would aim to emigrate – probably because learning Greek didn't offer any prospect of further movement outside the country. Using Greece as a transition point into Euroland via Patras to southern Italy hadn't become widespread.

Most of the foreigners in Greece were working expats, and we formed a good close-knit community. Many of us who lived in the northern suburbs of Athens would meet on Friday evenings throughout the year at a couple of hostelries, but usually at the Brown Sugar bar in Kifissias for a social evening of convivial drinking that would be followed by dinner at one of several local tavernas where the long-timers would always be well known by the bar owner and staff.

Athens was seen as a convenient staging post for businesses with Eastern European or Middle Eastern interests, usually civil engineering companies, pharmaceutical manufacturers, and, of course, shipping. As an employed expat in the financial services sector working for the largest and one of the best-known indigenous companies in the country, I found considerable resentment could be aroused if on being asked, 'How long are you in the country for?' at a petrol station or restaurant, I responded rather proudly, 'Quite a while, because I work here for InterAmerican!' So rather than responding in that way, we'd simply say we were over for a few weeks' holiday, and then all would be well!

Packing up the house and leaving was tough. The local daily English language paper, the *Athens News*, carried classified advertisements for both buyers and sellers of household goods, for which there was a ready demand. Life had been good despite the frustrations within the office. It was appropriate perhaps that on the day we left the flat, where the last days had been spent with friends nearby, to catch the early morning plane to London, the heavens opened and it simply poured with rain.

The experiment of adding an overseas dimension to my CV hadn't worked, and so I found myself applying for jobs for more than a year in London and the south-east on an almost daily basis. Usually these applications weren't acknowledged. Occasionally I would obtain an interview, and that would be as far as it would go. The usual excuses given for my lack of success were either that I was too experienced or that I lived too far away to be able to be able to work with sufficient flexibility. I knew but couldn't prove it that my age of fifty-two was considered too old – but they could have seen that from my CV. So I had to conclude they were farming me for ideas.

Chapter 12

Time to Go It Alone

A friend of mine named Robert Catcher, a rather maverick character with a creative marketing mind, had been telling me for a long time about his desire to create a business making waist belts (for trousers and skirts) which could be produced for any business in their corporate colours. So the market for these might be any club, team, association, manufacturer, or similar. The market had never been exploited before. It would be a unique promotional and marketing concept.

His sister-in-law Julia was able to stitch leather, and so Robert produced a number of prototype belts which I would use as samples in presentations to anyone who responded to my request to visit them. If multiple colours were needed, Robert would source striped web material. The only problem was that the manufacturer would require a minimum length order of 100 metres, sufficient for about seventy (unordered belts) for a full run, although they were prepared to produce lengths of about twenty metres for us to present belts in requested colours to potential buyers as samples.

We had visions of supplying school associations, clubs of all sorts, regiments and associations, sponsors and manufacturers, teams of all sorts – the list was endless and exciting. Although we never formally discussed it, Robert would in effect be responsible for belt production from the West Country where he and his sister-in-law lived, and I would be the marketer. Leather belts in several lengths for both men and women were individually stitched and embossed with a Fan Belts 'FB' logo device. Fabric belts were made of a woven canvas thread in the colours required by the customer and with stitched leather end-straps.

As time went on however, I also became involved in sourcing materials. We ordered suitable buckles (brass, silver, chrome) from the Britannia Buckle Company, a supplier in Homerton who had an extensive catalogue that included some sexually deviant bondage items which were exhibited at the London Sex Show!

I enthusiastically created a website using HTML for the text, a somewhat laborious process that was well beyond Robert's capabilities and certainly quite a brain stretch for me! I showed the site I had created using downloaded templates with on-line shopping to Robert at the Institute of Directors. I showed him, on my trusty Toshiba laptop that we were listed on Google under Fan Belts, partly because of the name but more importantly for the number of site links to which our site was affiliated. I had it connected to.

Google was new in 1998, and it was far and away the best Internet search engine for speed and relevant accuracy. I demonstrated what it could do. Robert was amazed. At this time he was barely familiar with computers and had only recently bought one. As a search engine Google soon superseded a number of other search engines of the day, which included Excite, Yahoo!, WebCrawler, Lycos, Infoseek, AltaVista, and Inktomi, many of which simply became extinct.

The first client of Fan Belts was the Pony Club of Great Britain. Robert had signed the deal with them at their head office in Stoneleigh, and we were invited to promote the belts at the Pony Club's annual three-day event in Shropshire in 1988. We set up a gazebo and signage, but hardly any belts were sold. This wasn't a good start, but we rationalised that riders and their parents were unwilling to buy the Pony Club belt (blue and gold) simply because the right size for a child this year would be too small next year! In fact we had thought that this would be a good source of repeat business, but clearly it wasn't.

The Secretary of the Lancing College Old Boys Association agreed to buy a few hundred pounds worth of our belts – a breakthrough, we thought, as they'd be worn on golf courses, arouse interest, at school reunions, arouse more interest, and so on and so on. But no more orders came. All the while I was keeping Robert informed of my activities and expenses which he refunded promptly.

Williams Formula 1 showed considerable interest. A visit to their UK head office at Grove near Wantage was arranged. It was a modern building with a number of world-championship-winning Formula

1 cars on display in the spacious lobby. It occurred to me what an extraordinary business Formula 1 is. It simply absorbs money from sponsors with no discernible end product, other than manufacturing a very fast car: millions of pounds absorbed and spent without a product: just technological innovation which one day may, just may, be adopted by the wider motor industry for private vehicles. Astonishing! Williams' requirement was for a carbon-fibre belt with a silver-plated buckle.

I found a supplier of carbon-fibre material and a selection of silver buckles, which together were made into finished samples. I presented these to the licensing and merchandising manager, Evy Bronneberg, a German lady in her early thirties who was normally based at BMW's (the chief sponsor of the team) head office in Munich. She was an attractive lady but as hard as they come in her demands. Cost wasn't much of a concern, however. Strange! We had costed these belts at £45 each for them to acquire, so the retail price would probably be in excess of £75. She wanted all the team, including the paddock crew and the drivers, to have at least one each. Not only that, but they would be for sale to any Williams F1 racing fan at all Grand Prix events all around the world. An order of several hundred looked in prospect. Hopefully all the other F1 teams would want to have it, and then other motor racing categories would get in on the act, and then other sports and so on. Perhaps we had found a really profitable niche. Things were exciting and looking good!

Our discussions were taking place in July, 1988 just after the British Grand Prix, so obviously our product wouldn't be available or needed until the Australian Grand Prix the following January. Delivery would be required in late November. This would not be a problem, or so I thought.

A problem did occur, however. Robert and Julia fell out after her marriage failed. Julia would have been responsible for ensuring that any belts ordered for any customer were made on time by her. She had recruited a team of sewers, all working from home who would be paid on a piece-time rate. But now she couldn't care a toss about Robert's business and didn't want to have anything more to do with it. The end result was that there were no belts, and the business venture was scuppered. At the time I had run up expenses of £5,000 and Robert decided he wasn't going to pay these, which had been our gentleman's agreement. That was the complete end to our twenty or more years of friendship. I politely wrote to him to say how disappointed I was, given first, that I knew he had recently sold his house and bought another one, and second that he knew that I had lost several thousand pounds of pension fund assets with the demise of Equitable Life. He said that he was sorry I had written to him in the way I had! We never spoke or communicated again.

At the same time I was involved with Fan Belts, my school advertised for a 'Marketing Person' to help rejuvenate the CH Club, an alumni club for Old Blues which all leavers could join as a right. The club had a number of regional sub-groups, each with a local coordinator. These regional groups were encouraged to meet several times a year, the frequency and location being determined by the members. My role was to reinvigorate some of the regions which had lapsed or were heading that way and to create new groups where none had existed before.

The role, which would be for two years, carried a salary of £400 per month plus travel costs, which felt like a fortune, and it would last for two years. I enjoyed the job greatly, working with and for the school with frequent visits to meet the club administrator, Wendy Kilner, a marvellous woman who just could not do enough for the club or the current pupils at the school. She had been in the post for nearly twenty years, and what she didn't know about the school and its machinations wasn't worth knowing.

New regional groups were set up in the West Country and the Solent area. Oxford and Cambridge area groups met at the universities. All the regions had their own characteristics. Of the new ones, the Solent area was the most tricky, as it covered both Portsmouth and Southampton, who wouldn't cross the tracks to have anything to do with the other, as well as the hinterland up to Winchester and halfway north to Newbury, where another regional group existed. The university town groups were a great success, Oxford being rather quicker off the mark than Cambridge. This was due in no small part to the energy and interest of the coordinator, Stephen Harrison, who was Professor of Latin Literature and Fellow and Tutor in Classics at Corpus Christi College. He was a thoroughly good man who enthused over this small but nevertheless significant link with Christ's Hospital.

The CH Club was reckoned to be the largest school alumni organisation in the country, almost certainly in terms of the number of regions, but quite possibly by the number of members also. Each region had an unspoken rule to arrange a dinner to mark Founder's Day in October each year, and I attended and spoke at a number of these. The Bath and Wells group (a well-established group, as opposed to the newly created Cotswold group next door), the Dorset group (another new group that met at the Crown Hotel in Blandford Forum), and the university-based groups all had excellent dinners, the last two in one or other of the university colleges.

On another occasion I attended and spoke at the Oxford group dinner and stayed overnight in rooms overlooking Corpus Christi quad. It was a lovely experience, one which I wished I had been able to enjoy much earlier in my life.

I completed my two year stint having satisfactorily fulfilled the role, in 1998.

Chapter 13

Self-Employed with a Greek Idea

In 1998 I could sense that finding permanent employment again was increasingly unlikely, and so I placed an advertisement in the local paper, the *Bexhill Observer*.

53: Too Old, Too Experienced?

That's what I'm told when I respond to job adverts, and I don't believe it! I am articulate, have initiative, and am capable of team playing and leading. I am a creative, computer=-literate marketer, well-travelled (on business) in Europe, Middle East, Far East, and a business builder for several major City institutions. Are YOU the employer who can use some or all of these and other skills in the service sector, in return for reasonable pay and a good deal of added value? I will work part or full-time for the employer who can offer both job and personal satisfaction. I can provide support, encouragement, knowledge, business insight, and career guidance to your own 'rising stars' without threatening their career objectives.

There was no response at all.

I found it hard to accept my position – unwanted, over-the-hill, and discarded. At my age, with my experience and knowledge, I couldn't possibly have come to the end of the line. Interviews came and went, and in retrospect there were occasions during these when I probably said more than was helpful to my cause. At one interview I asked a question of the Managing Director, who replied that the Chairman was the only person who could answer that question, and I would be meeting him later. At the time I thought this was a good thing, but clearly the MD felt I would be a threat. Needless to say, I wasn't offered the position. All through this career stage I had only ever wanted to support and encourage management. My days of wanting to 'run the show' were passed, and I would have been perfectly content to operate behind the scenes. Forty-something managers didn't see it that way!

When I was in Greece I had the foresight to think about the possibility, as an option, of running my own business, but not in financial services, if I was unsuccessful in returning to the City. A number of friends in Greece had plant pots on their terraces and patios supported on round wheeled saucers, and after my Intertrust contract had finished I made enquiries to find the manufacturer of these with a view to possibly importing them into the UK and selling them to garden centres. I had established that the UK garden market had an annual turnover of tens of billions of pounds and that the segment I was considering working in was a significant percentage of this. My research had taken me to the British Library, which contained an enormous amount of information and papers, as well as the Institute of Directors library which I had used previously.

I also commissioned Mintel do some Market Research and obtain statements from independent market reviewers about the potential size of the market for pots and trolleys. The results are shown at the end of this chapter. This informed opinion encouraged me to proceed with the idea.

On one of my research visits to Greece I was introduced to Efclides Horomides, one of two brothers who worked with their father in a substantial family-owned horticultural business not far from where we had been living in Ekali but to the west of the National Road. He was a jovial person in his early thirties with a young son he nicknamed Prince. His English was self-taught and more than good enough for us to get along well. He could see potential benefits in having me as his English agent once my new business had become established. He knew of a plastic injection mould business called Plastona that was based in Athens. He would arrange the manufacture of the stocks I needed. Efclides would also arrange transportation by road to the UK.

The first consignment consisted of an enormous truck load of packaged Plant Trolleys, and arrangements were made for them to be delivered to Castleham Industries. This was a printing and fulfilment business in a business park on the outskirts of Hastings, which employed handicapped people and was funded in part by Social Services. They had offered me free storage and despatch services because they thought that if they viewed the business positively, it would provide a steady volume of work experience for their staff. And for a while, Castleham offered a useful and very economical business benefit.

I decided the name of my business would be Withaph Limited, trading as Plant Trolleys. The name Withaph came to me as the name Stephens is spelt 'with a PH'!

I joined the Flowers & Plants Association based in Covent Garden to give the enterprise some credibility. Later I joined GIMA, the Garden Industry Manufacturers' Association, a trade body of which every major garden product manufacturer is a member, and I had the products tested by UKAS, the United Kingdom Accreditation Service near East Croydon railway station.

The tests were designed to demonstrate that the advertised carrying capacity or weight the trolleys could carry could be accredited. In order to do this, a sample of each of the four sizes I was proposing to market was subjected to a hydraulic pressure test. If the product could carry ten per cent more than the advertised weight, it could be accredited and certified as 'UKAS tested'. The laboratory in Leatherhead had never tested anything quite like this before. Being related in some way to the Lloyd's insurance market, their normal function is to test machinery used in the construction and shipping industries. Anyway, all the trolleys achieved their targets, and out of curiosity each was tested to destruction. This showed that the least strong trolley could carry twice its advertised load bearing tolerance, and the best nearly five times.

Armed with all this data, I sought a bank for the business. I wasn't looking for finance or equity participation, but I wanted small business banking and overdraft facilities. I prepared a business plan which included a significant amount of research into the growth and development of the garden business. This industry was being widely written about and was drawing a lot of comment at the time in leisure magazines and weekend newspaper gardening supplements. I visited the British Museum to look at various garden industry research papers and government reports.

I was able to put together a strong business case, with business projections worked out to almost the last penny using analysis techniques I had seen John Riley use at Sun Life.

NatWest and Lloyd's Lloyds Bank both immediately declined, which surprised me as I thought I had an excellent business model. I tried not to take their decision personally. HSBC, however, agreed because the lesson learned from the interviews with the other two banks had warned me to be prepared for the question, 'How do we get our money back if it all goes pear-shaped?' And the answer did turn out to be needed, as I describe later. HSBC extended their credit card facilities to me. This required me to have carbonated forms to use on a portable card-reader device. This had a fixed roller onto which I would write the sum being paid. A copy would be given to the customer, I'd keep a copy, and the card company would get another. This offer of this facility all helped restore my self-belief for the future.

One further element, which I thought important, remained before I was fully prepared to start trading. If possible, I wanted to get my products' design patented. This together with my UKAS accreditation would give me powerful product credibility. I went to the Patent Office in Chancery Lane. They believed I had a reasonable chance; neither they nor I could find a previously issued patent for the product concept.

I was put in contact with Swindells – what a name! – a firm of patent agents in Derby. Apparently a large part of their business consists of patenting Rolls Royce engine component designs worldwide, so my little project would be extremely small fry. Nevertheless, they gave me excellent service and were always punctual with their reports. Ultimately, however I did not proceed with their submissions as, on their advice, any design patent I obtained could easily be got around by a small modification to the design, and it would almost certainly ultimately become unenforceable in international markets. Even if we contested it, the costs would have been enormous

I built a website using a downloadable template that could be expanded to have several pages with on-line ordering (protected by Thawte security), which I found an interesting and intriguing experience, not least because of the requirements of the domain-hosting companies for high levels of security and site protection. The costs were not exorbitant. I began to accumulate site affiliates which allowed Plant Trolleys access to other garden-related sites in return for them having access to my site. In time I established relationships with what I regarded as likely interested on-line retailers. These included some 'silver surfer' sites, such as LaterLife, and garden-product specialists such as Greenfingers. I was enthusiastic and optimistic that I had found a commercial niche which could be developed and become profitable.

I printed labels showing relevant details about size and weight-bearing tolerances for each size, which included a barcode. The barcodes were obtained from GS1UK at a membership cost of £75 per year, and with their software I could identify each size and colour (terracotta, green, and white) on a barcode label. GS1UK issues what is known as a 'company prefix', which means that there are up to 1,000 unique barcode numbers allocated to each applicant. Initially, I needed just twelve! But the barcodes would make check-out and stock control at garden centres easy, and having them would prevent their non-existence being used as an excuse not to stock them. Learning about barcodes was interesting in itself. I learned that each country's barcodes start with a particular digit. All UK codes start with 5, France 3, and so on. The following digits add up to a predetermined number for the barcode licence holder.

The Plant Trolleys business started trading in 2001. I made sales by visiting garden centres in the South-East. The initial response was somewhat disappointing, though, as, unknown to me, products similar to mine had been marketed several years previously but without success. The redeeming feature for my products was that they were UKAS accredited, but what I hadn't realised or researched, very stupidly, were the margins that retailers operated on – effectively their commission: something I'd been all to well aware of in my investment marketing days. How silly! So, whilst my products had attractive sales price points (which I had set – possibly another error), the margin it left me meant that my turnover would have be many times bigger for me to hit the profitability I had hoped for. Bit by bit, however, I managed to find outlets to sell an initial supply.

I formed a good relationship with repeat business from several garden centres in the West Country and the Home Counties. Notable amongst these was Trago Mills, a family-owned business. It had served the West Country community from its three bases in Devon and Cornwall for some forty-four years, offering, it claimed, three million customers per annum the greatest range of discount goods anywhere in the UK. Little sophistication went into displaying items, but they offered everything at competitive prices for a clientele who probably sympathised with the owner's strong anti-European views. These were hard to avoid with humorous notices, placards, and statues in the car parks denouncing everything and anybody who stood for Europe

Distribution at Garden Shows was an obvious way to get sales at my full margin and hopefully raise interest from both the public and visiting commercial distributors. The first show I attended was the three-day Sussex County Show at Ardingly. The back seats of our Fiat Uno were removed and the entire space filled with plant trolleys: four sizes and three colours, terracotta, green, and white. In addition, I loaded other show essentials, such as signage, posters, leaflets, price lists, labels, and a trestle table and cover.

The show was due to start on a Friday, so Diane and I arrived on the Wednesday before. I was keen to see the lay of the land, find my allocated space, and generally find out as much as possible about being a trader as early as possible. Of course, we were one of the first to arrive, and all the other exhibitors there at that time were setting up big displays and stands that required days of work! Our position was inside an enormous shed with open sides at a high level, so it was draughty, and it had a considerable thickness of dusty floor covering suitable for a cow shed!

We duly set up the stand and the display, repositioning the table and posters a number of times, and then we wondered how safe it would be to leave it all. We returned each day to find everything exactly as we had left it and more stallholders and franchised catering vans arriving. Breakfast of a bacon and sausage butty, regardless of the time we arrived, was a daily highlight, along with a mug of tea that only tradespeople are capable of making – really good!

The takings over the three days were reasonable. We covered our costs and made a few hundred pounds profit. Visitor reaction to the product ranged from 'It'll never work' to 'Look what I have found! These are terrific – just what we wanted!' The overall experience had been worth the effort, and so we planned more participation at shows, mostly at places in the South-East.

It was at Ardingly that I discovered the National Traders Association. The street marketers of Pimlico, Middlesex Street, and Petticoat Lane, as well as street traders and market stallholders up and down the land belonged to this group, which offered discounts and benefits to members who displayed their membership plaque. I really wondered what I was doing and where I had found myself! It was all so removed from anything I had known or expected. My fellow stallholders were genuine people. All wanted the best for themselves. Most had travelled miles to be here and set up stalls and stands with various degrees of 'established business' presentation. They travelled the length and breadth of the country to promote their wares – some good, some ridiculous, some 'of the moment'. Their livelihoods depended on going from place to place, show to show, to display their wares, get sales, and pay their way. It was the equivalent of a travelling circus. But they were all helpful and interested, and they wanted me to succeed as a new business with a worthwhile product, albeit with my meagre presentation resources. I could not believe their spirit of goodwill. And I was now one of them! That was the reality!

The big business trade industry organisation, GIMA (Garden Industry Manufacturers Association), which I joined, had an annual three-day show at the Birmingham NEC which I attended twice. It involved considerable financial outlay, staying in an overly expensive B&B for the two-day build up and the three-day duration period, but this seemed unavoidable if the business was to be taken seriously by retailers. It gave me the opportunity to see what competition there was. It transpired that there was not much, but unfortunately it came from Sankey, one of the biggest producers of plastic-moulded garden items.

GIMA held monthly meetings at a country-house hotel in Warwickshire which I attended by driving up and down on the day, four hours each way. The great and the good from the manufacturing side were usually there, and I found the discussions and working groups very interesting. Everyone there, including the GIMA secretary, was very supportive and encouraging. In retrospect, their support indirectly encouraged me to stay with the project rather longer than I should, but more of that later. Through them I was given an entrée into the Japanese market. There was some initial progress, but then in a curiously Oriental way it went totally silent and came to nothing

In subsequent months and years I 'showed' at the Kent County Show a couple of times, at the Hop Farm near Paddock Wood, and at various country-house fairs, all of which were to varying degrees interesting and enjoyable if sometimes lonely when there was no trade for considerable periods. I can readily identify with stallholders at these and similar events who seem shunned by the attendees while the stalls nearby are being inundated with visitors and are taking money! The three most distant shows I attended were the Lincolnshire Show (the worst show I ever attended – I left a day early!), which I travelled to from the Repton house of one of my oldest mates from HYELM, Willie Welch; the RHS Show at Tatton Park in Lancashire, where I stayed in a B&B; and the RHS Hampton Court Palace Show.

Setting up the stall in a pre-booked three-metre square marquee in an avenue of similar marquees at Hampton Court was a new experience. Many of my neighbouring stallholders had done it all before. Queuing in a grassy field at five o'clock in the morning in late June just after sunrise to try to get reasonable access to the show site and my allocated space a couple of days before the public opening, when everyone else was intent on doing the same thing, was challenging – especially as a one-man band. Drivers would mix with the exhibitors, exchanging information and stories of where they had been and comparing one white van with another. Some thought they knew short cuts or better routes to different parts of the exhibition area. By and large everyone was very friendly and interested to see a new face.

The Hampton Court Show was a turning point in an unexpected way, both in the shorter and longer term. As a financially profitable experience it was excellent. A number of seasoned stallholders reckoned the display and product were good enough for long-term success, and as a result I followed up on interest shown by another stall's agent, who said he would like to take Plant Trolleys on as an additional product to his own product, a suspended 'flower tower'. At the same time I realised that my range of products would need to be increased, possibly with more mobile items, such as rectangular containers. Despite my misgivings, I went ahead with the agent. Robert Trevelyan-Thomas was a well-spoken man in his early thirties, a go-getting salesman who lived in Tiverton. He had been in the 'game' for several years and knew how to sell to all the right people. I paid Robert £150 per month, which was off-set against the commission he earned on the plant trolleys he sold.

Plant Trolleys were offered as 'Reader Offers' in the local paper, and reviews for them appeared in the *Sunday Telegraph* and various gardening magazines, which produced a flurry of enquiries. I found it somewhat curious that the trade never picked up the publicity in these nationally read media. It may have been a problem of distribution through wholesalers which I describe a little later.

The idea of Agency distribution hadn't occurred to me before. It had some appeal, not least potential nationwide distribution. It also added a layer of cost, however, but with several thousand pounds worth of stock being held in a warehouse (initially for free on the Castleham Industries estate in Hastings and later – more expense – at a monthly rental in a commercial warehouse, 'Azonic' in Rye), I was keener than ever to get them sold. Initially I tried to cover the South East, South West and Home Counties with agents, putting off limits retailers that Trevelyan-Thomas had identified. This obviously didn't go down too well with the new regional agents. I later appointed additional agents to cover other specific regions of the country with some success, but all the while I found myself in a learning process, and it wasn't proving easy to make the vital breakthrough.

Finding agents proved to be a trade-off. There were those who claimed to be capable of selling anything to anyone and had enormous product lists. And then there were those who for some reason had taken on a previous product within a small product portfolio and found it didn't sell and so would want to replace it with something that would. Obviously, as self-employed people they would only offer products they liked and could make money with. Quite a few agents claimed to know the specialist wholesalers well, and here we hit a conundrum.

Wholesalers, of which nationally less than half a dozen were potentially interested in my product, almost regardless of how appealing the product was, were reluctant to take on a new single-product supplier. They claimed that this would incur too much administration and costs that would be disproportionate to the amount of product sold. At the same time, agent distributors who had too many products to present to retailers would be unlikely to promote my product, however good it was, when they had known good-selling items to market and only limited time at their meetings. So I gave more time to supporting my agents, apart from Robert who seemed to make good headway.

Sometime in late 2001 I received an email enquiry from an American company based in New York State. The company was SourceOne (full title, SourceOne Marketing and Consulting, Inc.). Their proposal was that in return for a total licensing fee, paid in stages, totalling US$29,000 they would create a full Internet marketing and sales business plan, create TV advertising support across the nation (a sixty-second and ninety-second advertisement agreed by me in advance), and provide regular sub-agent trading activity and sales reporting. They would buy a significant consignment of plant trolleys at a price which they would set and I agreed to. As it happened, the profit margin was enormous. They would purchase a trolley that cost me US$2 for US$11.69 and retail it for rather more! Out of the US$29,000, they duly purchased over US$11,000 worth of goods as an offset payment against the licensing fee. If all went to plan, it should be possible to export plant trolley supplies directly to them from the manufacturers in Greece and take the margin. The future looked extremely bright. I did as much due diligence research as I could, following up references from existing supplier customers and bankers, and I had the business checked out by the British Consulate in New York. Dun & Bradstreet provided a favourable business report. Every piece of research came back positively. On the basis of these findings, I decided to proceed. It was an extremely exciting business prospect.

My contact was with Keith Phillips, who was enthusiastic and encouraging that together we would make significant sales. SourceOne was a significant mail order and Internet sales business. It had an extensive catalogue of goods for every need and purpose. Whilst most business came via its main office, it had several major subagents across the States who could respond more locally by holding their own stock supplied by SourceOne to supply demands and other requests. SourceOne had its administration office at 1359 Broadway, New York, and its distribution and warehouse facilities were at Valley Cottage and West Chester in upstate New York.

The significant consignment of stock was delivered to New York from the warehouse in Rye. The two advertisements for TV were shot on location in March 2002. They demonstrated the use and benefits of Plant Trolleys in and around the home. SourceOne accepted my requests for some small factual changes, and an advertising schedule was prepared, which I was assured were at times to catch the best audience attention based on SourceOne's knowledge of the market and expertise. It was agreed that detailed monthly sales statistics would be provided, and for a time these were supplied promptly.

Sales began to pick up encouragingly, and I could see from their website that the products were being featured prominently. After some months, however, I had to press for the sales feedback. Emails to Keith Phillips were not being answered as I had expected or as quickly as they had been, and telephone calls were going unanswered or messages were not being responded to. Not unnaturally, I became uneasy. Although I had been paid the very welcome sales profit margin for the sales that had been made, I could also see that the products were now being heavily discounted, which indicated some dissatisfaction by SourceOne in the pickup of sales for a new product for which they had had high expectations.

Ultimately I decided I had sufficient concerns about what was or wasn't happening, and enough was enough. I arranged a visit to see them in New York on 5th Avenue, in April 2004. Not being flush with cash, I booked the cheapest five day economy return fare I could, which included a Saturday overnight stay and Sunday return flight. I booked bed and breakfast accommodation in a basement room (with water dripping from the ceiling) in a house in Queens. I watched television most nights after eating cheaply in local restaurants, and I noticed that every commercial had a website address and rather peculiar telephone numbers made up of letters giving the company name. Neither of these marketing ideas had yet taken hold in the UK, but I thought they would do so soon enough. Hmm! Plant Trolleys could be 7536 887655397 or some abbreviation of that!

My appointment with Keith in his nineteenth-floor office of a twenty-one-storey building close to the Metropolitan Insurance Flatiron building was set for mid-morning the day after I arrived, a Thursday. I negotiated the Subway, found the rather unprepossessing building, and caught the lift up to a tiny suite of offices comprising a waiting room, Keith's office, his secretary's office, and a small kitchenette. None of this was quite what I had been expecting, and neither did it seem they were expecting me, so low-key was the welcome. After some delay, Keith, an unshaven and rather scruffy Jewish man, appeared and called me into his room overlooking the busy street below. There was just enough room for the two of us to sit facing each other across a desk covered with papers, used coffee mugs, and a computer screen.

The meeting lasted barely forty minutes. I gained absolutely no new information or feedback on our project. I was totally disheartened about the whole thing and thought what an utter waste of money the trip had been and would continue to be, as my flight tickets were unchangeable. I just wanted to get home as soon as possible. However, because of the inflexible tickets I had time on my hands in a city I didn't want to be in. I returned to my accommodation in Queens in pouring rain feeling utterly depressed. As I walked, I decided to take shelter in the Museum of the Moving Image, and what an experience that was! It exhibits a wide range of cinematic equipment, costumes, and artefacts of all sorts, and it held my attention until well past its official closing time, but the staff was happy to allow me to stay as long as I wanted. It was a very welcome diversion from the worries I now had.

I thought things through, and in my remaining time in the city, I again took a New York City bus tour, visited Ground Zero where the World Trade Center had only recently been destroyed (September 11, 2001), walked across and had a coffee overlooking the lake in Central Park, saw Strawberry Fields, went to the Frick Museum and the Natural History Museum, visited a garden show, and went to St Luke's, close to 5th Avenue, where I went to Holy Communion (BCP 1662) and was given a wonderful welcome.

SourceOne never made another consignment order, and despite all my best efforts, communication died away. I had not recovered anywhere near my outlay. Despite another business 'put down' I persisted back in Britain. I explored another idea for the business which was to try to become a partner with an existing manufacturer of plant pots. I tried with several and got closest to Stewart, the biggest. The idea was that Plant Trolleys would be offered by their sales team alongside the sale of Stewart pots. This seemed a logical concept, and I described it as 'bacon and eggs': one couldn't live without the other. Stewart had distribution agreements with several 'sheds' – jargon for the likes of B&Q and Homebase – for their pots and were keen enough on my idea to open negotiations with Homebase.

The requirement was that Stewart would buy my product, make their turn, and sell on to Homebase, who would make their mark up. The price points had been set by Homebase and were not much different from mine. The mathematics, however, just didn't work out. Homebase talked in terms of taking between 100,000 and 250,000 trolleys for each of the different product sizes, but my margin at the bottom of this tree was a loss of between 0.5p and 1.5p per item, so I didn't proceed. This may have been a mixed blessing. A number of trade-show exhibitors had warned me against doing business with these 'sheds', as they could make or break a business – the latter if they abruptly decided not to carry a product anymore. This would be particularly difficult if stock had been imported and warehoused *in anticipation* of repeat business and assuming that good sales had been achieved, so as to ensure speedy delivery. That would, however, have been suicidally risky.

I thought I had got around this problem by arranging for supplies to be transported directly to Stewart from Greece so that they took all the storage costs, and I would take my turn on the margin through normal invoicing. I also explored the possibility of having the trolleys made in the UK, and I visited several plastic-mould makers in Sussex who were all very enthused with the concept as a change from traditional industrial and product moulding. The cost for making moulds however was several thousand pounds each, but with the margins being obtained overall, these would not have been recovered for many years, and so that idea also came to nought.

Another idea was to broaden the range of products margins with better profit margins. I considered importing wheeled rectangular troughs, large flat bowls, and possibly Cretan pots. Samples were obtained and seemed very good. I didn't pursue that idea because of the fear of losing the large capital cost for acquisition and storage. The same reason ultimately held me back when looking at some plastic-coated wire-wheeled trolleys manufactured by KSP Engineering in Delhi. These were also very appealing products, seemingly strong and robust and cheaper than any Plant Trolley, but I sensed that the business of Withaph Limited wasn't strong enough to expand in this way.

I received a £5,000 direct order from a Scottish warehouse. This seemed a potentially life-saving bit of business, as it half-emptied the Rye warehouse, which was just what I wanted given my increasing awareness of costs and slow sales. The trolleys sent to Scotland were never paid for: the receiving business had gone bust within days of giving the order. Amazing! Plant Trolleys, which had been kept financially afloat with the proceeds of maturing traded endowment policies that had produced good returns as part of my retirement pot, began to really struggle. Trevelyan-Thomas, my principal agnt, threw in the towel, holding an unpaid-for supply of trolleys he had taken in advance of future sales. I never recovered the Scottish trolleys, and Robert's were collected from Devon after frequent, prolonged, and increasingly acrimonious telephone calls.

Another of my West Country accounts failed to pay for stock to the tune of almost£1,000, and I sensed that they were being unhelpful in acknowledging this. I decided to obtain payment in person and arrived at their premises near Looe to demand it. I didn't want to have to take the stock back. Their business was struggling, so I banked the cheque by immediately taking the cheque to the Callington (Devon) branch of Barclays where the cheque was drawn. Fortunately it didn't bounce, but the business did later go bust.

Collectively Plant Trolleys' business difficulties were a tipping point. The generally poor performance of Plant Trolleys as a business, was beginning to have what ultimately proved to be serious consequences for the mental health of my partner, Diane. It was something I hadn't seen coming, and when it did, I didn't know what to do about it. For the next unknown period I was going to have to think very seriously about how we could keep ourselves together as a couple. Diane was a deputy manager of a residential home, and despite her problems she kept turning up for work, dealing with a difficult manager and owner. For almost nine months she suffered severe mental depression, and although she was never quite suicidal, she endured terrible darkness, which in turn affected me. We took counselling separately, and although my depression was nothing approaching hers in its severity, she recovered more quickly than is usual thanks to some inspirational counselling and medication, quickly changed from the initial prescription that had created adverse effects. But as anyone who has had severe mental depression will say, you are never quite the same person after 'recovery'. Our change fortunately, was to bring us even closer together: to appreciate what we had had as people, not what we possessed materially.

HSBC had been keeping an eye on things and had accepted my rather too rosy picture for the future whenever we met to appraise things. They could see I had the financial resources to finance the growing overdraft which they happily allowed me. Not once did they question the business model, let alone offer suggestions about how things could be improved. My emotional commitment to the business had been overruling my head for quite a while, however, and when the overdraft built up, I funded the business from maturing endowment policies I had bought when at Intertrust to help fund my retirement.

I eventually decided to call it a day in August 2004. It was a typical example of a small businessman being ruled by his emotions and not his head. I should have pulled the plug at least a year previously and saved myself the loss of several tens of thousands of pounds.

In the early stages of setting up Plant Trolleys, I had envisaged the possibility of being employed as well as being a small business proprietor. I thought it would also look good on my CV having a collection of business activities. After all many people have several directorships, so why not me? How wrong I was. Quite obviously employers would be expecting all my time to be given to them. Who knows how many of my CVs were thrown out after reading this right at the start of it! By now I was a few years older and had already found that obtaining employment anywhere near home in Bexhill would be impossible. My outlook for re-employment was looking rather grim.

I sent job applications to local light-engineering businesses, funeral directors, a driver training instructor course near Tolworth, an invoice discounting business in Hastings, and various others, in addition to financial services businesses in the south of England and the City – all to no avail, and rarely acknowledged.

Eventually I saw an advertisement from Hastings Direct, a local motor insurance company, in the *Bexhill Observer* seeking call-centre personnel to respond to enquirers for motor insurance. The salary would be around £9,000 per annum. Money in rather than money out, I thought, and so I applied. I was given an aptitude test and a PC keyboard test, which I was told was an 'area of doubt', but I was accepted nevertheless to begin on 6 October 2004.

Mintel Market Research & Comment for 'Withaph Limited' – trading as 'Plant Trolleys'

Research – Commissioned by Withaph Limited

Because of the dearth of specific information about the sale of 'pots' – singly or potted up, Withaph Limited commissioned Mintel International to research this. A planned three-week exercise took almost three months to complete. Contacts were extremely reluctant to divulge privately held information even to Mintel, an independent Global market research company. However, sufficient raw data was accumulated, and together with more general previous 'garden industry' research from this company and others, some indicative conclusions have been drawn by Mintel for the pot market specifically, but with no distinction for whether they were single pots or potted-up.

In summary, the conclusions for pot sales in 1999 are as follows

1. Pots represent over 8% of garden industry sales by value (also confirmed by personal local research).

2. Sales estimates for the number of pots sold are in excess of 101 million. (See Mintel extract below.)

3. The most popular pot size is 12–14 ins. at the neck (47%) (i.e. more than half (53%) of the market for larger pots is likely to require plant trolleys (1 million+ units)).

4. Terracotta pots outsell all other pots (including plastic pots), having 38% of all pot sales by number and 40% by value.

5. Plastic pots have 37% of sales by number and 17% by value.

6. Glazed pots have 11% of sales by number and 19% by value.

7. Reconstituted stone pots have 7% of sales by number and 14% by value.

8. Wooden barrels and others have 7% of sales by number and 10% by value.
9. Latest available forecast figures show that 54% of the UK market for 'green goods' – the largest sector (£800m) of the market – are for sales of trees and shrubs (potential plant trolley users) and 31% plants.
10. No estimate can be made for the total number of pots currently in use.

Plant Pots

There are 24.7 million households in the UK, of which 20.5 million have gardens. The total adult population of the UK is 48 million.

Looking at the consumer research from the Garden Products Retailing report of January 1999, buyers of garden products can be broken down into five categories. Using these categories, we have estimated the number of pots they are likely to buy over the course of a year.

Type of Gardener	Percentage of Population	Population by Gardener type (million)	Unit number of pots bought	Total pots bought (million)
Keen	21%	10.1	6	60.6
Lackadaisical	20%	9.6	0.5	4.8
Entertained	14%	6.8	3	20.4
TV-inspired	16%	7.7	2	15.4
Uninterested	29%	13.9	0	0
Total	100%	48.0	11.5	101.2

Market Comment

The following is a brief selection of statements made in recent authoritative and independent reports which forecast changes for products and in the market itself. Positive trends are evident across all product categories.

Expenditure growth in excess of 4% in real terms from now until 2001 – the limit of current forecasts – is anticipated.

(Mintel, *Garden Products Retailing*, Jan. 1999)

There is a shift towards convenience gardening.

Garden design and plant selection are influenced by availability and fashion trends, and the renewed popularity for lifestyle gardening programmes has benefited plant sales.

Plant retailers have been able to add value through an increasingly large range of planted pots.

(Henley Centre, *Consumer and Leisure Futures*, No.3)

Those in the garden trade need to think about the variety of different niches, from specialist enthusiasts interested in particular types of garden to those who want an appealing garden with minimum time spent.

One niche worth talking to is those who will be approaching their 60's as the new Millennium begins. This group are of major potential to the garden market as many have considerable wealth ... There will also be more of them than in the past.

Given current levels of gardening within this age group, those involved in garden markets can expect a boost from the demographic and social trends that have conspired to create these healthy, wealthy, time rich, pensioners.

Keynote Ltd (*Garden Retailing*, 1997)

Future prospects for UK horticultural retailing look assured, with continued growth envisaged over the next decade.

'Garden Tools and Equipment' is a high-profile sector dominated by big brands and future market growth will be driven by new product developments, with the emphasis on added-value and convenience.

Design efforts have largely focused on improving ergonomics, which involve making use of the tool easier for the householder. Consequently new product launches in recent years have highlighted benefits of light weight and durability (important considerations for the growing numbers of gardeners aged 60+).

Pot and plant manufacturers have been running a number of joint promotions to stimulate further growth and hence extend sales after the main planting season ... The demand from the public for planted-up plants is clearly established and many within the trade believe that this is the big growth area ...

(Market Assessment Publications Limited, 1994–1998)

Chapter 14

My Hastings Battles

On October 6, 2004, I arrived at Hastings Directs' large building in Collington Avenue, Bexhill. Hastings Direct was a young motor insurance company and the largest employer in the town. The building had five floors, including a penthouse flat which was used by the founder and owner, an American named David Gundlach when he was in the building (most days, including some Saturdays). He also had a flat in Chelsea. I waited in the reception area on a faux leather sofa, with briefcase, suit, black shoes, and tie, and looked at an *Autocar* magazine and other motoring magazines left on the foyer table. Gradually more and more people arrived and stayed in the lobby area, and at about nine-thirty someone came along and said he would take us all up to the training room. This was on the second floor. There were about twenty of us.

Jay Wooten, who had collected us from the reception area, was going to 'train' us. The first session began with everyone introducing themselves. I was one of three people of a similar age, while the rest were considerably younger. Many of the others had been recruited from the local Job Centres, but had obviously passed the initial interview screening. Some of them were cocky, some seemed bright but nervous, and others not so bright but pretty. My two older colleagues, both men, had been employed within the insurance industry. I was surprised to learn that Richard Todd had been with Towry Law at one stage. The other gent, whose name I can't remember, had been a journalist and then editor of an insurance trade magazine.

The training course would last two weeks. It consisted of day-long information sessions with projected slides from Jay and some assistants.

All the information had to be noted – no hand-outs – and then learned for a test the following morning, which had a pass mark of eighty per cent. Every evening I would return home, desperately trying to remember the details we had been taught during the day, to be ready for the next day's test. Diane helped me hugely, but I could tell that my stress wasn't helping her own mental state. At the end of the course there would be a morning-long test on all that had been learned, with a pass mark of eighty per cent. From time to time I would have memories to my time at Bowrings and all my other employers, thinking, 'It has all come to this!' But I had tried with other job applications with financial businesses and been unsuccessful, so grab this chance, get your foot in the door, prove yourself, and get as far as you can!

To say that this training period was stressful would be an understatement. I tried to learn information by rote or in any other way that might work. I was never confident, but I usually passed the each morning's tests by a few percentage points. Some of the traineesus did rather well, while others would clearly not make the grade. For most, insurance terminology was alien. For me, being accepted at the end of the course would probably be the most important and critical period in my later working life. I just had to pass the final test.

Sadly, the guy who had been editor of an insurance magazine died during the second week of training. He had showed no stress indications and had been doing well enough each day, but obviously something had happened which triggered this tragedy.

Apart from having knowledge of motor insurance and its technicalities, I had had to learn the NATO phonetic alphabet. This was developed by the International Civil Aviation Organization (ICAO) in the 1950s and had been adopted by many other international and national organisations, including the North Atlantic Treaty Organization (NATO). It is an internationally understood way of confirming verbal word spelling between different but similar-sounding letters – for example, 'S' and 'F' (sierra, foxtrot), 'T', 'C', 'B', and 'D' ((tango, Charlie, bravo, delta), and so on. It was the only long-term benefit I was to gain from my time with the company!

When the final day of induction training came, after many, many sleepless nights, I took the final test. My mark was seventy-nine per cent! Jay reviewed my answers with me, trying to find an additional one per cent, but we couldn't. I thought, 'Well, this is it. I have tried my best and failed. What is the future now?' I felt depressed, disillusioned, and just plain down, but only for a moment.

'We want to recruit more people like you,' said Jay. 'You are close enough in your test, and I believe you have potential, so I am going to put you through. Nothing is to be said, okay?' We shook hands and I was in. Later that day I was taken to meet my team leader, aged about twenty-four and fellow team members, all under thirty years of age, and none of whom I thought I had much in common with, on any level. I would start work the following Monday morning. The following week I took my place at a desk on the south side of the building, from which the English Channel could be seen with the occasional ship heading westwards visible on the horizon. I wished I could be out there.

The salary was pitiful compared to my last earned-income employment in Greece, about twelve per cent. The years in between had been a series of financial, mental, and emotional struggles. At least my days without the certainty of employment income, when I walked dejectedly with my head down, looking at pavement slabs so as not to see goods in shop windows: when even buying a second-hand shirt from a local charity shop for three pounds felt like (and was) an extravagance, had ended. But other nightmares were to come.

As with every department in the business except for Underwriting and Finance, the department I was in, Customer Services worked a rota system, which meant that every four weeks I was required to work on Saturdays. The hours would be the same, nine to five-thirty with an hour for lunch in the in-house canteen. One week out of four would be worked as 'lates', which meant working from eleven to eight with a lunch hour at four o'clock! I hated these non-standard weeks, although I tried to rationalise it all by thinking of all the people who work unsocial hours and weekends. I never could get my head around it. Apart from anything else, none of our friends was 'inconvenienced' in this way, although at the time Diane was working these unsocial hours and more as deputy manager of a local care home.

It was well known that the local job centres would direct young unemployed people to work at 'Hastings' – the name by which the company was known – knowing that they would get the benefit of an albeit inconsistent management style, which didn't tolerate personal laxness in time-keeping, dress, or application, but usually turned a blind eye to bad language and alcohol use on and off site. Many of the youngsters joined the business with poor personal histories, family problems, financial problems, or even with criminal records for such things as GBH and theft. Junior staff retention was abysmal. Towards the end of my six years with the company, efforts were being made to improve the quality of staff recruitment, and clamp down on the drink problem. It was a bit like working in a social correction centre.

My teammates were representative of most of the Customer Services sales force. They were young (mostly under twenty-three), educated to a very low level, living mostly locally in Hastings, Bexhill, and Eastbourne, and for many this was their first job. Some had trouble with simple mental arithmetic (ten per cent of thirty, for example). Their language amongst themselves was dreadful despite management's efforts to control it, and standards of dress were often inappropriate – especially among the young girls, who seemed to view being there as an opportunity to find and maintain relationships. Sprinkled amongst them were a few older folk like myself who for one reason or another found themselves with nowhere better to go.

Many newly recruited youngsters never settled to the rigours of working, even if the style of team management was unprofessional, and so they left, usually of their own volition, but not infrequently at management's insistence. They would be dismissed for poor performance or sometimes for dishonest behaviour either within the business or in conducting business with customers.

When I started, the business was just eight years old and there was only a handful of staff had been with the business since it all began in 1998. My team leader, Adam Floyd, reported to a floor manager, Karl Jones. Adam was one of about eight team leaders, each team having up to twelve members. Our job in the call centre was to take incoming telephone calls from the public who wanted quotations for car or motor bike insurance, or later for home insurance. There was no cold calling, which was a relief. Our conversations could be listened to ('monitored') and recorded in the event that there was a customer complaint. Detailed notes had to be kept in each phone answerer's 'diary notepad' on the bulky desktop computers everyone had, and a system for checking accuracy and following correct procedures was followed.

Our office was the entire length of an office block that had originally been built for the East Sussex Health Authority, who had somehow obtained planning permission for a six-storey office block in the middle of a respectable residential area near the centre of Bexhill. The whole building and an annex were occupied by the business. One floor could accommodate some eighty people and was overseen by a floor manager. Julie Birchall was ours. She sat at her desk just behind me shouting instructions and orders so loudly she could be heard by incoming callers. Like a fish wife she'd call out her commands. 'Get on the phone!' 'Why are you on "not ready"?' (This referred to an option on the phones that the team leader or floor manager could use to monitor how much time you spent unable to take calls, whilst making on-screen notes of conversations and actions, or simply blowing your nose.) 'There are twelve calls in the queue!' (This implied that existing calls should be terminated quickly, or that if you were on 'not ready', you should get back to work.) All of this would be on top of your own team leader's constant monitoring of everyone's work, behaviour, and punctuality throughout each and every day.

We were allowed two daily breaks, one in the morning and one in the afternoon of either ten or fifteen minutes depending on how busy we were. I spent this time in the ground-floor internet café where there were a dozen or so screens with access to the Internet. They were seriously censored; there was no access to travel or financial websites, for example.

Within a few weeks of joining, Diane's mental condition worsened, and one day I received a call from her to say she had gone home early from her work. I had already assessed that I was unlikely to get much sympathy from the floor manager that day and that it would go without saying that if I took time off, I wouldn't be paid and would have to make up the time. Instead of talking to Adam, I decided to talk directly to Karl, who had a reputation for being extremely hard. When I approached his desk, he motioned me to sit down, and I explained the problem and said that I wanted to go home. To my great surprise and eternal gratitude he immediately said, 'Yes, take as much time as you need.' Karl said that he had once been a mental counsellor and understood the need for me to be at home. It proved to be the most personally considerate moment of my six years with the company.

In our teams we were expected to be able to take calls for at least ninety-five per cent of our time in the office, and woe betide you if you failed this first measure! Other measures included sales targets of so many closed sales per week (each one noted on a team board for all to see). We were encouraged to tell all the team of our achievements, and at the end of each day our productivity in selling a policy or ancillaries was duly noted to go towards the monthly target on which a modest commission would be added to our basic salary. Ancillaries included insurance coverage for legal cover, breakdowns or personal accidents.

From time to time I was withdrawn from this customer-service role to give aptitude tests to potential new recruits. This was not a little bizarre, given that most of the test consisted of giving a PC test to ensure candidates could use a keyboard and screen, which had been an area of doubt about my own 'skill set' (to use the modern jargon) when I had joined!

Occasionally teams would be shuffled about with some members being replaced by others, and occasionally a whole team would be moved to another area previously occupied by another team, sometimes on a different floor. It became apparent that team leaders (TLs) had considerable influence on who stayed and who went from the company. The whole enterprise was managed on a target-based system measured by productivity on which the TL would receive override commission. They were only interested in high achievers unless there was some other factor which they felt desirable – anything from being able to access cheap cigarettes, playfulness at weekends, or just 'eye-candy'.

Not infrequently, customers would call with questions about their insurance policies which had to be referred to another department. These calls caused them frustration and cost us valuable sales time. Later an automatic system was installed that would more immediately direct calls to the right department. Staff were routinely humbled by a TL's accusations of improper or inadequate business performance without so much as a 'please' or a 'thank you'. Humiliation and mental bullying were the order of the day, and although we all moaned about it in the twice-a-day break periods, nothing could be done. Union representation was just not to be countenanced or tolerated, even though on a number of occasions people who had been sacked took the company to tribunal.

The customer services 'experience', however, taught me that being abrasive when complaining to a call centre of any business is not the best way to achieve satisfaction. We worked under tremendous pressure, often dealing with identical problems and queries repeatedly day in, day out. The best way to obtain cooperation is to be polite, courteous, and tolerant. Who knows? You might be talking to someone who has just finished their initial training course and is terrified at the prospect of dealing directly with the public, just as we all were when we started.

Not surprisingly, staff morale was low to non-existent, not just within Customer Services but, as I discovered throughout my six years' time within Hastings Direct, in all departments. Staff management was very heavy-handed and for the most part insensitive. A colleague who had a hip replacement had to make up the time he had taken for the operation and recovery! Indeed, illness of any sort had to have the time made up with extra working shifts, once the statutory time had been taken. Doctors' notes counted for little.

In September 2006 the company was sold by its founder and principal shareholder to IAG (Insurance Australia Group) – a significant insurance company with interests around the world but until then, not in the UK. Hastings Direct was perceived as offering potential for significant expansion and growth, along with another acquired insurer, Equity Red Star. IAG introduced a firm of management consultants, PCP, to the business with the brief to look at ways to cut costs – as always dressed up in management speak to 'deliver improvements within and outside the business'. Over a short period of just a few months the head count dropped significantly: from board level to the post room. In a management effort to improve morale, 'dress-down days' were introduced for the last working Friday of each month. Normally the dress code was quite strict – jackets and ties, no jeans or trainers for the men, and no bare flesh, plunging neck lines, or overly high heels for the women. Breaching this code meant being sent home to change and making up the time lost within a week. Ties could only be removed when the temperature in the office reached twenty-seven degrees centigrade! There was no air-conditioning. 'Dress-down days' unleashed a complete reversal of all this, with trainers, jeans (sometimes torn), football shirts on the young men and clothes suitable for a disco being worn by the young women.

In due course I moved from Customer Services to Policy Services, where my role was to service existing policies at renewal, amendment, or cancellation. Again, the work pressure was intense with so many 'pieces of work' expected to be completed against a department average per day. Woe betide you if you fell short with 'disciplinaries' being handed out! My record was that I never received one of these, but if an employee received three within a year and there was considered to be no prospect of improvement, he or she would be fired and walked out of the building there and then accompanied by a TL.

Respite from this employment nightmare came one day when I was asked if I would take on a requirement of the Financial Services Authority, our Industry Regulator to prepare User, and Product Manuals. The Legal and Compliance Department – a comparatively new department – was newly staffed by experienced industry lawyers and technicians who were aghast that the business had lasted so long since its beginning without such manuals, let alone formal compliance. The FSA had informed the business that it was unsatisfactory not to have these. It was all so typical of the off-the-cuff way the business had been run. Writing these manuals was an opportunity to use the knowledge I had acquired over four years in an environment away from the high-pressure, task-driven, target-focussed atmosphere I had endured. And it was a fun time too, offering opportunities to get about the building and talk with some intelligent and interesting people, mostly in IT, who provided the support and systems which made the business function. I was back in a creative role!

The initial expectation was that this secondment would last three months. However, the production of six tomes covering New Business, Renewals, and General Administration to describe the process and the procedure for each of these business areas took almost two years, not least because each manual had to be accepted not just by the department it had been written for but also by the Legal and Compliance Department.

This period was followed by my return to Policy Services, but this was only for a short while. The business needed to test new products prior to offering them on line for the first time. Known as UAT (User Acceptance Testing), this involved system testing the products for motor, bike, and home insurance policies on a test system programme and trying to find anomalies or faults in the system. Endless and repetitive tests were made and the results reported to the IT Department and Underwriting Department. But it was all still handled in a rather half-hearted way, with access to test systems programmes sometimes denied, and feedback from results testing slow.

The time came to put a small team together to undertake the corporate UAT task, and I was asked to set this up. I requested a dedicated office or test area and basic computer hardware and software to run what would effectively be a parallel universe with separate support and computer systems as a basic requirement. Office space was found in one of the Training Department rooms with PCs installed. Only now were flat-screen PCs becoming the norm. How they had changed from their early bulky size! On the Friday before my selected team and I were due to start, I asked that all the PCs should have Microsoft Office software installed and have Internet access. This would be required in order to make comparative studies with leading competitors as part of the role. Shades of my broking past, looking at competitive rates, as in my Towry Law days, gave me some job satisfaction, at last.

The IT Department assured me that everything would be in place for the new UAT office space by the following Monday. What I hadn't expected was for there to be a problem in moving Microsoft user licences from one PC to another within the business, given that throughout the building, because of many redundancies, there were now many unused PCs. Having been told that this was the way to avoid having to pay £300 or so for new licenses, I was told that it wasn't my role to offer solutions to problems even if I had identified the problem! Because of this intrusion (as it was seen) I was taken off UAT work and returned to Policy Services.

PCP identified seven employees they wished to see go from Policy Services out of twenty-four, but they also offered voluntary redundancy to the entire department, despite the fact that at times our back-load amounted to three weeks work! The back-load was seasonal, so whilst it was never seen as desirable, it was always regarded as being manageable. Their list of seven compulsory redundancies included me, probably because I had been doing work outside the department at intervals. I received my redundancy notice in a letter dated November 12, 2007. Unfortunately for me, no other department had taken me under their wing either, even though the UAT work had significant commercial importance for the company's future.

The list of staff put under review included virtually all those who had the most service and experience (and probably were paid the most). It was a catastrophic period, not just for the department but for the company, and it came at a time when IAG discovered that because of inadequate due diligence when bidding for the company, they had acquired an unpaid tax bill of £15 million. Sorting out this mess meant staff having to be taken off normal duties and 'fire-fighting'. In fact, the company should have written to the affected policyholders, who had been issued with inaccurately calculated premiums for their policies and offered compensation, but instead they chose to cancel and reissue policies. This was a process designed to antagonise the policyholders affected and was a total PR disaster.

While the statutory redundancy consultation procedures were followed, significant numbers of staff chose to take voluntary redundancy anyway. It seemed like a good idea to get out of a company with what appeared to be at best an uncertain future, when main board members were also being shown the door or choosing to walk out anyway. Seeing colleagues go was enough to deeply unsettle many staff all across the company. This uncertainty resulted in the department being under-staffed. As a consequence, I was invited to continue employment within Policy Services, with my redundancy notice withdrawn, even though I had not actively used its work procedures for several months, having been involved with so many special corporate projects, some of which had necessitated me attending Board committee meetings.

Eventually PCP left the building. It then became pretty obvious that under the new buy out by management, the business had almost been brought to its knees. Studious efforts began to be made to improve working conditions, including new office furniture, redecoration, blinds at the south-facing windows, air-conditioning, security boxes for personal possessions (none of which were allowed in the office areas), and, they said, a pay review. In fact, three attempts were made to bring in new pay structures over a period of eight months, but it was still all so unprofessional. Quarterly staff meetings were organised to encourage staff participation in the decision-making process, but they were actually used for gathering information and ideas to be re-presented again at a later meeting. An outside catering company was brought in to manage the revamped ground-floor staff canteen, now known as Harry's Bar, which even had a cash machine installed!

One of management's stated aims was to turn the company around sufficiently well to enable it to seek a stock market listing, management hoped, in three years' time. Shares would be issued to all staff members with more than three years employment remaining, which ruled me out. Despite my written submissions that the future of the company was being built on the efforts of those who had been working there in the past, and offering an ex-employees association with an annual lunch at which shareholders could be apprised of company developments and plans, none of these ideas was taken on board.

Needless to say, I was relieved to be back in the fold after considerable support from Susan French, a senior manager who had been with the company since its beginning. The prospect of redundancy two and half years before retirement was distinctly unattractive, with minimal prospects for finding work again anywhere else. Even so, I did apply for and failed to land alternative employment in other local businesses. So I resumed being monitored and assessed against targets that I had difficulty meeting, not least because the methodology of measuring 'performance' had changed from being simply one of measuring 'productivity' (the number of pieces of work completed against a department standard) to one which measured individual productivity or performance against a department average plus 120 per cent.

I felt so strongly about the way the department was managed that I wrote a note to the floor's manager pointing out the scope for unfairly manipulating team members' performances by the type of work distributed each day to each of us. In this way it was possible to influence bonus payments for exceeding targets and, conversely, to minimise bonus payments or even make them unreachable for staff who were not liked personally by the team leader. This could lead to disciplinaries and ultimately dismissal. It was worthy of exposure more broadly than being kept snugly within the building, but it was impossible to imagine a way to do that anonymously. Disliked or unpopular members of staff were frequently moved from team to team. It wasn't difficult to see how these decisions were being made.

This department target average obviously changed weekly – strangely, always upwards – as section staff became more proficient or systems enhancements were introduced. Anyone falling to ninety-five per cent of the department average could be assured of a good dressing down, with disciplinaries being issued if targets were missed too frequently. After a few months I requested to work part time, and surprisingly and thankfully, my request was accepted. I thought management would prefer to see me leave once and for all, since I was rather opinionated. However, my new hours would be eight till one daily without shifts or weekends for my last eighteen months. I could not believe how lucky I was.

As retirement loomed I began to make my personal preparations, particularly for my own pension arrangements. The company had its own money-purchase-with-profits scheme, which was changed to a Standard Life unitised scheme. This shoe-horned people into a variety of predetermined funds considered the best ones for the future pensioners at each stage of career. I chose to make my own fund choices, looking for on-going capital growth while it was still invested, not the bond-based security route favoured by the external consultants. Indeed, later in retirement, I continued what the investment community would consider a high-risk investment profile, looking for capital gain and income growth on the basis that I might live another twenty or more years. What good would there be in having retirement savings in so-called 'safe investments' over this period of time? If a typical lifetime consists of 1,000 months of which three hundred are spent sleeping, and three hundred working, I wanted to be able to enjoy the balance!

Even my retirement date could result in a salary deduction from my last month's payment if the holiday I had taken in that year, as a proportion of the year's entitlement, had been exceeded, such was the inbuilt callousness to staff by middle management, who hadn't yet caught up with the emergence of a slightly more enlightened approach from the top.

To arrange my pension resources, even after being involved in the loss of several tens of thousands of pounds with the demise of Equitable Life in 2000, I went to Bristol to meet a consultant from Hargreaves Lansdown in smart purpose-built offices close to the city centre. It was a company which had always specialised in offering investment advice.

Hargreaves Lansdown was established in 1981 by Peter Hargreaves and Stephen Lansdown, both of whom I had met many times in my Slater, Walker days. From its beginnings in modest offices in a residential area of Clifton in Bristol, by 30 September 2013 Hargreaves had become one of the leading providers of investment management products and services to private investors in the UK, with £39.3 billion of assets under administration held on behalf of private investors. Later I corresponded with Peter, who remembered not only me but also Jim Slater and Tim Miller – names for me to conjure with!

About four months before my retirement date (12 July), Human Resources invited me to discuss my time with Hastings Direct, and I didn't pull any punches. They looked at my CV and reviewed my work and performance in the company. I was asked if I would consider staying on if a specialist role could be found. I said that I would consider that, but only prior to my leaving date. I said that if I walked out of the door without an offer, I wouldn't be coming back.

My final period, whilst still attached to Policy Services, was to be seconded to another business area which required assistance with generating renewal quotes for customers whose previous underwriter was no longer willing to take on the business; this was known as 'rebroking'. This insurance market reaction was due entirely to the original costly error by Hanover and resulted in a new procedure for taking on underwriters for the Hastings Direct underwriting panel. It was rather similar to the collective underwriting slips used at Lloyds all those years ago! I found the new work routine acceptable, and was able to do sufficient work not to be disciplined, thus maintaining my (rare) unblemished employment record.

Finally it came to say 'goodbye' to my work colleagues in the Policy Services team on my last morning. They were mostly good hardworking young men and women (including the great-great-grandson of Bill Voce the 1930s fast bowling England test cricketer). I told them that in a working life you may be lucky to have three or four breaks to make real advance and progress. It may not be with the same company, and such opportunities are created, not given. When they occur, I said, take them and never look back.

Financially my monthly earned income at the end of my working life was the same as when I had started work forty-seven years earlier, adjusted for inflation. It was equivalent to the £28 6s 8d (£28.33) per month after tax I had earned in 1963. At least I had, at the end, managed to save some of the hard-earned cash to retire relatively comfortably at sixty-five years of age. I was so grateful for being able to earn something each month during my twilight working years. It was money in, rather than money out, but it had been a battle to keep my self-respect through all the personal indignities and overhanging dismissal threats.

My RDP (running down period) was at an end. I was glad to hand in my security pass. (We were never given one of these when I started!) I walked through the security doors from the office and then those of the building for the last time, at about one o'clock. I knew that throughout my working career I had always done my best. I had had the opportunity to think outside the box, to innovate, to have some fun, to travel a large part of the world, and to be successful most of the time whilst meeting many people whose company I enjoyed.

Quite by chance, and independent of Hastings Direct, I was selected to be one of a handful of people to be interviewed by Prunella Gee. As an actress she had once performed with, amongst others, Sidney Poitier and Michael Caine and later with Sean Connery in a James Bond film, *Never Say Never Again*. Having left the world of acting, she was now writing a thesis for a postgraduate doctorate on the subject of retirement at Birkbeck College, to record how people, selected at random, were preparing for this life-changing moment and what their thoughts about it were. Prunella invited me three times to talk and record my thoughts, some of them changing as the date approached and passed, about my situation at three-monthly intervals before, at the moment of, and after retirement.

They were interesting discussions, but sadly I never saw her paper which she had said I would. Being also a counsellor, she was interested in a personal trait which she had never experienced before and which I only realised I had when talking with her. It is that, unless there is absolutely no alternative, I never choose to retrace my steps exactly or repeat something even in routine actions (going shopping on foot or by car or driving somewhere, for example). Being forced to do so because I might have forgotten something really irritates me no end! I also really dislike repeating myself in conversation, whether it's my fault in speaking quietly, or unclearly or because of inattention by the listener. Pru said she'd like to explore the reasons for this behaviour, but she never did. Are there any clues within this memoir?

On my retirement day I felt, at the end, a tremendous sense of relief. It was as if the wind inside me of my pent-up worries and concerns of my last working years could now be expelled, like a deflating balloon. Hopefully I could now look forward to a few years of good retirement without pressures of either managing or being managed. My future wife, Diane, who had stood by me in the last difficult years and at great cost to her for a while, and I, made a good start to that and celebrated with a short break beginning that hot sunny afternoon at a wonderful hotel, South Lodge at Lower Beeding not far from Christ's Hospital.

I had completed the circle.

About the Book

This memoir tracks how George became involved in an area of business that grew from one of several million pounds to one of many billions. He observes with some humour how life was, and how it changed in his working years, both inside and outside his office.

George was an ideas man, creating and developing investment products for private individuals initially and later for institutions. He had product and marketing ideas that were literally ahead of their time. Many of them are now widely available. When they were new, they attracted press headlines. 'Stirs up a Hornet's Nest,' said the *Financial Times* about an innovative way to remunerate stockbrokers in the 1970s.

He describes businesses, the work environment and people he encountered in most of the eleven countries in Europe, two Scandinavian, seven Middle Eastern, and three in South-East Asia, as well as the United States, where he operated before becoming an expatriate. On returning to the UK, he attempted more innovative ideas, outside the world of finance, before his final and most difficult employment period.

Old customs and traditions became disguised by modern technology, but the creative flow kept coming right to the end of an inventive, absorbing, and socially beneficial career.

Lightning Source UK Ltd.
Milton Keynes UK
UKOW05f2252210714

235522UK00002B/101/P